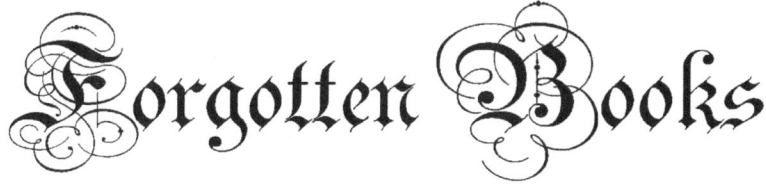

ISBN 978-1-334-03911-9
PIBN 10638277

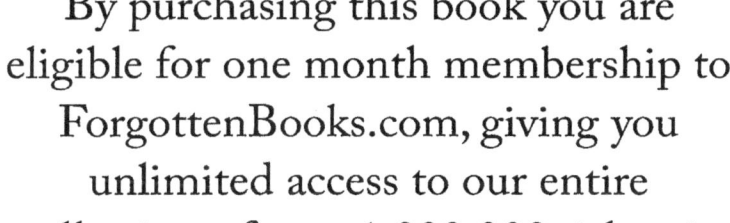

His Life and Works

With a Catalogue of His Pictures,

By

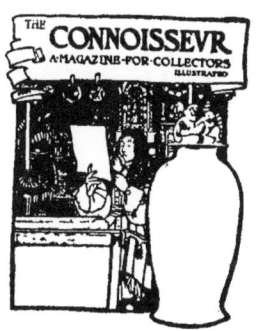

LONDON:

PUBLISHED BY

(OTTO LIMITED).

———

1911

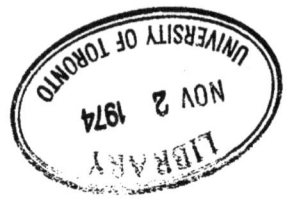

Preface.

" WE cannot know enough about Sir Henry Raeburn. He was a great artist and a splendid type of man," were the words used by a friend when told that I had been commissioned to write a short life of the Scots artist. Up to comparatively recent days little was known of Raeburn. Indeed, when the exhibition of his works was held at the French Gallery last winter, there still were at least two people who had never heard his name, for they addressed a letter to him at the Gallery, asking him if he were a relation, and whether he could tell them anything of a long lost parent. An excuse may be accepted for this ignorance, but none for the critics who, surely owing to lack of knowledge of his work, dub Raeburn as a parodist of Lawrence, or dismiss his claim by relegating him to a chapter headed "The Contemporaries of Lawrence." But of later days a more intimate study of his achievement has banished neglect and raised him, as we shall see, to one of the highest places in Art. In 1863 his portraits were held in so little repute that a fine " Sir Walter Scott as a Boy " was bought in at £3 5s., and at the sale of his pictures in 1887 forty-nine of them realised only £6,000. Since then the Scott portrait fetched 1,000 guineas, and two of the portraits sold in 1887, the " Lady Raeburn " and the artist's own portrait, now in the Scottish National Gallery, made between them in the Tweedmouth Sale, 13,200 guineas—ten times the combined price of 1887.

But Raeburn's greatest triumph was on May 19th of this year when Messrs. Duveen paid 22,300 guineas for his splendid portrait of " Mrs. Robertson Williamson," and again July 14th the same firm gave 14,000 guineas for a very beautiful portrait of " Lady Janet Sinclair," who married James Traill, of Hobbister and Rattar. In another part of this volume will be found a description of these two pictures and an account of their sale at Christie's.

My main object in writing this book was to supply fresh information about Raeburn and his paintings, information of importance that is absent from the standard work and subsequent monographs dealing with him and his Art. In the memoirs of Raeburn there is an unaccountable dearth of letters by him, though Cunningham, his earliest biographer declares that the artist " maintained an intercourse by letters with some of the first literary men of his age," yet he gives portions only of two letters written by Raeburn. Sir Walter Armstrong, in his " Sir Henry Raeburn," published in 1901, states that Raeburn "kept no diaries and no accounts, and wrote no letters, so that in his case the usual channels of information do not exist." But I am able to show that he did keep accounts (see Chap. VI.) and I have been fortunate to bring together for the first time in any monograph on Raeburn, about thirty letters. Nine of these documents were brought to light by myself, and have never before been published in a life of the artist. In the list of pictures will be found about 1,000 works, which far exceeds the number hitherto recorded. Of course the list does not give a complete account of his achievements. During last year several works were disposed of at auction which appeared to me so doubtful, that I have not ascribed them to Raeburn. On the whole, however, I think there are few known portraits of merit omitted from my list. In its preparation, Mr. James L. Caw, Director of the National Gallery of Scotland; Mr. W. Roberts; Mr. D. Croal Thomson, of the French Gallery; Messrs. Colnaghi & Co., Messrs. J. J. Duveen, Sir George Cooper, and others, gave me much help, for which I thank them. I also owe gratitude to Mr. C. Fairfax Murray, Mr. James L. Caw, Mr. W. Roberts, and the Buchanan Society, of Glasgow, for permission to use letters under their control.

July, 1911.   J. G.

SIR HENRY RAEBURN, R.A.

INTRODUCTION.

"THERE never was an artistic period. Art happens," said Whistler. There certainly was not an artistic period in Scotland from the Reformation, until Henry Raeburn "happened" from the chaos that followed the iconoclasm of Knox and his adherents. Nor did art suffer alone. The spirit that caused the destruction of the splendid cathedrals and abbeys, with their decoration, crushed for a long period the literature of the north country. But conditions changed and art and literature once more flourished in Scotland, the one culminating in the genius of Robert Burns, the other in the work of Sir Henry Raeburn. For centuries, internecine strife between Church and State, King and Covenant, kept Scotland in the direst poverty. It was otherwise in Italy during the Renaissance. Art, religion and politics were indissolubly associated, and wealth followed in their train. Towns waged war against each other, Pope and Emperor in bloodly strife sought power, votes were controlled by sword and spear, party hatred culminated in the murder of candidates, the clash of arms was seldom absent in street and palace. So intense was the frenzy that some of the younger men waited neither for helmet nor cuirass, but in their sarks they mounted their steeds and charged the stubborn pikemen who lurked in dark corners, or rode through showers of arrows, winged from high windows, until their ranks were reduced to a few bleeding, worn-out figures, ready for prison or death. If the fortunes of the day were on their side, they took possession of lordly palazzo and desecrated the Cross because God, as they thought, had favoured the enemy. Yet, amid all the tempestuous carnage, art— "Italy's heritage from antiquity"—grew throughout the land. Artists themselves, when neither fighting nor planning fortifications, as did Niccolo at Naples and at Gaeto, and Michael Angelo at Florence, were carving votive images, painting the story of Christ, tender representations of the Madonna and angels, or raising to skies, ringing with the sounds of laughter or strife, magnificent campanile, church, and dome. And when a great work was created, when the Madonna of Cimabue* arose lifelike amid the rigid and bloodless Byzantine effigies, the youths and maidens of Florence, in a temporary period of peace, carried the painting in triumph to the transept of Santa Maria Novella. Splendid cities grew. Arnolfo built a new and glorious Florence; the Siena that fascinates was created; on grass-covered ruins the Popes rebuilt Rome with the treasure derived from vicious and victorious war.

It was not until after the union of the crowns that the material resources of Scotland began to be developed. At intervals, the Civil War

---

* The advocates of the Sienese Schools say that it was Duccio, the Sienese, not Cimabue, who painted this Madonna.

and other troubles arrested progress, but at the end of the rebellion of '45 trade, commerce, and wealth, grew with amazing rapidity. Artistic taste among the *nouveaux riches*, however, remained dormant for a considerable time. Lord Cockburn wrote that "Scotland was neither rich enough nor old enough for the rise of merchants princely in their taste." Many years before the beginning of the Nineteenth Century, however a new spirit moved the social and religious life of Scotland. Without losing any of their native force, Scotsmen gradually became refined under the influence of more humane and generous ideas. Calvinistic puritanism and the exalted austerity of the covenanters were fusing into a condition of greater tolerance. This freedom of thought, growing with increasing prosperity, gradually quickened the intellectual life of the nation, and when, in 1802, the *Edinburgh Review* was founded, the Scottish capital had become the literary and artistic centre of the country, attracting by its brilliance men of the standing of Sydney Smith and Thomas de Quincey.

It was in this general awakening that Raeburn came, as it were "full armed from the brains of Jove"—he received no training of any consequence in the evolution of his genius ; his own personality and the remarkable men and women of his time supplying the impetus for the development of his art. Much has been written about the source of his inspiration. Before Raeburn there were good painters born in Scotland, but none of them showed any marked national style, no individual force. They painted noble lords, proud lairds, and their ladies, but in a fashion formed in England or on the Continent.

George Jameson, the "Scottish Vandyck," was the first known native artist, he preceding Hogarth, by about a hundred years. Born in Aberdeen on the 8th of February, 1587, Jameson was the son of an architect. An instinct for art began to show itself early in his life, and while still a youngster, he won local fame as a painter. His parents encouraged the youth. We are told on doubtful authority that he was sent to Antwerp to study in the studio of Rubens, where, it is said, Vandyck was among his fellow students. How long he remained abroad is not known. But on his return to Scotland, he began his professional career in Aberdeen, ultimately removing to Edinburgh, where he was soon busy with commissions from both factions in the party strife. He himself was a Royalist. His name is found on a privy council register of 1641 as a "malcontent" opposed to the Covenanters. Three years after this date Jameson died in the Scottish capital, leaving a considerable number of portraits, among them those of the great rivals Argyll and Montrose.

Of his successor, John Scougal, little is known. He was popular, but his work is not marked by any strong individuality, which makes it difficult to distinguish his portraits among those of the period that are without recorded parentage. Sir John Medina, a Fleming of Spanish origin, cannot, of course, be classed as a Scottish artist. He manufactured portraits of the Scottish nobility in the manner of Lely, adopting the custom of the time of adding heads to bodies supplied by costume painters like Vanhaken, who we know was retained by two artists to give his "exclusive and estimable" services at a salary of £800 a year. The result of this combination was deplorable. All English portraits had, according to the Abbe le Blanc, a family likeness. "The most sensible difference to

it the end of the rebellion of
:h amazing rapidity. Artistic
:r, remained dormant for a
at " Scotland was neither rich
hants princely in their taste."
xeenth Century, however a new
otland. Without losing any of
ne refined under the influence
istic puritanism and the exalted
into a condition of greater
with increasing prosperity,
ie nation, and when, in 1802, the
capital had become the literary
by its brilliance men of the
: Quincey.
baeburn came, as it were " full
received no training of any
s ; his own personality and the
supplying the impetus for the
en about the source of his
good painters born in Scotland,
ional style, no individual force.
if their ladies, but in a fashion

ck," was the first known native
ndred years. Born in Aberdeen
the son of an architect. An
lly in his life, and while still a
. His parents encouraged the
that he was sent to Antwerp to
is said, Vandyck was among his
abroad is not known. But on his
nal career in Aberdeen, ultimately
busy with commissions from
self was a Royalist. His name is
I as a " malcontent " opposed to
date Jameson died in the Scottish
I portraits, among them those of

: is known. He was popular, but
ig individuality, which makes it
mong those of the period that
hn Medina, a Fleming of Spanish
Scottish artist. He manufactured
: manner of Lely, adopting the
lies supplied by costume painters
ired by two artists to give his
alary of £800 a year. The result
English portraits had, according
. The most sensible difference to

WILLIAM FERGUSON, OF KILSIE

be observed betw
the left, in othe
same neck, and

    Medina's fac
and they need m
of Thomas Man
only by birth a
and has no natio
on the art of hi
had decided arti
of Cairnie, nea
sold his ancestr
in Edinburgh m
became a fashio
may be made to
of Scottish pa
Nories, the ■
artist.

    Pictorial ai
career not bec
Italians of the
became plumb
for a professi
of the penny
of Art, after a
quickening. ■
and supplied :
becoming a fr
revenge, and a
regularly with
church and ■
warranted ■
trenchant or
death and ma
emotion that
stored with
the necessity
temperament,
" a Campbell
sought for re
change houses
    In this co
inspired the ■
" Honest ■
Oliphant, " the
glad of sometl
to the wigmak
printed a new
brought in fresh
a witty letter ■

be observed between them was that in some, the heads were turned to the left, in others, to the right. These effigies had the same flesh, the same neck, and the same arms, the same attitude."

Medina's feebleness was still further reduced by his son and grandson, and they need not be considered, nor shall I do more than mention the art of Thomas Murray (1666-1724) and Joseph Michael Wright, both Scottish only by birth and name. Their principal work was executed in London, and has no national character. John Alexander (1690-1760) left no impress on the art of his country, but his contemporary, William Aikman (1682-1731) had decided artistic talent. He came of a good stock of Forfarshire lairds, of Cairnie, near Arbroath. His enthusiasm for art was so great that he sold his ancestral land in order to go to Rome to study, afterwards settling in Edinburgh in 1712. About eleven years later he went to London and became a fashionable painter of refined taste. He died in 1731. Reference may be made to Jeremiah Davidson, or Davison, who was born in England of Scottish parents; William Ferguson, John Smibert, and the two Nories, the house decorators, who trained more than one successful artist.

Pictorial art was not yet a living thing in Scotland, Art was chosen as a career not because of any great innate impulse like that which moved the Italians of the Renaissance. Some men become painters just as others became plumbers. Most of the artists of the time might have "tossed" for a profession and been equally successful in whichever métier the fall of the penny decreed for them. But the way was clearing. The spirit of Art, after a long sleep, was beginning to rub its eyes, its feelings were quickening. Material prosperity created the desire for intellectual culture and supplied the means for its acquisition. The Scottish capital was becoming a free place—free from great passion and hatred, feuds and revenge, and zeal that cried for blood and fire. Its streets no longer rang regularly with the sound of war, the clash of the steel of rival factions, of church and state. It was in the main, a city of peace, of hard work that warranted leisure. People were not afraid to express their thoughts in trenchant or witty language. Laughter and revelry were common where death and moaning had often been. It was in this Edinburgh of brighter emotion that Allan Ramsay began his career as a poet. His mind well stored with the folksongs of his own countryside, he at first did not feel the necessity for personal expression. But the wig-maker was of a joyous temperament, and when he tired of curling the hair of a "Hepburna" or "a Campbella," or fitting the wig of a Lord or a rubicund advocate, he sought for relaxation among the gay souls who frequented the clubs or change houses in the Canongate or Luckenbooths.

In this congenial company and atmosphere, the muse of Scottish poetry inspired the first important poet of the revival to "lisp in numbers." Soon "Honest Allan's" songs became famous. "By-and-bye," says Mrs. Oliphant, "the good-wives in their high lodgings, floor over floor, ever glad of something new, learnt to send one of the bairns with a penny to the wigmaker's shop in the afternoon to see if Allan Ramsay had printed a new poem; and received with rapture the damp broad-sheet brought in fresh from the press, with a fable or a song in ' gude braid Scots,' or a witty letter to some answering rhymster full of local names and things."

Thus Allan's fame was spread, until it reached the ears of writers and lawyers, professors and clergy. His business instinct widened with the growth of his poetic fame. Bookselling was added to his other trade, and, before long, he removed to the Luckenbooths, which was then a sort of Piccadilly or Bond Street, and devoted himself entirely to Bookselling. In 1726 he opened the first circulating library in Scotland, and his shop became a meeting place for the eminent people of the day. When the Duchess of Queensberry brought the poet Gay to Edinburgh, he was among Ramsay's most frequent visitors at the shop which was adorned with medallions of Ben Jonson and Drummond, of Hawthornden. Ramsay's celebrity attained its zenith when he produced "The Gentle Shepherd," one of the most exquisite pastorals in the Scottish dialect. The poem won extraordinary popularity, yet, for all its beauty, few but students now read the story of Jenny and Peggy, who talk so delightfully amid the charming scenery of Hobby's Howe.

Despite this freedom, peace and gaiety, there were still strong elements of political and religious unrest in Scotland, which found vent in the frenzy of the Porteous Mob in Edinburgh, and in the Jacobite risings of 1745. A certain section of the clergy were still stultified by ideas so narrow that Ramsay's attempt to spread knowledge by means of a circulating library was banned, and when, in 1736, he built a theatre in Carruther's Close it was closed by the magistrates. But as Mr. James L. Caw says in his admirable volume, "Scottish Painting, Past and Present," "opposition could not withstand the quickening sense of life for ever. It only postponed the inevitable. Art had its share, a small one to be sure, in this little renaissance of the joy of life." As we have seen, Aikman was the most popular painter of his time in Edinburgh (1712-1723). At £10 each he painted the notable men and women of the Scottish capital. Among his most important achievements are the portrait of his cousin, Sir John Clerk in his robes as Baron of Exchequer, a bust of the Sixth Earl of Lauderdale, and the best likeness ever painted of Allan Ramsay, the poet. Aikman's own image, by himself, is in the Uffizi, Florence. Apart from a certain insight into character, his work has no suggestion of nationality. A year after Aikman settled in Edinburgh, there was born to the author of the "Gentle Shepherd" a son, that was destined to be the greatest of Scottish painters prior to Raeburn. The lad was named after his father, who encouraged him in his love of art. From his twelfth year young Allan studied drawing alone, or in the studios of friendly artists, for up to 1729 there was no school or academy of art in Edinburgh. At that period, however, interest in art had grown to such an extent that the "School of St. Luke," was inaugurated. But the movement was premature, and the school soon ceased to exist.

Young Ramsay, then in his sixteenth year, was one of the working members. When he was about twenty, he went to London and studied at St. Martin's Lane Academy under Hogarth, and later, in the studio of Hans Huyssing—a Swedish painter. His stay in London was brief. "The seat of the beast beyond the Alps," as the elder Ramsay called Rome, was the Mecca to which all artists of the period made a pilgrimage, and, in 1736, the young painter went to the Eternal City. If the French Academy, Solemina and Imperiale, did their best to denationalise his art and dwarf his personality, yet he acquired a considerable knowledge of drawing and painting, and on his return to Edinburgh in 1738, he, for eighteen years, easily held the first place as a portrait painter. A man of great refinement and culture, Ramsay mingled with the leading men of Scotland, and when, in 1756, he finally removed to London, his courtly manners and scholarly attainments, more than his art, won him favour with the king and queen and society generally. He was made portrait painter to the court in 1767, and after that date he seldom produced a portrait without the aid of his numerous assistants. Most of his fellow artists and contemporary critics thought but little of his work. Reynolds commended his sense, but not his art. Northcote thought his manner "dry and timid," though he and Walpole praised his portraits of women for their elegance. This quality, and his method of painting, are, unmistakably, of Gaelic origin.

The Fair Woman Exhibition at the Grafton Gallery last year included a very beautiful portrait of "Lady Susan Fox-Strangeways," which might have passed for the work of an Eighteenth Century French artist. His drawings also have much of the charm and grace that distinguish those of Watteau and Quentin Latour. Altogether, his art is now held in higher repute than it was in his lifetime. On the other hand, in contemporary literary circles, he was much esteemed. Voltaire and Rousseau were his friends. The latter's portrait by him hangs in the National Portrait Gallery of Scotland. Dr. Johnson says: "You will not find a man in whose conversation there is more instruction, more information, or more elegance, than in Ramsay's."

Ramsay had reached his forty-third year when Raeburn was born in 1756. At that date there was as yet no sign of any Scottish artist of individual force, of purely national expression. But the country was quickening æsthetically. "A blast o' Janwar wind blew hansel" on Robert Burns in 1759. Eleven years later came James Hogg, the "Ettrick Shepherd," who wrote "Bonnie Kilmeny," a poem of exquisite fancy; in the following year the triad was completed by the birth of Sir Walter Scott, so that in the course of sixteen years nature gave to Scotland four men, who were to raise that nation from obscurity to a place among the greatest in the hierarchy of literature and art.

It is interesting to note the character of these forms of artistic expression, the pictorial and the literary. Burns, Hogg and Scott, though they sang and wrote of eternal things, were, to a great extent, retrospective. They came, as it were, from the past, lest it should be forgotten. Their's were the voices long hushed by the silence enforced by repression and poverty which were "wearin' awa' like snaw wreaths" in a glorious thaw.

Imagination, fancy, romance, transfused the different phases of life they represented in song or story. It was otherwise with Raeburn. He had nothing immediate to do with the past, save to prepare for it by leaving something noble and enduring to the future. No painter ever had a better opportunity of fulfilling a destined purpose. In the course of his forty years of working life Scotland was in the forefront in Philosophy, Literature, Poetry, Science, Law and Commerce. The dawn had more than justified its promise. Scottish intellect won admiration all over the world. Strong minds were fortified by strong bodies, and it fell to Raeburn to commemorate the men and women of this mighty period. With the exception of Burns and Hogg, he painted from life the portraits of all the eminent Scotsmen of his generation, and, in the following pages, I shall attempt to show how nobly he performed his appointed task. But before passing to consider his life and work, it may be of interest to glance at the condition of art in England and on the Continent at the date of his birth.

We have seen how art stood in Scotland about the middle of the Eighteenth Century. Allan Ramsay was the one native artist of distinction —David Allan, Wilkie's precursor in genre painting, was twelve years old in 1756, and the only place where academic training could be obtained was at the school established in Glasgow in 1753 by the Brothers Foulis. The Trustees' Academy was not opened in Edinburgh until 1760.

Across the border, Hogarth had long since broken with the convention that denationalised English art, Joshua Reynolds had moved to Great Newport Street, and was so busy that he began to keep the diaries that are now so valuable; Gainsborough was preparing himself in Ipswich for the great achievements of later years. Watteau was dead, but his influence moved in the work of Fragonard; Latour and Perronneau were producing magnificent pastels of their fellow countrymen; Carle van Loo was rector of the Academie des Beaux Arts, Paris; Drouais was emulating Boucher and Nattier in painting the portraits of members of the court of Louis Quinze; Chardin, was immortalising the *petite bourgeoisie* and painting *natures mortes* with a breadth and veracity that excelled the work of the earlier Flemish and Dutch artists; while Greuze was delighting the heart of Diderot with his exposition of the melodramatic philosophy of the day in pictures like " Le Malediction Paternelle," and " Le Fils Puni."

Across the Alps, Longhi was giving to or receiving hints from Hogarth; Canale and Guardi were commemorating the glory of Venice; and Tiepolo was surpassing all decorators with his superb mural and easel paintings. But it was not they who dominated art in Italy. This power belonged to second-rate painters like Pompeo Battoni and Rafael Mengs, the art pontiffs of Rome, during many years. In Holland and Flanders, artists were trying to mix, shall I say, wine with the lees of Seventeenth Century Dutch and Flemish art, and Spain was waiting for the ten year old Goya to revive its artistic glory.

With one or two exceptions, the names of the foreign artists mentioned in this brief summary suggest that art on the continent had become anæmic in consequence of a period of artificial and cloying nourishment, and offered little inspiration to nascent genius. In England a healthier influence was apparent. The spirit of Rubens, Vandyck, Watteau and the Venetians (Velasquez was not yet recognised) was quickening the soul of Hogarth, Reynolds and Gainsborough. Scotland was still *retardataire*. The elements for the fructification of the artistic temperament were ready, when Raeburn came. They at once began to act on his genius, and their impulse never left him—he was greatest at the end of his life.

iod. With the exception of
■ portraits of all the eminent
wing pages, I shall attempt to
ted task. But before passing
of interest to glance at the
next at the date of his birth.
tland about the middle of the
e one native artist of distinction
xainting, was twelve years old in
ining could be obtained was at
by the Brothers Foulis. The
pargu until 1760.
nce broken with the convention
Reynolds had moved to Great
gan to keep the diaries that are
aring himself in Ipswich for the
:eau was dead, but his influence
and Perronneau were producing
nen; Carle van Loo was rector of
mi was emulating Boucher and
rs of the court of Louis Quinze;
poisie and painting *natures mortes*
the work of the earlier Flemish
ighting the heart of Diderot with
osophy of the day in pictures
■ Fils Puni."
ı or receiving hints from Hogarth;
the glory of Venice; and Tiepolo
arb mural and easel paintings. But
:. This power belonged to second-
Rafael Mengs, the art pontiffs of
ud Flanders, artists were trying to
Seventeenth Century Dutch and
the ten year old Goya to revive its

ies of the foreign artists mentioned
ı the continent had become anæmic
ud cloying nourishment, and offered
England a healthier influence was
ick, Watteau and the Venetians
■ quickening the soul of Hogarth,
mmm still *retardataire*. The elements
:rament were ready, when Raeburn
genius, and their impulse never left
ik.

THE earlier fami

On one occasion

" There, a relat

Morrison, in hi:

" On a ride wi

Raeburn, we ri

and from this i

other hand, W

describes it as a

Sir Walter Scot

the Scottish bor

from the Hill

himself " ▮▮

from a burn ▮

Motto : " ▮▮

different accou

on both sides

country ▮▮

brought peace

cultivating thei

1715, one of tl

charming ▮▮

time a suburb o

its closeness t

Edinburgh in ▮

. a very worthy

lady. Two ▮▮

born on the 4th

the elder was a

and continued l

of Eminent Sco

gave his brothe

Whatever Wi

was a pupil at

Christ's H▮▮

1765, we read t

by Sarah Sand

Henry, son of I

both dead."

" Jingling Geo

fairly successfi

—most boys ▮

4th of June,

CHAPTER I.

BIRTH AND EARLY DAYS.

THE earlier family history of Sir Henry Raeburn is more or less conjectural. On one occasion Sir Walter Scott, in referring to a field near Selkirk, said: "There, a relation of my own, a Scott of Raeburn, fought a dual," and Morrison, in his "Reminiscences," published in *Tait's Magazine*, says that "On a ride with Sir Walter Scott to call on his relation, Mr. Scott, of Raeburn, we visited the Eildon Tree." Sir Walter was then at Abbotsford, and from this it has been inferred that Raeburn was in Tweedale. On the other hand, William Raeburn Andrew, Sir Henry Raeburn's great grandson, describes it as a hill-farm in Annandale, still held, when he wrote in 1886, by Sir Walter Scott's family. There seems to be no doubt that this spot is on the Scottish borderland—the painter's forefathers probably taking their name from the Hill farm of Raeburn, hence the reason for Sir Henry styling himself " Raeburn of that ilk." On his shield is a rae of roe-deer drinking from a burn or stream at its feet. The crest is a roe's head, with the Motto: " Robur in Deo." His ancestors were, probably, bonnet-lairds. In different accounts we read of them as reivers, who raided their neighbours on both sides of the Border; and as soldiers of war who fought their country battles against the invading English, until the union of the crowns brought peace. Then they laid down the sword for the plough-share, cultivating their land in peace until, perhaps, about the troublous time of 1715, one of their number, Robert Raeburn, gave up pastoral life in the charming border country for milling or yarn boiling in Stockbridge, at that time a suburb of Edinburgh. That spot was probably chosen because of its closeness to the Water of Leith, and of the growing importance of Edinburgh in trade and commerce. Robert Raeburn, who, we are told, was a very worthy man, married Ann Elder, described as a tender, motherly lady. Two sons came of the marriage, William, born in 1744, and Henry, born on the 4th March, 1756. Unfortunately, they were left orphans when the elder was a lad of sixteen or seventeen, but he had real Scottish grit and continued his father's business. In Chamber's Biographical "Dictionary of Eminent Scotsmen " it is stated that William, with heartfelt satisfaction, gave his brother Henry " the scanty, but usual, education of the period." Whatever William did for his younger brother, it is certain that Henry was a pupil at Heriot's Hospital, an institution similar in character to Christ's Hospital. In the minutes of the hospital board, dated 15th April, 1765, we read that a presentation was laid before the Governors, " granted by Sarah Sandilands, relict of Thomas Durham, of Boghead, in favour of Henry, son of Robert Raeburn, Burgess and Freeman, whose parents are both dead." At this institution, founded by George Heriot (Scott's " Jingling Geordie ") the famous goldsmith, young Raeburn's career was fairly successful. He was fond of drawing figures on his slate or copybook —most boys are—but he did not neglect his ordinary studies, for, on the 4th of June, 1770, Henry Raeburn and Francis Ronaldson were each awarded for their skill in writing, etc., the sum of one pound, five shillings sterling accruing from Dean of Guild Heriot's Mortification. In the following year Henry was again considered best entitled to a similar reward. It was at this period that he is supposed to have left school and was apprenticed to Mr. Gilliland, the goldsmith, whose shop was located in a dark close in the Luckenbooths, near by St. Giles's Church.

The craft of the goldsmith in Scotland is of old date. As early as 1457 the maker's mark identified pieces of Edinburgh origin; from 1457 to 1681 the standard mark was formed of the deacon's initials; the assay master's from 1681 to 1759, which was then superseded by the thistle, "the town mark of a castle" from 1483, the date letter from 1681-2, and the duty mark of the Sovereigns' heads from 1784, as in England. Cripps gives a long list of Edinburgh deacons' names from 1525 to 1682, which shows that the art was practised without a break throughout the Reformation and revolutionary epochs. Many of the objects produced, were, unfortunately, destroyed in troublous times, but there is still much old Scottish silver in existence, but owners will not part with it, except at enormous prices. Recently, a piece of Tudor, or Sixteenth Century date, passed to a Scottish collection at £5,000, while the following account of a sale of a "Quaigh," which appeared in the *Morning Post* of March 25th, 1909, also gives an idea of the value of old Scots silverwork:

> "'The linguists were much concerned yesterday at Christie's,' says the chronicler. 'A Scotch Quaigh' was announced for sale. The Cataloguer's knowledge of the value of this vessel was revealed in the 'small caps.' heading, and the only person who reached near to the correct pronunciation of the word was Mr. Anderson (a Scot). The vessel is synonymous with the Gaelic cuach, the old Irish cuach, the Greek kavka the Welsh cawg, and probably the latin caucus, and is, in reality, a drinking cup which in earlier, times, was made of wooden staves. Hence the radiating lines which characterise the bowl in question. Sir John Fowlis mentions a quech weighing '18 ounces and 10 drops'; in 'Marmion' we read the 'quaighs were deep, the liquor strong'; Mrs. Carlyle wrote in 1849 that 'in passing a cooper's shop . . . . I stept in and bought two little quaighs'; while Queen Victoria, in ' More Leaves,' refers to 'a silver quaigh out of which Prince Charles Edward drank.' The quaigh is otherwise familiar in literature. For instance, Smollett, in ' Humphrey Clinker' says 'the spirits were drunk out of a silver quaff.'
>
> "This introduction is necessary to the report of the sale at Christie's of a silver quaigh weighing 14 oz. 12 dwt., and bearing the Glasgow hall mark of 1665. The maker was probably modest Thomas Moncurr, and the cup may well be the first piece of silver plate emanating from the Western Scottish Metropolis. Certainly, there is no larger nor earlier piece known. Mr. Holms, of Paisley, has a smaller and later quaigh, and others still smaller have been sold. The cup purchased yesterday by Messrs. Crichton at £28 an ounce may, therefore, be considered 'unique.' The design is simple—conventional thistles, roses, flowers, etc.—the silver of the purest, and its quality and ornament indicates its Carlovian origin. It measures 7·⅝ in. diameter of bowl by 11¼ in. wide. The maker's mark is T.M., with crown above, pellet between, and heart below in shaped shield, twice repeated. On the lip the following letters are engraved: 'M.R.S.C.L.' The exact price may be given, £408 16s. (560s. per oz.)."

This reference to old silver will show that young Raeburn, in selecting a trade or craft of great historic importance in Scotland, was emulating the sculptors of the Italian Renaissance, Donatello, Verrochio, and Cellini to name but three who were famous goldsmiths. Gainsborough, also, began life in London as a gold or silversmith, and the practice was of considerable service to him, as it must have been to Raeburn, in developing his sense of design and sureness of hand and eye. Apart from this impetus, the Scot had, in all likelihood, an opportunity of seeing in Gilliland's shop specimens of pictorial art in the shape of miniatures which came to be set in gold or silver. At any rate, we know that it was in "painting in little" that his genius first found expression. There is no evidence to show where he received his early training in draughtsmanship. While still at Heriot's he may have spent some of his spare hours at the Trustees' Academy, under the direction of Delacour (an imitator of Watteau) and Pavillon, and, during his apprenticeship, Alexander Runciman, then Director of the Academy, may have given him advice. Wherever he was taught he seems early to have acquired a certain facility and sureness of drawing which grew speedily to maturity. There is some proof of this in "A Tribute to the memory of Sir Henry Raeburn," made in a speech by Dr. Andrew Duncan, shortly after the painter's death. Charles Darwin, a son of Dr. Erasmus Darwin, author of the "Botanic Garden," a now forgotten poem, and uncle of Charles Robert Darwin, of natural history fame, was a pupil in the medical class of Dr. Duncan. In the dissecting room the student contracted blood-poisoning and died, it is supposed, about 1778, when he was twenty years old.

"On the death of young Darwin," says Dr. Duncan, "I was anxious to retain some slight token in remembrance of my highly-esteemed young friend, and, for that purpose, I obtained a small portion of his hair. I applied to Mr. Gilliland to have it preserved in a mourning ring. He told me that one of his present apprentices was a young man of great genius, and could prepare for me in hair a memorial that would demonstrate both taste and art. Young Raeburn was immediately called, and proposed to execute on a small trinket, which might be hung at a watch, a muse weeping over an urn, marked with the initials of Charles Darwin. The trinket was finished by Raeburn in a manner which, to me, afforded manifest proof of very superior genius, and I still preserve it as a memorial of the singular and early merit both of Darwin and Raeburn." If Dr. Duncan's story may be accepted, then Raeburn was twenty-two years of age at the time this commission was executed, and still an apprentice to Gilliland. Mr. James L. Caw, on the authority of Miss Deuchar, avers that her Great-Great-Grandfather, David Deuchar, who was a seal engraver and etcher, called to see Raeburn's master not long after the apprenticeship had begun, and found the youth drawing a portrait of himself. Deuchar, seeing signs of promise in the sketch, and finding that Raeburn had not received any training, offered to give him an hour's teaching after business hours, once or twice a week. The offer was accepted, and, before long, it was apparent to Deuchar that the lad's talent lay in the direction of portrait painting. On the strength of this conviction he spoke to "the mild and worthy" Gilliland, and the result of the consultation was that Raeburn and David Martin (1737-98), the leading portrait painter in Scotland, were introduced. There is some confusion about these statements. Martin did not settle in Edinburgh until 1775, so that Raeburn had been at least three years with Gilliland previous to his meeting with Martin. By that time the lad had painted many miniatures, among them those of Deuchar and Dr. Andrew Wood, the former, if mechanical, having a certain sense of character expressed with considerable decision, while the latter, evidently the later of the two, shows a distinct advance in colour and freedom of modelling. An admirable miniature was lately acquired by Mr. J. L. Caw for his own collection, which he is fully justified in believing to be an early work by Raeburn, executed during his apprenticeship with Gilliland, the silversmith, It resembles in every way his authenic "paintings in little" of that period. The eyes, in particular, have a vivacity of expression unusual in the work of his contemporaries, and the modelling shows keen observation and considerable knowledge of structure. Raeburn and Martin soon separated, jealousy on the part of the elder man being hinted at as the cause of the severance. Martin was an indifferent painter, whose style was formed on that of Ramsay, in whose London factory he assisted his master to produce puppet-like copies of the effigies of the King and Queen and their courtiers. Martin, aware of his own weakness and the lad's fresh outlook and individual expression, seemingly did everything to prevent him from acquiring any knowledge of his profession. He lent him pictures to copy, but gave him no technical advice. He had to discover everything for himself ; how to prepare his colours, place them on his palette, and, as Cunningham says, to apply them "according to the rules of art as taught in the academies . . . . Raeburn had to make experiments, and drudge to acquire what belongs to the mechanical labour and not to the Genius of Art." But all this drudgery was a blessing in disguise. For had Martin revealed to the youth what he considered to be the masonic secrets of the artistic profession it might have taken Raeburn a long time, despite his originality, to free his genius from the trammels of a cart-horse convention. So that Raeburn acted wisely in leaving Martin when the latter accused him of selling a copy of a picture which he, Raeburn, had made. Martin's resentment, it is stated, did not diminish after they parted, for when Raeburn returned from the eternal city in 1787, Martin remarked that " the lad in George Street painted better before he went to Rome." I am inclined to doubt this saying chiefly on the score that Raeburn was no longer a lad at this period, he having reached his thirty-first year, and been married some nine years. The story may be set down as merely a repetition of what Hudson said to Reynolds : " By G—, Reynolds, you don't paint so well as when you left England." Whatever feeling actuated Martin, Raeburn, in later life, spoke of his kindness at their first meeting and with approval of his portraits, which Cunningham says were to Raeburn what the Verses of Fergusson were to Burns, and the result was not dissimilar." The comparison is good, though it must be added that Fergusson was a far finer artist in words than was Martin in paint. The contact with Martin evidently affected Raeburn in one very important way. It gave him the impetus to break with the confinement of miniature for the breadth and force of painting on a life-size canvas. In the year following his probable meeting with Martin, Raeburn produced in 1776 his portrait of George Chambers, of Pittencrief, now the property of Dunfermline Town Council, a remarkable work for a youth of twenty who had no academic training that we know of, and whose eye and hand had been but lately limited to the space of a few inches of ivory or card.

The story that Raeburn was hard up in his youth is somewhat apocryphal. He was an orphan, but from the time he left school he began to earn money, and we may suppose that his brother William was reaping a fair reward for his labours in the yarn-boiling business, and that, if necessary,

by Mr. J. L. Caw for his own
believing to be an early work by
⬛ with Gilliland, the silversmith,
paintings in little" of that period,
expression unusual in the work of
▮rs keen observation and consider-
⬛ Martin soon separ²ted, jealousy
at as the cause of the severance.
▬▬ style was formed on that of
assisted his master to produce
▬g and Queen and their courtiers.
⬛ the lad's fresh outlook and
▬▬▬g to prevent him from acquir-
▮ent him pictures to copy, but gave
▬er everyth'ng for himself; how to
▬tte, and, as Cunningham says, to
▮ art as taught in the academies
▬▬ts, and drudge to acquire what
⬛ to the Genius of Art." But all

For had Martin revealed to the
masonic secrets of the artistic
▮ a long time, despite his originality,
▮ of a cart-horse convention. So
▮ Martin when the latter accused
▮ which he, Raeburn, had made.
▬t diminish after they parted, for
⬛ city in 1787, Martin remarked that
▮ before he went to Rome." I am
⬛ the score that Raeburn was no
▬ched his thirty-first year, and been
▬y be set down as merely a repetition
▮y G—, Reynolds, you don't paint so
▬hatever feeling actuated Martin,
▬ees at their first meeting and with
▬am says were to Raeburn what the
⬛ the result was not dissimilar." The
▬ded that Fergusson was a far finer
⬛ The contact with Martin evidently
▮ way. It gave him the impetus to
▮ for the breadth and force of paint-
▮ following his probable meeting with
▬s portrait of George Chambers, of
▬rmline Town Council, a remarkable
▮ academic training that we know of,
▬tely limited to the space of a few

⬛ up in his youth is somewhat
▬▬ the time he left school he began
▬ his brother William was reaping a
▬▬▬g business, and that, if necessary,

he would share his ■
economy had to be α
paint or canvas wa■
question is told by C
fact. Raeburn bec■
afterwards known ■
wit. Both were the
Clerk, of Eldin, and
may be that Clerk
regulation allowance
shortage he invited
Raeburn arrived, :
placing on the tabl
other, three potatoes

"Is this a'" ?

"Ay," she qu■

"A'," he ■■■■■
a gentleman was ■
potatoes?"

Humble fare. I
those days. "The
sumptuously on r
quarters, where ■
members of the "!
a "groat and a ha■
marrow bones in I
imposed" on the ■

The social ■■■
the excess of freed
earlier years its li
"fashionable to ;
Sunday was ■■■
disgraceful to be ■
chronicler relates :
Rome, "attendan■
relaxation; fram
with them; the ■
evenings they are .
disused; and it ■
number the Rev. J
the old playhouse ■
zealots drove him
the "cave of the
Post Office the ■
graphic phrases I
period. It was be
and good fellowshi;
drink."

he would share his fortune, however small, to help young Henry. No doubt, economy had to be considered, but the want of a meal or money to buy paint or canvas was not the lot of Raeburn. A story bearing on this question is told by Cunningham, whose fiction is frequently not founded on fact. Raeburn became acquainted with a young advocate, John Clerk, afterwards known as Lord Eldin, who was famous as a lawyer, cynic and wit. Both were then poor, the gossip goes, though Clerk was a son of John Clerk, of Eldin, and grandson of Sir John Clerk, of Penicuik. The truth may be that Clerk was a young spendthrift and soon exhausted his regulation allowance of pocket money. On one of the occasions of financial shortage he invited the artist to dine with him at his lodgings. When Raeburn arrived, no doubt, feeling very hungry, the landlady was placing on the table two plates; on one were three herrings, on the other, three potatoes.

"Is this a'"? cried Clerk in anger.

"Ay," she quietly replied, "it's a'"!

"A'," he answered, with emphasis, "didn't I tell you, wumman, that a gentleman was to dine wi' me, and that ye were to get six herrin' and six potatoes?"

Humble fare, like this, was not uncommon even among the well-to-do of those days. "They knew how to combine thrift and pleasure. They supped sumptuously on rizzered haddies, or sheep-head and trotters in lowly quarters, where they could themselves keep an eye on the cooking." The members of the "Spendthrift Club" were debarred from paying more than a "groat and a half" on supper. The "Marrow Bones Club" feasted on marrow bones in the belief that "a large quantity of drink could be super-imposed" on the top of that savoury dish.

The social habits of Edinburgh in Raeburn's day were characterised by the excess of freedom that comes after a long period of repression. In his earlier years its life was, to a great extent, still decorous. In 1763 it was "fashionable to go to church, and people were interested in religion. Sunday was observed strictly by all ranks as a day of devotion; it was disgraceful to be seen in the streets during the time of worship." The same chronicler relates that twenty years later, two years before Raeburn went to Rome, "attendance at church is much neglected; Sunday is made a day of relaxation; families think it ungenteel to take their domestics to church with them; the streets are often crowded in the time of worship, and in the evenings they are often loose and riotous. Family worship is almost totally disused; and it is even wearing out among the clergy." One of the number the Rev. John Home wrote a play "Douglas" which was acted in the old playhouse in the Canongate amid the applause of other ministers. The zealots drove him from his kirk, but in a brief time on the north side of the "cave of the winds" there rose on the site of the present General Post Office the first regularly licensed theatre in Edinburgh. In a few graphic phrases Henley sums up the Scottish Capital of the latter period. It was he says "a centre of conviviality—a city of clubs and talk and oo fellowship—a city of harlotry and high jinks—a city above all, of drink." d

"Whare Couthie chiels at e'enin' meet
Their hizzin' craigs and mous to weet."

If the moral, social and intellectual life of Edinburgh was changing, the physical aspects of the city also were beginning to move with the mutability of human progress. The population of the Scottish capital was outgrowing the space of the romantic ridge running from the castle to Holyrood. At the date of Raeburn's birth, it was no longer necessary for strategic reasons to confine Edinburgh to the limits of this picturesque barrier that still stretches between the Border and the Highlands. The wealthy classes grew tired of climbing up tortuous flights of dark stairs to dingy small rooms in lofty tenements, "where they could shake hands with their neighbours on the other side of the close." It was not uncommon in those days for all the members of a well-to-do family to sleep in the same chamber, the children with their nurse occupying beds which were laid down each night on the floor while the house-maid slept on the bottom of the kitchen dresser, and if there was a man-servant he had to find apartments elsewhere. The nobility, gentry and the thriving merchants, the ladies of rank, and the wives of tradesmen were no longer content with these uncomfortable conditions. Peace opened the way to the expansion of social ambition, and individual independence. Prosperity supplied the gold to vault ambition and gild independence. This imposing "temple of the winds," with its long dirty alleys, had served its day. It had played a great part in Scottish history. Feud and foray were ended; English invaders no longer stormed the "high altar" of the Temple, the last enemies of freedom, the "unco guid" of the kirk were diminishing. The city might now with safety break down its northern ramparts. The time was past:

> " How when a mountain chief his bugle blew,
> Both field and forest, dingle, cliff and dell,
> And solitary heath the signal knew."

The swamp of the Nor' Loch could now be filled up. Zealots and heretics, witches and gipsies were no longer drowned in its marshy wilderness of water. Instead of a means of defence it was an offence, a "pest bed," that must be cleaned. But it took a long stretch of years to effect this purpose. As late as 1816 there remained a portion of the Nor' Loch which was described by Lord Cockburn as a filthy impassable swamp, "the receptacle of many sewers and seemingly of all the worried cats, the drowned dogs and blackguardism of the city."

The foundation of the magnificent Edinburgh of to-day was laid about 1765, when Raeburn was nine years old. On a plan of the city of that period, says Mr. John Geddie in his excellent "Romantic Edinburgh," there is traced at the bottom of that "hollow of the winds" which divided what is now known as the New Town from the Old, the solitary pier of a bridge. "It is the footprint of Old Edinburgh setting out for fresh woods and pastures new.

But it took seven years to complete the spanning of the newly reclaimed and unstable soil. On the north side there were then but few buildings on the bare land, and the scanty population consisted chiefly of wastrels, the flotsam and jetsam of life—poachers and smugglers, linkboys and beggars who made the neighbourhood not altogether safe, at night time in particular. By-and-bye, however, the new town grew—a new town that bore no resemblance to the old pile opposite. The architecture of Greece and Rome was imitated. Domes shot up triumphantly to the sky, Corinthian columns stood erect and proud as if mocking the decrepit tenements on the hill, and huge, dull Georgian houses were built for the big folks who came crowding across the North Bridge leaving "auld Reekie" to its poverty and squalor. Certain members of the aristocracy, gentry and the learned classes were "sweer" to flit from their old homes and haunts. They were loath to forsake the laughter and jest, the convivial clubs and the drinking "howffs" for the snug rectitude of Hanoverian Edinburgh. In time, like sheep, they followed the lead. Lord and lady, lawyer and philosopher, famous doctor and historian and literary men flocked to the more spacious if less inspiring pens of the New Town. Had it not been for men of taste like Lord Cockburn and Henry Mackenzie, the "man of feeling," the Edinburgh—that is, the Princes Street of to-day, would have borne a far different aspect. They protested against the erection of a large block of buildings on whose site now towers a huge railway hotel despite spirited opposition. From this point westward, however, Princes Street has been saved from the vandals. The glorious view to the south will remain for all time. The "Poem of Princes Street," as Alexander Smith called it will continue to move in its present noble rhythm, now joyous with sunshine, now moist with wind-driven rain, or grey with the "haar" trailing ghost-like from the north sea. "The puppets of the busy and many-coloured hour," will continue to flaunt the fine clothes and gaze across the ravine, where "time has piled the Old Town ridge on ridge, grey as a rocky coast, washed and worn by the foam of centuries; peaked and jagged by gable and roof; windowed from basement to cope; the whole surmounted by St. Giles's airy crown. The new is there looking to the old. Two times are brought face to face, and are yet separated by a thousand years."

I wonder why this city "half as old as time," this "Poem of Princes Street," has never inspired a landscape painter as the great men of Raeburn's day inspired him. Many have tried to represent the old and the new, but of all artists who have made the attempt in paint, none has been so deeply endowed with the historic sense, the spirit of age and romance as Sir George Reid. He is a worthy successor to Raeburn, as a realistic painter of strong, intellectual Scotsman, but in landscape his art is all emotion and his finest efforts are his illustrations to Mrs. Oliphant's "Royal Edinburgh." No one has given a better pictorial translation of Sir Walter Scott's description of Edinburgh in "Guy Mannering," than has Sir George Reid in his drawing "St. Giles from Princes Street." Here we have the suggestion of eternally changing bustle : A spectacle which, though composed of the most vulgar materials, when they are separately considered, has a striking and powerful effect on the imagination. In this beautiful picture we see the extraordinary height of the houses marked by lights which glimmer irregularly along their front, ascending high among the attics and seeming at length to twinkle in the middle sky. Some day, perhaps, a great Scots landscape painter will come—a Turner not a Canaletto—and do in paint what Sir George Reid has achieved in monochrome.

CHAPTER II.

GOOD fortune came to Raeburn on his marriage to a wealthy widow. Allan Cunningham with his usual leaning to romance tells a story of Raeburn's first meeting with his future wife that is almost similar to the tale he told about Gainsborough's courtship. The young Scots artist was out in a wood one day sketching when he saw a charming lady whose figure he introduced into his picture. Whether she was conscious of this honour to her beauty we are not assured. At any rate not long after this alleged incident a little lady of demure and winsome appearance called at Raeburn's studio and asked if he would paint her portrait. He remembered the face, became interested and no doubt was more courteous than usual. The commission was accepted with pleasure, the sitting began at once. While the artist painted his visitor watched his dark eyes and handsome face grow animated as the work proceeded. He noted perhaps, that his visitor was no longer a girl—she was indeed twelve years older than himself. But she looked very pleasant, her soft dark eyes had a certain allure, her full yet graceful figure appealed to his sense of form. With each sitting the artist and his model unconsciously opened out to the other's attraction and in the end, within the short period of a month the pair were married. Thus at twenty-two Raeburn, says Cunningham, had won " an affectionate wife and a handsome dowry " which was quite true, but the manner of their meeting and courtship, as Fulcher showed in the case of the Gainsborough story, was more prosaic in character. The lady who became his wife lived in Deanhaugh House which stood so close to his own residence, that the artist and his future spouse must have known each other. He must have been aware that she was a widow of the name of Leslie; his local fame had surely reached her long before their marriage. She was Ann Edgar, daughter of Peter Edgar, Laird of Bridgelands, Peebles-shire, and factor to the Earl of Selkirk. About 1768 she married James Leslie of Balquhun, who, while abroad, was created a Count. At his death she was left with a boy, who was accidentally drowned, two girls and considerable property. Raeburn was a shrewd practical person but too sincere and manly to have jumped at a *marriage de convenance*; his sensitive temperament would have rebelled at the idea of binding himself for life to a widow twelve years older than himself with two children, in order to gain some worldly pelf. At the time of his marriage he must have been earning more than enough to keep himself, while consciousness of his growing artistic power would strengthen his spirit of independence. I believe, therefore, that the marriage was a real love match and their after life fully justifies this faith. Raeburn's great grandson, Mr. Andrew, says that the artist " fell in love with his sitter and made a very fine portrait of her." Nothing is known of this portrait, the only certain likeness of her being the magnificent canvas which brought 8,000 guineas in the Tweedmouth sale at Christie's in 1905. This picture, now the property of Sir Ernest Cassel, represents her as a

typically Scots
quiet, intense, y
and in the tende
Ferrier, eldest
professor P
account of the

"More
childhood at
was in those
was reached
where we lived
old house was
pear trees, and
part of which
the right of this
houses.

"In this
very intimate
some years bet
and his wife w
The great
impressive app
dark hair, at
well remember
the small
him. His
while he held
your opinion
with consternat
vainly attempti
what delight
tea-table,
place of securi
which Sir H
play to
managed to di
and always
extinct. I ca
tormented
had fled for
inventions at
bed-pillows at
she would
it a magnifice
with these w
ye; no' g
any mair.'
at the least
throw out
colours, in

typically Scots lady of forty-five. The face is strong but kindly, with a quiet, intense, yet motherly passion working in the full well-formed mouth and in the tender honest eyes. Their life was ideal in its happiness. Mrs. Ferrier, eldest daughter of "Christopher North," and then widow of professor Ferrier, of St. Andrews, gave Dr. John Brown a most delightful account of the Raeburn family at St. Bernard's House.

"More than half a Century ago" she says "I was frequently in my childhood at St. Bernard's House, on the banks of the water of Leith, which was in those days green and smooth to the river's edge. This old house was reached by a broad avenue of trees and shrubbery from Ann Street, where we lived for some years; this would be about 1820. This interesting old house was surrounded by large green fields, a fine orchard of apple and pear trees, and leading from this was another avenue of old stately elms, part of which still remains with the rookery in St. Bernard's crescent. On the right of this avenue was a nice old garden, well stocked and with hot-houses.

"In this ancient mansion lived the Raeburn family, with whom we were very intimate as children likewise. School companions, though there were some years between our ages. Sir Henry and Lady Raeburn, and their son and his wife with three children, comprised the family party at this time. The great portrait-painter, as far as I can recollect him, had a very impressive appearance, his full, dark, lustrous eyes, with ample brow and dark hair, at this time scant. His tall frame had a dignified aspect. I can well remember him, seated in an armchair in the evening, at the fireside of the small drawing room, newspaper in his hand, with his family around him. His usual mode of address to us when we were spending the evenings, while he held out his hand with a kind smile, was 'well my dears, what is your opinion of things in general to-day?' These words always filled us with consternation, and we all huddled together like a flock of scared sheep, vainly attempting some answer by gazing from one to the other; and with what delight and sense of freedom we were led away to be seated at the tea-table, covered with cookies, bread and butter and jelly! From this place of security we stole now and then a fearful glance at the armchair in which Sir Henry reclined. After tea we were permitted to go away for play to another room, we made as much noise as we liked, and generally managed to disturb old Lady Raeburn. This old lady was quite a character, and always spoke in broad Scotch; then common among the old families, now extinct. I can never forget the manner in which we uproarous creatures tormented her, flinging open the door of her snug little room, whither she had fled for a little quiet from our incessant provocations and unwearied inventions at amusement, which usually reached the climax by throwing bed-pillows at her and nearly smothering her small figure. At this juncture she would rise up, and, opening the door of a cupboard, would bring out of it a magnificent bunch of grapes which she endeavoured to divide among us with these words of entreaty, 'Hoot, hoot, bairns, here's some grapes for ye; no' gang awa' an' behave yersels, like gude bairns, and dinna deave me any mair.' For a short time the remedy effected a lull in the storm, which, at the least hint, was ready to set in with renewed vigour. She would then throw out of a wardrobe shawls, turbans, bonnets, and gear of all sorts and colours, in which we arranged ourselves to hold our court, Anne Raeburn, being very often our queen." Miss Ferrier continuing her narrative gives a graphic description of a "Cuddy Headrigg" sort of a man who was fed and supported by the family. His name was Barclay, but he was familiarly known as "Shelley" because his chief duty was the shelling of peas. This old half-witted creature was short of stature and of most miserable aspect. On his head an old grey hat crushed over his face, which was grizzly with unshaven beard. He wore a long-tailed coat, probably one of Sir Henry's, and always had a long stick in his hand.

We wished to be very familiar with him, but were never at our ease, owing to his strange appearance and his shuffling gait. He exercised a great fascination over us and we used to ask him to tell us stories, although he was nearly idiotic, "silly," to use a common Scotch phrase. He often said, as he turned round and pointed to the banks of the river, "Oo aye, bairns, I can well remember Adam and Eve skelpin' aboot naket amang the gowans on the braes there."

This picture is of Sir Henry's life near its close, but it represents his family environment throughout his career, from the time of his marriage, when he removed to Deanhaugh House, which belonged to the Leslie property, until his death at St. Bernard's in 1823. When Raeburn left Deanhaugh about 1809 Mrs. Ann Inglis, one of his step-daughters, whose husband died in India, occupied the house with her two boys Henry Raeburn Inglis and Charles James Leslie Inglis. The former who was deaf and dumb was the original of the artist's Royal Academy diploma picture, the "Boy and the Rabbit." By the time of their mother's death, the house had fallen on degenerate days. The rapid growth of Edinburgh spread houses all around it, and the mansion was divided into tenements. In this condition it remained for many years "as something that now had no right to be there," before it was "swept away to make room for the extension of Leslie Place."

The happy domestic conditions just described are perhaps more essential to painters—portrait painters, at least, than to poets who "learn in suffering what they teach in song," which is sweetest when it tells of "saddest thought." The portrait painter must assume happiness and seem fairly comfortable before he can hope to attract wealthy sitters. The ramshackle studio or leaky mansard in the clouds; the unkempt hair and shabby clothes may not interfere with the creation of great works of imagination, but lord this, or lady that, and the *nouveaux riches* prefer the comfort of pleasant well-furnished rooms when sitting for their portraits, and this Raeburn was now able to give. He made noble use of the fortune that came with his marriage. It spurred him to high endeavour, brought out the best qualities of his independent nature and enabled him to concentrate them in producing great portraits of great people. The early years of his married life must have been an ideal period for him both as a man and an artist. A perfect wife, splendid health, many friends and numerous commissions were his. What more could mortal desire? Ambition! That also inspired his heart and brain. Rome with its glorious traditions, its masterpieces, was ever in his mind. But with the caution of his race he waited until he was absolutely certain of himself, sure that nothing but the greatest art could influence him. Of the work actually achieved before he left for the Eternal City little is definitely known.

There are no dates on his portraits of that time to relieve the doubt. The " Chalmers of Pittencrieff" is the one canvas about which there is absolute certainty. It was painted in 1776, and shows an elderly man sitting in a chair by a window through which is seen a ruined abbey. The lighting of the figure is somewhat arbitrary. No light from the window touches the head, body or legs. The illumination comes from the opposite direction. This is a dangerous experiment, which was frequently employed by Raeburn in after days. In the " Mrs. Ferguson of Raith and children " (1780-81) a similar method of lighting is repeated. The mother and her boy and girl placed in a landscape, form a harmony limited to brown and white. " William Ferguson and his third son," " Major Buchanan " and " Robert Dundas of Arniston," are also accepted by some critics as having been painted before the Roman visit. Mr. James L. Caw, however, ascribes the Dundas picture to 1787, the year of the judge's death and of Raeburn's return to Edinburgh. These early works are chiefly remarkable for clear vision and direct painting, the precise well-considered touch that was to develop with such force and express character in bold deft masses of light and shade. There was yet little attempt at subtle modelling or at blocking out the planes of the face with almost sculptural relief. The colour is thin in substance and quality, the surface flat and void of artistic interest as might have been expected from one who had but recently, perhaps, still was working on the small space of a miniature. Their merit however, appealed to Sir Joshua Reynolds if we are to believe Cunningham. When in 1785 Raeburn and his wife stopped at London on their way to Rome, the Scot showed some of his portraits to Sir Joshua which at once won his favour. Raeburn " ever afterwards," says the biographer, mentioned the name of Sir Joshua with much respect—related how he counselled him to study at Rome, and worship Michael Angelo in the Sistine Chapel ; and how he took him aside, as they were about to separate, and whispered, " young man I know nothing about your circumstances ; young painters are seldom rich ; but if money be necessary for your studies abroad, say so, and you shall not want it." This generous offer Raeburn declined with due thanks. If this story is true it, to some extent, absolves Sir Joshua from the charge of parsimony and avarice that Cunningham elsewhere allows to pass without much enquiry or dismissal. It would be futile to discuss the Englishman's attitude to Raeburn on the strength of Allan's tale. We may be sure Sir Joshua was kind to Raeburn and would give him good advice. It is even quite probable that the great man allowed the young artist to work for some time in his studio. But of that there is no record. All we are sure of is that Reynolds and Raeburn met in London, and that the future work of the younger man betrays no sign of Sir Joshua's artistic influence. Of his residence and labour in Rome there is not more evidence. Goethe was in Rome at the time of Raeburn's visit, but if they ever met—it is quite possible they did—no reference to the fact was made by either the poet or the painter, although the former in his " letters from Italy " praises the mock-classic work of Raeburn's compatriot, Jacob More. Gavin Hamilton was another Scoto-Roman artist who had considerable vogue in the Eternal City. We are told he lived in grand style, "maintaining much of the dignity and state of the great old Italian masters," and that he helped to decorate Prince Borghese's villa. Raeburn made his acquaintance, but Hamilton's feeble art was of little value to the young student. Far greater service was rendered to Raeburn by James Byres, of Tonley, who advised him never to paint anything without having the object in front of him. Byres who was a man of strong character and refined taste, served as an officer in Lord Ogilviès regiment in the French army. In Rome he was known as the Cicerone, and Sir Walter Armstrong says, "his chief title to fame is the fact that he was once the owner of the Portland vase." But he had another and greater distinction. He inspired Raeburn to paint one of his greatest portraits of age—the "James Byres of Tonley," shown at the Raeburn exhibition in the French Gallery last winter.

We are entirely in the dark as to the nature of Raeburn's studies during his eighteen months stay in Rome. That he was not idle may be granted. Yet save for one portrait which I saw at the French Gallery some time ago, there is nothing I can point to as having been achieved in Rome. The picture in question was a likeness of a fresh looking lady of about forty, wearing a blue dress with a black shawl round her shoulders, one end of it thrown over her head. In my opinion this may be a portrait of Mrs. Raeburn painted in Rome in the style of Largilliere. The face has a resemblance to the face in Sir Ernest Cassel's picture of her, already referred to, and the colour of the flesh, and flat, shadowless treatment recall the "Mrs. Ferguson and her children," which has, however, greater vivacity. The dress and general arrangement do not suggest Raeburn. They are essentially French, and the only probable explanation of this curious pastiche is, that Raeburn may have visited the French Academy at Rome, and been impressed by some work there, and painted the canvas in question as a souvenir of his wife's visit to Rome, and the temporary influence of Largilliere. Of course, this is conjecture, but I feel certain that the face is unmistakably by Raeburn, and in no other portrait of his that I know are there similar costume, arrangement and colour. This hypothesis is the only new thing to be added to previous accounts of his sojourn in Rome, which ended in 1787.

■ was of little value to the young
■ to Raeburn by James Byres,
int anything without having the
a man of strong character and
Ogilvies regiment in the French
crone, and Sir Walter Armstrong
hat he was once the owner of the
greater distinction. He inspired
traits of age—the " James Byres
tion in the French Gallery last

the nature of Raeburn's studies
:. That he was not idle may be
■ I saw at the French Gallery
t to as having been achieved in
reness of a fresh looking lady of
black shawl round her shoulders,
my opinion this may be a portrait
style of Largilliere. The face has
t Cassel's picture of her, already
■ and flat, shadowless treatment
drea," which has, however, greater
nest do not suggest Raeburn. They
obable explanation of this curious
ed the French Academy at Rome,
, and painted the canvas in question
■ and the temporary influence of
■ but I feel certain that the face
other portrait of his that I know
and colour. This hypothesis is the
t accounts of his sojourn in Rome,

On his return
welcome, and
influence the
development of
David Martin
to him by Ca
contemporarie
in George Stre
from Rome. I
there in his thi
his time. The
the "big folk
whose older b
lingered in ▆
their wit and l

Raeburn's
first Edinburg
Street, in St. ▪
poet for a ▪▪
from there to :
the bookseller
second edition
that Burns "
James M'Leha
the poet and ▮
of Burns, ▆
sever." In ▆
immortalised
masonic meet
eulogistic not
Blair, Profes
Ferguson's ▮
ry Dugald S
'dignified pl
'I never saw
incredible th

But evi
Raeburn eve
Duchess of ▮
It must be n
in Novembe
painter was
the north.

CHAPTER III.

Portraits of Burns and Scott.

On his return to Edinburgh, Raeburn's old friends gave him a hearty welcome, and were anxious to know how he had fared in Rome; what influence the art and life of the Eternal City had exercised in the development of his talent. We have already seen what his former master David Martin is said to have thought in this respect. The opinion given to him by Cunningham mattered little then and less now, for Martin's contemporaries forsook him and crowded to Raeburn's newly opened studio in George Street and we know that he did paint better after he came back from Rome. In George Street and neighbourhood, when Raeburn settled there in his thirty-first year, were the houses of the most eminent men of his time. The Old Town had been almost abandoned as the residence of the "big folk" of the Scottish capital. Some of the more conservative, whose older blood was slower to respond to the impulse of the newer life, lingered in the lofty houses and brightened the clubs and dingy closes with their wit and laughter and rich hued costumes.

Raeburn's removal to George Street corresponds with the date of the first Edinburgh edition of Burn's Poems. It was in the vicinity of George Street, in St. James' Square, behind what is now the Royal Bank, that the poet for a time lodged with William Cruikshank. He made many errands from there to 5 George Street, the premises of Creech, in order to induce the bookseller to come to a definite settlement about the payment for the second edition of the "Poems." It was while staying in St. James' Square that Burns "spied" Clarinda, who had been deserted by her husband James M'Lehose. The long intimacy and inflated correspondence between the poet and this lady are well-known; their final severance by the marriage of Burns, produced one of his finest lyrics—"Ae fond kiss and then we sever." In Edinburgh Burns made the friendship of many of the men immortalised by Raeburn. He was introduced to Henry Erskine at a masonic meeting, Henry Mackenzie the "man of feeling" wrote a very eulogistic notice of his poems in the "Lounger," he was received by Robert Blair, Professor Gregory, Fraser Tytler and Adam Ferguson. It was at Ferguson's house that Walter Scott, then a lad of sixteen, brought thither by Dugald Stewart, saw Burns and he afterwards spoke of the poet's "dignified plainness and simplicity" of his eyes which "literally glowed." "I never saw such another eye in any human head," said Scott. It seems incredible that Burns and Raeburn never met.

But evidently they never shook each other by the hand, nor did Raeburn ever see the eloquent eyes, the great personality that carried the Duchess of Gordon "off her feet." Why they never met we cannot explain. It must be remembered, however, that when Burns first went to Edinburgh in November, 1786, Raeburn was in Rome, and about the time when the painter was settling in his George Street studio, the poet was touring in the north. Yet the pair must have been living near to each other in

Edinburgh for a considerable period; the same people were their friends and surely Raeburn would be eager to paint the expressive face of Burns. But one thing is certain. Raeburn never painted a portrait of Burns from life as some people have thought. Of this statement there is ample proof in a series of letters from Raeburn to Cadell and Davies, the London publishers, which is now the property of Mr. C. Fairfax Murray. Alexander Nasmyth painted three portraits of Burns. The original is in the National Portrait Gallery of Scotland. The one painted for George Thomson is in the National Portrait Gallery, where it is catalogued as having been painted by Nasmyth and retouched by Raeburn. But there is no authority for this statement.

Here are the letters referred to and they seem fully to prove that Burns and Raeburn never met:—

(1)

HENRY RAEBURN TO CADELL AND DAVIES.

EDINBURGH, 14*th*, *November*, 1803.

GENTLEMEN,

According to your order transmitted to me by Mr. Cunningham, I have finished a copy of Burns the poet, from the original portrait painted by Mr. Nasmyth. I have shown it to Mr. Cunningham, who thinks it very like him, and I hope it will also meet with your approbation. I am ready to send it whenever you please to order me.

Smacks leave this for London twice a week. I have frequently sent pictures by that mode of conveyance, and they always went safe.

I am, Gentlemen,
Your most obedient Servant,
(Signed) HENRY RAEBURN.

(2)

YORK PLACE, EDINBURGH,
1*st*, *December*, 1803.

GENTLEMEN,

I enclose you a receipt for a case containing Burns's portrait, and I have no doubt you will get it soon and safe; and I flatter myself with the hope of its meeting with your approbation, than which, I assure you, nothing will give me more pleasure.

I have twenty guineas for a portrait the size of Burns. I do not wish you to remit the money to me, for, as I have money to pay in London, I shall, after receiving your permission, draw upon you for the amount.

I am, with much respect, Gentlemen,
Your most obedient Servant,
(Signed) HENRY RAEBURN.

(3)

EDINBURGH, 22*nd*, *February*, 1804.

GENTLEMEN,

Nothing could be more gratifying to me than the approbation you expressed of the copy I made for you of Robert Burns.

I hope you will be equally pleased with the portrait I now send you by the orders of Mr. Henry MacKenzie. It is shipped on board the " Glasgow," William Liburn, master, and I have no doubt you will receive it safe.

I am, respectfully, Gentlemen,
Your most obedient Servant,
(Signed) HENRY RAEBURN.

When Burns was in Edinburgh, Sir Walter Scott was a boy of fifteen or sixteen, and, though it is not recorded in Lockhart's " Life," Raeburn it appears painted Scott's portrait about this time. Mr. W. Roberts in an article on the "Portraits of Sir Walter Scott" in *Chambers' Journal* last January, refers to the subject:—

"As Sir Henry Raeburn was fifteen years older than Scott, it is quite possible that he may have painted the latter 'as a youth'; but there is no record of this in Lockhart, and any such portrait must be accepted with reservation. There is, however, such a portrait in existence; it was in the W. Russell sale of 1863, and was bought in at three pounds five shillings, for it reappeared in the same collector's sale in 1884, when it advanced to one hundred and fifty guineas; and once more in Lord Tweedmouth's sale, June 3rd, 1905, when it brought one thousand guineas. In the catalogue it is stated to have been formerly in the possession of the poet Campbell. This portrait (29 in. by 24 in.) shows Scott as a young man in brown coat, with pink vest and white stock. In a sale held on May 8th, 1897, there was another portrait by Raeburn of Scott 'when a boy in Highland costume' (30 in. by 28 in.), which realised one hundred and fifteen guineas." The Tweedmouth portrait which was certainly by Raeburn, had a strong resemblance to Scott; the Highland costume portrait I never saw.

The properly authentic portraits of Scott by Raeburn may here be considered, though they take us a long way out of a chronological record of the artist's work. In Mr. James L. Caw's list he gives six portraits. These are the Tweedmouth portrait, the Buccleugh, the Maxwell Scott, the Earl of Howe, the Arthur Sanderson and the replica which belonged to the late Baroness Burdett Coutts. The Buccleugh portrait was painted in 1808 for Constable, the publisher. Scott is shown at full length seated on a ruined wall with his English bull-terrier "Camp" at his feet. In the distance are Hermitage Castle and the Liddesdale hills. He is dressed in black and wears Hessian boots. It will be recalled that on the day of "Camp's" death Sir Walter wrote that he could not dine out because "a very dear friend" had died. This "noble portrait" as Lockhart calls it also won praise from Dr. John Brown who asks if there was ever "a more poetic portrait of a poet." Further testimony to the truth of the likeness is afforded by Mr. J. B. S. Morritt, of Rokeby Hall, where the discredited "Venus" came from. Scott was a great friend of Morritt, and frequently visited the latter at his English home. "His person" says Morritt, "at the time may be exactly known from Raeburn's picture, which had just been executed for his bookseller, Constable, and which was a most faithful likeness of him and his dog 'Camp.' The literal fidelity of the portraiture, however, is its principal merit. The expression is serious and contemplative, very unlike the hilarity and vivacity, then habitual to his speaking face, but quite true to what it was in absence of such excitement. His features struck me at first as commonplace and heavy, but they were almost always lighted up by the flashes of the mind within."

On the 12th January, 1809, Scott wrote to the Constables, expressing a wish that the portrait should be his own, and that the expense of the picture and any engraving of it should be borne by him. The portrait was engraved by C. Turner, in 1810, and the following announcement of the projected mezzotint appeared in the *Gentlemen's Magazine*, December, 1809.

"Mr. Gromek will shortly publish a whole length portrait of Sir Walter Scott, from the admired picture painted by Raeburn, for Constable of Edinburgh, which appeared in the last exhibition of Scottish paintings. The Print will be 20 × 24."

This note shows that the portrait was exhibited a second time—it appeared in the Royal Academy, in 1810.

In 1809, Raeburn again painted a full length portrait of Scott, which has a curious history. Mr. David Douglas, editor and publisher of that most noble and pathetic of all human documents, Scott's *Journal*, says that at the time of Scott's Novelist's financial troubles, the picture was placed in the keeping of Mr. James Skene, of Rubislaw. "Mr. Skene tells us," writes Mr. D. Douglas, "that when No. 39 Castle Street, was displenished in 1826, Scott sent him the full-length portrait of himself by Raeburn, now at Abbotsford, saying that he did not hesitate to claim his protection for the picture, which was threatened to be paraded under the hammer of the auctioneer, and he felt that Skene's interposition to turn aside that buffet, might admit of being justified." In a letter dated, Abbotsford, the 16th January, 1831, Scott asks Skene to have the portrait copied, and to send the copy to Abbotsford. In accordance with this wish made when Scott's health began to fail, Skene had "an absolute facsimile" of it painted, which he kept to himself, he sending the original to Scott.

Scott's opinion of Raeburn's portraits appears to have varied. About April, 1819, the Duke of Buccleugh wrote to Sir Walter saying, "my prodigious undertaking of a west wing at Bowhill is begun. A library of forty-one feet by twenty-one, is to be added to the present drawing-room. A space for one picture is reserved over the fireplace, and in this warm situation I intend to place the Guardian of Literature. I should be happy to have my friend 'Maida' appear. It is now almost proverbial 'Walter Scott and his dog.' Raeburn should be warned that I am as well acquainted with my friend's hands and arms as with his nose—and Vandyck was of my opinion. Many of R's. works are shamefully finished—the face studied, but everything else neglected. This is a fair opportunity of producing something really worthy of his skill."

To this uncompromising and curious criticism, Scott replied from Abbotsford, on the 15th of April, 1819. He said he would be proud and happy to sit but, "I hesitate a little about Raeburn, unless your Grace is quite determined. He has very much to do ; works just now chiefly for cash, poor fellow, as he can have but a few years to make money ; and has twice already made a very chowder-headed person of me. I should like much (always with your approbation) to try Allan, who is a man of real genius, and has made one or two glorious portraits, though his predilection is to the historical branch of art."

This is a strange letter to come from Sir Walter Scott. The suggestion of greed on the part of Raeburn is unfair, as we know that he was most generous. He, like Scott himself, lost his entire fortune as we shall see later. It is also unjust to hint that Raeburn was producing mere "pot boilers" at this period. Some of his best works were painted about 1819. That Scott's idea of art was meagre, is shown by his preference for Sir William Allan, the historical painter. This projected portrait was apparently never painted, and as we have seen the Duke had to wait until the Ballantyne failure, which involved Scott to the extent of £130,000, when he secured the "chowder-headed" Constable portrait which now hangs at Bowhill.

was exhibited a second time—it

█ length portrait of Scott, which
▓▓, editor and publisher of that
documents, Scott's *Journal*, says
:nancial troubles, the picture was
e, of Rubislaw. "Mr. Skene tells
▓en No. 39 Castle Street, was
full-length portrait of himself by
█ be did not hesitate to claim his
▓eatened to be paraded under the
that Skene's interposition to turn
█ justified." In a letter dated,
█ asks Skene to have the portrait
▓▓▓ord. In accordance with this
to fail, Skene had "an absolute
: to himself, be sending the original

▓▓ appears to have varied. About
▓rote to Sir Walter saying, "my
at Bowhill is begun. A library of
▓ded to the present drawing-room.
▓r the fireplace, and in this warm
█ of Literature. I should be happy
t is now almost proverbial 'Walter
warned that I am as well acquainted
▓ his nose—and Vandyck was of my
▓▓▓y finished—the face studied, but
·opportunity of producing something

▓▓▓ criticism, Scott replied from
l. He said he would be proud and
▓▓ut Raeburn, unless your Grace is
to do; works just now chiefly for
few years to make money; and has
▓▓ded person of me. I should like
to try Allan, who is a man of real
▓▓▓ portraits, though his predilection

▓▓e from Sir Walter Scott. The
▓▓▓urn is unfair, as we know that he
▓▓▓self, lost his entire fortune as we
▓ hint that Raeburn was producing
S▓▓e of his best works were painted
▓rt was meagre, is shown by his
▓▓ historical painter. This projected
▓ and as we have seen the Duke had
w▓▓h involved Scott to the extent of
▓▓r-headed" Constable portrait which

JAMES CAMPBELL

If we are to
Walter changed
in his " Re...
declined again t...
he had already
sitter, and he ▮
" Not only my...
preparing his ...
tried to get Sc...
often that I ▮
Raeburn's old ▮
beggars. Even
more of the po...
what he is ...
down, and Sir ...
two would be ▮
This was in ▮
find a client ▮
copy, Sir Walter
it may find its ▮
" After two
highly pleased."
of me were in ...
a very disagre...
expression of S.
is evidently ▮
16th June, ▮
from Sir H▮
he ever painted,
A noble repres...
mouth that has ...
Morrison ▮
Montagu, and ...
son, Henry ▮
says, that Lord
picture on his ...
on the 27th ▮
Edinburgh in ...
remains that ...
the Montagu ▮
passed from the
portrait was re...
not believe the
example. Lockh...
but which gro...
deep and fine '

If we are to believe Morrison, the friend of Scott and Raeburn, Sir Walter changed his opinion about his own portraits by the artist. Morrison in his "Reminiscences," says, that the artist expressed regret that Scott declined again to sit to him, as he thought the two portraits of the novelist he had already painted were heavy in appearance. Scott was a restless sitter, and he found it difficult to realise the features in animated expression. "Not only myself, but my very dog growls when he observes a painter preparing his palette," declared Scott. According to Morrison when he tried to get Scott to sit once more, the latter said, "I have been painted so often that I am sick of the thing, especially since, with the exception of Raeburn's old portrait, I can only see so many old shoemakers, or bluegown beggars. Even Lawrence whose portrait is in progress, has been thinking more of the poet than the man. 'The poet's eye in fine frenzy rolling' is what he is aiming at; but I anticipate a failure. Raeburn's portrait looks down, and Sir Thomas's too much up. I think that something between the two would be better. I hate attitudes." In the end Scott agreed to sit. This was in 1822. At the first sitting, Scott told Raeburn that he might find a client for the portrait, to which Raeburn replied : "You may for a copy, Sir Walter, but the portrait I am now painting is for myself, although it may find its way, in time, into your own family."

"After two or three sittings," continues Morrison, "Sir Walter was highly pleased." "I wish," he said to Raeburn, "none but your portraits of me were in existence." A portrait may be strikingly like, and yet have a very disagreeable look. This reported appreciation differs from the expression of Scott's opinions in his letter quoted above. The third portrait is evidently the one referred to in Scott's *Journal*. The entry dated, 16th June, 1826, reads : "I got yesterday a present of two engravings from Sir Henry Raeburn's portrait of me, which (poor fellow) was the last he ever painted, and certainly not his worst." No! It is one of his best. A noble representation of a "bluff man of the world—with his pleasant mouth that has a *burr* on it," says Dr. John Brown.

Morrison states that a copy of this portrait was made for Lord Montagu, and that the "original is in the possession of the painter's only son, Henry Raeburn, Esq., of St. Bernards." On the other hand, Lockhart says, that Lord Montagu asked Scott to sit "without delay for a smaller picture on his own behalf." To this request Scott promptly sent a reply on the 27th March, 1822, heartily agreeing to sit when he returned to Edinburgh in May. This discrepancy is a trifle perplexing, but the fact remains that Raeburn painted two half-length portraits of Sir Walter : the Montagu version belongs to the Earl of Howe, and the other which passed from the Raeburn family to Mr. Arthur Sanderson. The Sanderson portrait was recently sold in London. I saw it on that occasion and could not believe that it came from the brush of Raeburn. Of the Montagu example, Lockhart wrote, "A massive strong likeness heavy at first sight, but which grows into favour upon better acquaintance—the eyes very deep and fine."

CHAPTER IV.

DEVELOPMENT AND METHOD.

RAEBURN'S art shows no very distinctive periods. His study in Rome brought him in touch with the work of the Continental schools but on his return to Edinburgh in 1787 there was little or no evidence of foreign influence.

His knowledge of structure was greater, his hand more certain, and the problems of light and shade, as suggested perhaps, by the Bolognese painters added interest to his essays. In short he came back from the Eternal City the best equipped artist in Scotland of that time, and his merits were soon recognised and appreciated. Before long all Edinburgh was eager to be immortalised by the virile brush of the young artist. His introduction to the public came, it appears through a commission from the Harveian Society to paint a portrait of William Inglis, one of its original members who was noted as "the chief restorer of the *Ludi Apollinaris* at Edinburgh, games annually celebrated on the links of Leith, at which there is an admirable combination of healthful exercise and social mirth."

This portrait was followed by another of the society's President, Alexander Wood, and about this time came the likeness of Professor Andrew Duncan, already mentioned as an early patron. This work is the property of the Royal Medical Society, and some thirty years later he produced a second portrait of Dr. Duncan for the Royal College of Surgeons. Other early works are the portraits of "Lord President Dundas," "Principal Hill of St. Andrews," and "John Clerk," his friend of the "Herrin'" legend, and afterwards Lord Eldin, of whom he painted a superb image with a "Crouching Venus" set on the table.

It is not till we come to the portraits of "William Ferguson of Kilrie," as a boy, and the "Sir John and Lady Clerk," recently acquired by Mr. Otto Beit, that any marked change is found in his method. His colour is more assertive, sometimes to garishness, and the handling is surer and more fluent. But it is in the distribution of light and shade that we see any real development. He is no longer content with ordinary studio lighting. Light for its own sake is introduced, though it in no way deprives the subjects of their importance. It not only enhances the pictorial effect but it brings out in more striking fashion the characteristic features of his sitters. The "William Ferguson" is one of Raeburn's most charming pictures of boyhood. How beautifully the light falling over the right shoulder models the soft round cheek and the fine clear cut nose; and follows the negligé lines of the white shirt front which shows the full grace of the well-formed neck. The wistful eyes, the parted lips and the natural poise of the aristocratic head represents Raeburn's genius in its most sympathetic mood.

The "John Clerk and his wife," if less tenderly alluring, is of nobler aspect, and has a certain pathetic interest. Husband and wife, no longer young, stand in a landscape; he pointing to some place or object in the distance, perhaps recalling some early joy when the fires of life still burned ardently in their hearts. But the sentimental side of the subject need not be discussed. It is the artistic difficulties so admirably overcome that demand attention. The light comes from the left behind the figures, catching the side of the lady's face and her white muslin dress, and outlining Sir John's shoulder, arm and his body on the right. His face is in shadow, but the light refracted from his wife's dress plays with great subtlety over the planes. This happy conception is carried out with masterly ingenuity. These pictures which date before 1790, were followed by two others "Master Hay," and "Raeburn's Son on Horseback" 1796, which present similar effects of lighting. Both were exhibited at the French Gallery, Pall Mall, last year and won high praise. The "Master Hay" has considerable charm and the poise of the boy in the second canvas is unaffected and natural. But the lighting is somewhat theatrical.

Other Ferguson portraits are those of "Sir Ronald and Robert Ferguson practising Archery," a very winsome picture which shows a brief spell of rest in the artist's technical development, though there is a certain pleasing motive in its design. Two years later in 1791, came the "General Sir Ronald Ferguson" in sportsman's costume. Here, if the arrangement is somewhat conventional we find more expressive modelling, a more generous brush applied with greater ease. In 1795 the same gentleman figures in an equestrian portrait in which are noticed an absence of sharply divided masses of light and shade. Roundness is secured by subtle gradation of light, the just appreciation of values.

But the picture that marked in the highest degree Raeburn's progress in his early period is the "Dr. Nathaniel Spens" painted in 1791 for the Royal Archers Company, Edinburgh. This is a work of extraordinary insight and skill. Here his perceptive faculties are employed with amazing precision and graphic expression. The keen eager eyes directing the arrow to its flight; the firm mouth, purposeful nose and chin are presented with a power hitherto unknown in Scottish art. The whole body of the archer suggests force, nervous tension. How masterly the light is manœuvred. From the starting mass of white waistcoat it moves over the white belts with their silver mountings, touches the gloved hands and the feather of the arrow, throws the shadow of bow-string on the ruddy face and passes to rest amid the half tones of the sky beyond the autumn trees. No wonder that this work created something like a sensation when it was exhibited in Burlington House in 1875. Up to that date Raeburn was little more than a name classed in "The School of Lawrence"—the irony of it!

About five years after the "Spens," came an even finer achievement— the famous portrait of Sir John Sinclair of Ulbster. In this magnificent canvas are concentrated the spirit, and character of the Highlands and the Highlanders. The forceful face, the strong erect figure, clad in the swaggering costume of boisterous hues, bring to mind visions of stirring days, great victories and noble defeats. Some critics prefer the quieter dignity of the "Spens," but as a display of executive skill, the "Sinclair" is Raeburn's *chef d'oeuvre* and indeed, stands unrivalled in British art in its fearless and brilliant brush work. The "Macnab" painted about the same time has similar qualities and it is said that Sir Thomas Lawrence characterised it as the best representation of a human being he had ever seen. This dour-faced laird, dressed in the Highland costume of the Breadalbane Fencibles makes a splendid defiant figure set in a mountain landscape. It is now at the Rome International Exhibition.

I may here refer to a fourth important portrait of a Highlander "Colonel Alastair Macdonall of Glengarry" though it was painted long after the others; about 1812. This canvas when I saw it last December was placed too high in the Scottish National Gallery for a proper examination of its qualities which seemed to be somewhat obscured by a dull haze spread over the surface. Cleaning or revarnishing would perhaps remove the opacity. In his volume on the "Scottish School of Painting" Mr. W. D. McKay speaks very highly of this portrait. He considers it to be freer from some of Raeburn's mannerisms "notably those which arise from the constant use of a very high light." The sidelight and the nature of the background suggests to Mr. McKay that the picture was painted in the chieftain's own hall at Invergarry. In this surmise he is apparently correct, for the owner of the picture—Mr. J. Cunninghame of Balgourie—says that the shield hanging on the wall in the background is among the Glengarry guns, arms, etc., in his possession. Further he writes: "From enquiries I have made of relations, I am quite convinced that the painting was done at the chief's own house." Mr. Cunninghame also clears up the doubt about the date of the picture which was stated to be 1800 in the catalogue of the Raeburn Exhibition of 1876.

Glengarry was born in 1774, however, and the picture shows a man of more years than twenty-six, so I may conclude that the picture was produced about 1812, the year of its exhibition in London. Mr. McKay says of the canvas that "there may not be such palpable feats of brushwork as characterise the painting of those earlier portraits, but surely there is a strength in its reticence which goes beyond either." The picture certainly is suave and dignified in poise, while there is solidity in its less resourceful handling, but it has not the allure of the impetuous craftsmanship of the "Sinclair" or the "Macnab."

The Pre-Roman "Mrs. Ferguson and children," the "Spens," "Sinclair" and the "Macnab" have a landscape setting as have many of his later portraits. Morrison reports the following conversation between Scott and Raeburn, on the question of backgrounds.

"I wish," said Sir Walter, "that you would let us have a little more finishing in the backgrounds. Sir Thomas Lawrence, I understand, employs a landscape painter."

"Of that I do not approve," replied Raeburn. "Landscape in the background of a portrait ought to be nothing more than the shadow of a landscape: effect is all that is wanted. Nothing ought to divert the eye from the main object—the face; and it ought to be something in the style of Milton's ' Death ' :—

> The other shape—
> If shape it might be called that shape had none
> Distinguishable in member, joint or limb,
> Or substance might be call'd that shadow seem'd
> For each seem'd either."

"I am at present painting an Admiral and had some thought of asking my friend, the Minister of Duddingston, to paint me the sea ; but, on second

■ the Highland costume of the
. defiant figure set in a mountain
tional Exhibition.

ortant portrait of a Highlander
" though it was painted long after
hen I saw it last December was
Gallery for a proper examination
at obscured by a dull haze spread
ing would perhaps remove the
I School of Painting" Mr. W. D.
it. He considers it to be freer
tably those which arise from the
sidelight and the nature of the
t the picture was painted in the
a surmise he is apparently correct,
ninghame of Balgourie—says that
ground is among the Glengarry
ther be writes: "From enquiries
ced that the painting was done
nghame also clears up the doubt
; stated to be 1800 in the catalogue

er, and the picture shows a man of
ry conclude that the picture was
exhibition in London. Mr. McKay
be such palpable feats of brushwork
rher portraits, but surely there is a
d either." The picture certainly
ere is solidity in its less resourceful
the impetuous craftsmanship of the

■ and children," the "Spens,"
I landscape setting as have many of
the following conversation between
backgrounds.
you would let us have a little more
■ Lawrence, I understand, employs

d Raeburn. "Landscape in the
oothing more than the shadow of a
■ Nothing ought to divert the eye
■ ought to be something in the style

that shape had none
er, joint or limb,
d that shadow seem'd
either."

■ and had some thought of asking
■ to paint me the sea; but, on second

thoughts, I am a
picture in the clear

The conventi
portraits. The
sitters and it is
request of his
backgrounds say
to Raeburn: "I
have made in yo
beautiful. Then
a systematic h
fair play . .
great interest in
year, you persis
Pursue your pur

Raeburn
friends on cer
backgrounds we
better settings
mountain lands
gorgeous hues

Of course
Reynolds, were
Raeburn's styl
and theatrical
natural simplici
on occasion

Between th
Balfour" (Sing
represented in
saxpence under
the picture's
hame; Round
Hanley, with
used to tell
his hospitable
of the old L
heard of this,
bottles of whi
£30, and two
also, and pro
was fulfilled."

Another
painted in t
was bought
in the splend
is to be con
art. Dr.
of the port
quoted.

thoughts, I am afraid that Mr. Thomson's sea might put my part of the picture in the shade."

The convention of the period demanded landscape backgrounds for portraits. The scenic setting appealed to the vanity or supposed taste of sitters and it is said that Raeburn adopted the prevailing fashion at the request of his clients and the critics, the latter objecting to his azure backgrounds says Cunningham. One member of the Royal Academy wrote to Raeburn: "I congratulate you on the great improvement which you have made in your backgrounds . . . your pictures are now altogether beautiful. There is no beautiful head and finely executed figure ruined by a systematic background; everything is in harmony, and your subject has fair play . . . I beg you to pardon this forwardness; I have ever felt a great interest in your reputation, and been much mortified when, year after year, you persisted in a manner that was so disadvantageous to your fame. Pursue your *present plan*, and your immortality is certain."

Raeburn may have changed his backgrounds at the request of his friends on certain occasions, but, I am inclined to think that his backgrounds were chosen according to the character of the subject. What better settings could be imagined for a " Sinclair " or a " Macnab " than the mountain landscape that throws out their imposing figures and repeats the gorgeous hues of their costume.

Of course in many cases his landscape backgrounds, like those of Reynolds, were flimsy and artificial, and as R. A. M. Stevenson says Raeburn's style " was incompatible with pretty elegance, spotty colouring, and theatrical disposition of the canvas. It went best with the solemn, natural simplicity of Velasquez, the Dutchman and the Flemings." Yet all on occasion used landscape backgrounds.

Between the " Spens " and " Sinclair," came the portrait of " James Balfour " (Singing Jamie), executed for the Golfer's Hall, Leith. He is represented in the act of singing his favourite ditty, "When I hae a saxpence under my thoom." Dr. John Brown tells an interesting story of the picture's history. "You hear the refrain—'Toddlin' hame, toddlin' hame ; Round as a neep (turnip), she cam' toddlin' hame.' Mr. Melville, of Hanley, with whom have perished so many of the best Edinburgh stories, used to tell how he got this picture, which for many years hung and sang in his hospitable dining-room. It was bought at the selling-off of the effects of the old Leith Golf-house, by a drunken caddie for 30/-. Mr. Melville heard of this, went to the ancient creature, and got it for 40/- and two bottles of whisky. James Stewart, of Dunearn, offered him (Mr. Melville) £80, and two pipes of wine for it, but in vain. Sir David Wilkie coveted it also, and promised to pay for it by a picture of his own, but died before this was fulfilled."

Another portrait of this period is the " Mrs. Barbara Murchison," painted in 1793. This picture, once the property of Mr. R. F. Murchison, was bought by Messrs. Colnaghi and Co., at Christie's, in 1903, and is now in the splendid art gallery at Budapest, whose director Dr. Gabriel de Terry is to be congratulated on securing an example so characteristic of Raeburn's art. Dr. de Terry's opinion of the picture printed along with a reproduction of e portrait in the *Burlington Magazine*, Vol. XII., page 250, may be quoted.

"The young woman," he says, "represented almost full face, has something so motherly in her ample, soft contours, that she attracts one immediately. She has the languid, somewhat phlegmatic movement of a woman who is rather fully developed for her years, and who knows very well that this healthy *embonpoint* becomes her. She sits calmly gazing contemplatively from her beautiful dark eyes; on her high white forehead curl the locks of her rich brown hair. Her gently-rounded cheeks, her full lips, her white neck and plump arms, so enchantingly modelled all speak of youth, the height of summer and harvest time. She is dressed all in white, in that short-waisted costume which is artistically so attractive, and has a permanent value above all other fashions. The picture is broadly and freely painted, especially the landscape background."

This eulogy is well-deserved. There is no better Raeburn in any Continental gallery. The artist himself was pleased with the picture as will be seen by the following letter:—

> DEAR SIR,
> I have this day sent Mrs. Murchison's portrait carefully packed up on board the "Three Friends," now directed to the care of Mr. Inglis, Inverness. I hope you will receive it safe. Inclosed you have the ship-master's receipt.
> I took particular pains in finishing Mrs. Murchison's picture, and flatter myself it will meet with your approbation. Mr. Liddell, the frame-maker, says that besides this one there is a small oval frame due, that went about your picture which I had reduced and altered, I mean the picture which was painted by Mr. Battoni—and which was sent to some lady in town here.
> I hope you will forgive me for having been so long in finishing this picture. I assure you it did not proceed from neglect, the truth is I could not get it overtaken. I have been much pressed for pictures which have been still longer in the house than yours, and even now, yours is finished before the turn.
> I had the pleasure some time ago of seeing an addition to your family announced in the papers, I did in my own mind congratulate you upon it.
> I hope Mrs. Murchison is well, may I beg you would make my most respectful compts. to her, and that you would believe me with best wishes, and much respect.
> My dear Sir,
> Yours most obedt. servant,
> HENRY RAEBURN.
>
> EDIN., 18th May, 1793.
> To KENNETH MURCHISON, Esqr.
> of Farradale by
> Inverness.

Among other portraits painted before the end of the century, are the beautiful "Mrs. Campbell of Ballimore," in the National Gallery of Scotland, the "Mrs. Newbigging," recently shown at Messrs. Agnew's Galleries; the splendid "Captain David Burret," "Lady Stewart of Coltness," "Admiral Lord Duncan" (1798), "Professor Robinson" (c. 1798), and the "Macdonald of Clanronald" (c. 1800). "John Tait and grandchild" is generally believed to be the work of 1798, or 1799, but a letter which appears in Miss Emily Robertson's volume, on the correspondence of her father, Andrew Robertson, the miniaturist, proves this date to be wrong. Her father, a native of Aberdeen, went to Edinburgh at the age of sixteen to study under Nasmyth, but "being very desirous of seeing Raeburn's pictures," he bravely knocked at his door, "armed with a shilling for his servant." Raeburn received the youth with much kindness, and when he had learned that Andrew wished to copy some of his portraits he prepared a small studio for him.

"The first picture I copied," says Robertson, "was an old gentleman, a half length of Mr. John Tait, advocate, with a blazing warm sky on one side, close to the head, which I thought injured the effect. I never dreamed there was any harm in altering it, and lowering the tone. Raeburn stared at my copy and frowned, then at me and smiled, saying, 'I see you have improved upon my composition.' 'Yes, I think it is an improvement; don't you think it is?' He then laughed heartily at my simplicity, and asked me to dine with his family next day at his picturesque and delightful villa at Stockbridge, but he never forgot the joke of my altering his composition. Some years after, I saw the picture again and found that he had adopted my alteration. This enabled me to turn the joke against him, but he said he 'did so, merely to oblige me.'" This epistle gives a delightful glimpse of the great painter, and the incident it describes happened in 1793, three years before the child in the picture was born, thus proving that his portrait was introduced about 1800. A matter of considerable interest is the discovery of Robertson's miniature of the picture in its original condition. Mr. Dudley Heath, in an article in the *Connoisseur*, says, that the miniature was the property of a lady in Sussex, who sold it with some sketches, and other miniatures to a Brighton dealer, from whom it passed to the collection of Mr. Lionel Moseley. On the back of the miniature is inscribed in Robertson's handwriting: "John Tait, Esq., Edinburgh, a copy after Raeburn; before I came to London." The figure of Tait in the miniature, is identical with the original, save that the right arm is lowered, and the hand holds a large hat, and of course the child is absent. A curious thing is noticed in the altered picture—the old man has two right hands, Raeburn, without thinking, having turned the left hand into a right hand.

We have now followed Raeburn's progress for thirteen years, that is, since his return from Rome. After that event we have found his style mature. It is characterised by greater care, analytical perception, more generous application of pigment, and richer colour. Problems of lighting have also been successfully solved, but not generally adopted, chiefly, no doubt because sitters did not care to have their favourite features perhaps lost in obscurity. Now and again he went back to the broader, less searching modelling of his pre-Roman days, but his instinct for essentials is keener, his eye more certain, his hand readier to execute with full brush and fluent touches, portraits like the beautiful "Mrs. Campbell of Ballimore," and the wonderful "Professor Robison" (c. 1798). Of the latter, Dr. John Brown says, "Did you ever see a dressing-gown so glorified? and the night cap, and the look of steady speculation in the eyes—a philosopher all over." In the later work of his life, from 1800 to his death in 1823, we shall find a steady development, greater appreciation of form, more incisive drawing, subtler modelling, tenderer colour, and a more expressive distribution of light and shade. But in all cases he adapted his methods to suit the character and temperament of his sitters.

By 1785 increased practice made it necessary for him to move to a larger studio, but as he could not secure anything suitable he built one for himself in York Place. Cunningham tells us that the painting rooms were on the street floor above the area; the first floor was a spacious gallery lighted from the top, measuring fifty-five feet long, thirty-five feet wide, and forty feet high. Raeburn's habits of work required considerable space, and this huge room gave him ample freedom of movement. Cunningham gives an admirable description of the painter's technical methods and manner of procedure. " The motions of the artist were as regular as those of a clock. He rose at seven, during summer, took breakfast about eight with his wife and children, walked into George Street, and was ready for a sitter by nine; and of sitters he generally had, for many years, not fewer than three or four a day. To these he gave an hour and half each. He seldom kept a sitter more than two hours, unless the person happened— and that was often the case—to be gifted with more than common talents. He then felt himself happy, and never failed to detain the party until the arrival of a new sitter intimated that he must be gone. For a head size he generally required four or five sittings; and he preferred painting the head and hands to any other part of the body; assigning as a reason that they required less consideration. A fold of drapery, or the natural ease which the casting of a mantle over the shoulder demanded, occasioned him more perplexing study than a head full of thought and imagination. Such was the intuition with which he penetrated at once to the mind, that the first sitting rarely came to a close without his having seized strongly on the character and disposition of the individual. He never drew in his heads, or indeed any part of the body, with chalk—a system practised by Sir Thomas Lawrence—but began with the brush at once. The forehead, chin, nose and mouth were his first touches. He always painted standing, and never used a stick for resting his hand on; for such was his accuracy of eye, and steadiness of nerve, that he could introduce the most delicate of touches, or the almost mechanical regularity of line, without aid, or other contrivance than fair off-hand dexterity. He remained in his painting room till a little after five o'clock, when he walked home, and dined at six. . . From one who knew him in his youthful days, and sat to him when he rose to fame, I have this description of his way of going to work. ' He spoke a few words to me in his usual brief and kindly way—evidently to put me into an agreeable mood; and then having placed me in a chair on a platform at the end of his painting-room, in the posture required, set up his easel beside me with a canvas ready to receive the colour. When he saw all was right, he took his palette and his brush, retreated back step by step, with his face towards me, till he was nigh the other end of the room; he stood and studied for a minute more, then came up to the canvas, and, without looking at me, wrought upon it with colour for some time. Having done this he retreated in the same manner, studied my looks at that distance for another minute, then came hastily up to the canvas and painted for a few minutes more. . . I may add,' continues the story, 'that I found him well-informed, with no professional pedantry about him; indeed, no one could have imagined him a painter until he took up the brush and palette; he conversed with me upon mechanics and shipbuildings, and if I can depend upon my own imperfect judgment, he had studied ship-architecture with great success. On one of the days of my sitting he had to dine with me at the house of a mutual friend; our hour was six, and you know how punctual to time we in the north are; he painted at my portrait till within a quarter of an hour of the time, threw down his palette and brushes, went into a little closet, and in five minutes sallied out to dinner in a trim worthy of the first company. I sat six times, and two hours

:edom of movement. Cunningham
painter's technical methods and
the artist were as regular as those
summer, took breakfast about eight
George Street, and was ready for a
had, for many years, not fewer
: gave an hour and half each. He
unless the person happened—
with more than common talents.
ed to detain the party until the
must be gone. For a head size be
and he preferred painting the head
y; assigning as a reason that they
drapery, or the natural ease which
er demanded, occasioned him more
ought and imagination. Such was
at once to the mind, that the first
his having seized strongly on the
He never drew in his heads,
: chalk—a system practised by Sir
: brush at once. The forehead, chin,
. He always painted standing, and
on; for such was his accuracy of
could introduce the most delicate of
larity of line, without aid, or other
. He remained in his painting room
ed home, and dined at six. . .
days, and sat to him when he rose
of going to work. 'He spoke a
kindly way—evidently to put me
having placed me in a chair on a
in the posture required, set up his
. receive the colour. When he saw
brush, retreated back step by step,
nigh the other end of the room; he
then came up to the canvas, and,
with colour for some time. Having
, studied my looks at that distance
up to the canvas and painted for a
' continues the story, 'that I found
pedantry about him; indeed, no
ter until he took up the brush and
mechanics and shipbuildings, and if I
judgment, he had studied ship-
. one of the days of my sitting he had
friend; our hour was six, and you
north are; he painted at my portrait
the time, threw down his palette and
in five minutes sallied out to dinner in
I sat six times, and two hours

together.' " ▪
methods. "L▪
high platform, ▪
nostrils. The
hanging like p▪
Raeburn and I

Sir Walt▪
Raeburn, I ▪
was rich, and
went to cont▪
the necessary
him, in my ▪
picture; whi▪
which I ▪
given as re▪
palette was▪
times yellow
crimson lake
a compositio▪
were ground
for use." T▪
light, and th▪
twill."

I am ▪
tells us when

Dear ▪
I ha▪
London—
2 lbs. ▪
desired ▪
I a▪

John ▪
I▪
I have
Arbroath ▪
established

together.'" Dr. John Brown supplies a somewhat similar account of his methods. "Like Sir Joshua," he says, "Raeburn placed his sitters on a high platform, shortening the features, and giving a pigeon-hole view of the nostrils. The notion is that people should be painted as if they were hanging like pictures on the wall, a Newgate notion, but it was Sir Joshua's. Raeburn and I have had good-humoured disputes about this."

Sir Walter Scott adds to the picture by declaring, "I never knew Raeburn, I may say, till the painting of my last portrait. His conversation was rich, and he told his story well. His manly stride backwards, as he went to contemplate his work at a proper distance, and, when resolved on the necessary point to be touched, his step forward was magnificent. I see him, in my mind's eye, with his hand under his chin, contemplating his picture; which position always brought me in mind of a figure of Jupiter which I have somewhere seen." At this point a list of his colours may be given as recorded by Alexander Fraser, R.S.A., in *The Portfolio*, 'His palette was a simple one; his colours were vermilion, raw sienna (but sometimes yellow ochre instead), Prussian blue, burnt sienna, ivory black, crimson lake, white of course, and the medium he used was 'gumption,' a composition of sugar of lead, mastic varnish, and linseed oil. The colours were ground by a servant in his own house and put into small pots ready for use." To this Mr. J. L. Caw adds "that his studio had a very high side light, and that he painted on half-primed canvas with a definitely marked twill."

I am able to supplement these statements with a letter, in which he tells us where he bought his painting materials.

EDINBURGH, 10*th October*, 1822.

DEAR SIR,

I have according to your request ordered from Middleton, 81 St. Martin's Lane, London—the gent with whom I deal—16¾ cloth the same as I use, 4 oz. vermilion, and 2 lbs. flake white, which last I should imagine would not serve you long. I have desired the case to be addressed—according to your instructions.   . .

I sincerely wish you all success.

Believe me always,
My dear sir,
Most faithfully yours,
HENRY RAEBURN.

JOHN MORRISON, Esq.,
Annan.

I have also discovered that this particular kind of canvas was woven at Arbroath under the encouragement of the British Linen Bank which was established to stimulate British Linen industry.

CHAPTER V.

THE portrait of Professor Robison referred to in the last chapter, is generally regarded as the culmination of Raeburn's summary, "square touch" style, when the modelling of his faces was described in clear cut, decisive patches without suavity or fusion. But in time subtlety crept into his handling. It is not yet very evident in the "Lord Chief Baron Montgomery," of 1801, nor in the vigorous presentment of "Rolland of Gask," and the fine manly effigy of "Professor Wilson" (Christopher North) (1805), in the National Portrait Gallery of Scotland. But about 1808 came the masterly "Dr. Alexander Adam," now in the National Gallery of Scotland. Adam who was dubbed the "Scottish Arnold," was the much loved rector of the Royal high school of Edinburgh, and among his pupils were Walter Scott, Jeffrey, Brougham, and Cockburn. The portrait which was a commission from a number of his scholars, shows Dr. Adams seated in gown and black dress, his right hand extended, his face set in a curious kindly smile. The attitude reminded Dr. John Brown of the story of the rector when on his death-bed. Raising his hand, he said: "But it grows dark, boys; you may go." The characterisation is remarkable; the craftsmanship direct and without swagger is entirely in harmony with the simple kindly "dominie." Almost contemporary with this canvas is the extraordinary portrait of "Lord Newton." "Full-blooded," says Dr. John Brown, "taurine with potential vigour. His head is painted with a Rabelaisian richness; you cannot but believe, that when you look at the vast countenance, the tales of his feats in thinking and in drinking, and in general capacity of body and mind." Lord Newton was well named "the mighty." Raeburn's portrait fully warrants the epithet. What a great head it is. Huge and rubicund, and blocked-out as if from a mass of red sandstone. The knit brows, the heavy inquisitive eyes, strong nose and firm mouth denote uncompromising will, the flabby flesh and double chin, the "taurine" aspect created by high living. The handling is masterly, the whole effect superb. Another splendid work of this period is the portrait of "James Byres of Tonley," his friend of the Roman days who advised Raeburn never to paint anything but what he saw. This picture which was shown at the French Gallery last winter, forms a striking contrast to the "Newton." The "Tonley" is distinguished by the qualities of his finest work. There is a reverence in the touch, a tender fusion of the tones, a roundness of modelling, absent in the impetuous craftsmanship of the other canvas. The "Tonley" takes its place among the great portraits of aged men—with those of Rembrandt and Hals. Here is the noble pathos of one who has passed his sixtieth birthday suggested with consummate art. How tenderly the grey hair silvers the fine head; the dark eyes are dulled, the lips have lost much of their force, but they still have significance.

We know from the following letter that this portrait was painted about 1809. It was sent to Cadell and Davies, the firm to whose order Raeburn painted a copy of Nasmyth's bust-portrait of Robert Burns. The latter also proves that Raeburn contributed to the " British Gallery of Contemporary Portraits, which was a series of 150 engravings of the 'most eminent persons now living, or lately deceased in Great Britain and Ireland.'" This publication was issued in twenty-five numbers at 25/- each, by Cadell and Davies, between 1809 and 1816.

To Messrs. Cadell and Davies, London.

Edinburgh, *August 24th*, 1809.

Gentlemen,

    I am ashamed of not having acknowledged the receipt of your two first numbers of your " British Gallery," etc. I have Mr. John Clerk, of Eldin, Mr. Henry Mackenzie, and Mr. Byres, of Tonley, ready to send up to you. I know not if you are acquainted with the last-mentioned gentleman; he is a man of great general information, a profound antiquary, and one of the best judges perhaps of everything connected with art in Great Britain. He resided for upwards of thirty years in Rome, and is personally known to almost all the nobility and wealthy people of England who have travelled during that period.

    These three I could send you immediately, but I have a portrait of the late Sir William Forbes, of Pitsligo, if you wish it. He was a gentleman universally known and respected in Scotland. I believe I could also get you a portrait of Dr. J. Hamilton, senior, first physician to the Royal Infirmary, a gentleman very eminent in his profession, and who has lately published a medical work that has done him great credit. On your answer I shall send you a case containing the above in the meantime. I have a portrait of our present Lord President Blair; the proprietor, Mr. (Alexander) Maconochie, his son-in-law, and one of your subscribers, is not unwilling that it should be engraved, but does not like to part with the picture. I shall talk to him again about it. Mr. Cromack (Cromek) lately sent off a portrait of Walter Scott. He means to publish a print of him by itself. I believe you do not like any portrait of which there is already a print, or from which it is intended there shall be a print, but if you wish to have that, as I cannot see that your publication will injure the sale of his print, I suppose he will have no objection to let you have it, or Mr. Constable, whose property it is. I have a head of Dugald Stuart (Stewart); it is the property of Lord Woodhouselee. I shall speak to him, and have no doubt he will let you have it; but there was a print lately done from it, and on that account you will perhaps not wish to have it. There may be some objections, too, on that account to the Lord President, for I believe there are some thoughts of having a separate print of him.

    I am, Gentlemen, your most obedient servant,

        (Signed) HENRY RABBURN.

P.S.—On reading this letter over I find in some parts it is not very correct, but you will understand what I mean.

        (Initialed) H. R.

The portrait of Scott mentioned was the full-length painted for Archibald Constable in 1808 and exhibited at the Royal Academy two years later. It will be seen that the portraits of " Dugald Stewart," " Dr. J. Hamilton " and " Lord Blair " date before 1809.

In the French Gallery exhibition also was a splendid portrait of " Professor George Joseph Bell," the property of the Hon. Ewen Charteris, which was perhaps painted about 1810, the year in which Raeburn painted the portrait of the " Mrs. Bell " referred to in the following letter.

To George Joseph Bell, Esq.

St. Bernards, *8th December*, 1810.

My Dear Sir,

I return you my best thanks for the very handsome manner in which you have paid me for Mrs. Bell's picture. You have enclosed 25 guineas, I return you five of them, which I have no right to accept, my price having been raised since I painted that picture, and my obligations to you are such, that, were it not for the peculiar situation in which I find myself at present, and the great demand I have for money, I believe (great as the regard is which I have for you) I would almost have quarrelled with you sooner than I would have accepted of one farthing.

I had the misfortune late on Thursday night to lose my brother unexpectedly—a most excellent and worthy man, to whom I was much attached. I ought to have sent you an intimation, as one I believe interested in what befalls me; but many escaped me.

Believe me, with most sincere esteem and regard, ever yours,

(Signed) HENRY RAEBURN.

This epistle is of particular interest; it gives an idea of Raeburn's prices at the time and corrects a mistake as to the death of his brother which was made by Andrews in his biographer and repeated by Sir Walter Armstrong, R. A. M. Stevenson and E. Pinnington. The passage in which the mistake occurs in Andrew's book is as follows : " About this time (1787-8, he was now in his thirty-second year) Raeburn removed with his family Deanhaugh to the neighbouring estate of St. Bernards which he had succeeded to on the death of his elder brother William." A little research would have revealed the fact that in Edinburgh directories of 1801, 1809 appears the name of " William Raeburn, yarn boiler, Stockbridge," and in the *Edinburgh Evening Courant* of Thursday the 13th December, 1810, we read : " Died on the 6th December, Mr. William Raeburn, manufacturer, Stockbridge." Apart from this proof there are the title deeds of St. Bernards which show that Raeburn purchased the estate from the trustees of Mrs. Margaret Ross in 1809.

Other portraits of this period are the incomparable "Mrs. James Campbell" and the scarcely less fine portrait of "Mrs. Tod," exhibited at the French Gallery. The latter which was previously unknown has the plastic structure, the liquid purity, the intimate statement of character that marks all great portraiture. In this work, temperament and will are evident. She had been a generous hostess. Her guests would be given abundance of the best things in her larder, and though like Mrs. Poyser, she would not have allowed her mind to dribble like a leaky barrel, there would have been no scandal.

In 1810 Raeburn seriously thought of removing to London, the reason given by some writer being financial disaster, following the failure in 1808 of the firm of " Henry Raeburn, and Company, merchants, Shore, Leith," which consisted of Henry Raeburn, Junior, and James Philip Juglis who had married Ann Leslie, the artist's step-daughter. The nature of the business is not known, but in all likelihood it had to do with shipping. Raeburn was fond of ships and knew something of shipbuilding and in his own bankruptcy proceedings he was described as "Portrait painter and underwriter," which, as Mr. Caw suggests, that the business was in the nature of marine insurance. In the "crash" Raeburn lost all his money. Alexander Cunningham in a letter written on the 16th February, 1808, says: " I had a walk of three hours on Sunday with my worthy friend, Raeburn. He had realised £17,000, which is all gone. He has offered a small

ery handsome manner in which you have
enclosed 25 guineas, I return you five of
price having been raised since I painted
: such, hat, were it not for the peculiar
▮ the great demand I have for money, I
: for you) I would almost have quarrelled
of one farthing.

it to lose my brother unexpectedly—a most
▮ attached. I ought to have sent you an
it befalls me; but many escaped me.
eem and regard, ever yours,

    (Signed) HENRY RAEBURN.

▮; it gives an idea of Raeburn's
se as to the death of his brother
spher and repeated by Sir Walter
▮nsington. The passage in which
▮follows: "About this time (1787-8,
Raeburn removed with his family
▮ of St. Bernards which he had
rother William." A little research
▮dinburgh directories of 1801, 1809
▮, yarn boiler, Stockbridge," and in
▮day the 13th December, 1810, we
lr. William Raeburn, manufacturer,
' there are the title deeds of St.
chased the estate from the trustees

▮ the incomparable "Mrs. James
ortrait of "Mrs. Tod," exhibited at
was previously unknown has the
▮mate statement of character that
▮ temperament and will are evident.
▮ guests would be given abundance
▮ like Mrs. Poyser, she would not
▮ barrel, there would have been

t of removing to London, the reason
isaster, following the failure in 1808
▮ompany, merchants, Shore, Leith,"
unior, and James Philip Juglis who
step-daughter. The nature of the
▮▮owed it had to do with shipping.
something of shipbuilding and in his
described as "Portrait painter and
▮gests, that the business was in the
"crash." Raeburn lost all his money.
ten on the 16th February, 1808, says:
▮ with my worthy friend, Raeburn.
all gone. He has offered a small

composition, w
fate in Londor
I feel the tea
London, but t
Henry Raebu
doubt the art
and finance.
St. Bernards
of life as a
favour. He
"without a
noted in his
London and
Sir David en
had come to
prospect of
Beechey."

Anothe
"who happ
David "we
Gentlemen
dinner be m
health was
Despite Wi
return to ▮
have been a
that the fut
Scot's ▮▮▮
once droppe
Royal Acad
competition.
long after
President o
light. Law
his position
was wise i
that he pro
filled the ▮
have pass
thus have

Raeb
brilliant v
Newton, ▮
pictures t
beginning
of Bucha
believed ▮
origin of
effigy of l
doubts I

composition, which he is in hopes will be accepted.   He quits this to try his fate in London, which I trust in God will be successful.   While I write this I feel the tear start."   Raeburn may have intended at that time to go to London, but though he received his discharge in June, 1808, the affairs of Henry Raeburn and Company were not settled until March, 1810, and no doubt the artist delayed his projected change until he was at ease in mind and finance.   Within a year after the failure he was in a position to purchase St. Bernards and by the spring of 1810 he felt rich enough to risk the cost of life as a fashionable portrait painter in London.   The time was in his favour.   Hoppner died on the 23rd of January, 1810, and left Lawrence "without a rival."   On the 2nd of March of that year Sir David Wilkie noted in his *Journal* that he had heard of Raeburn's intention of coming to London and that he was to occupy Hoppner's house.   On the 12th of May, Sir David entered : " Had a call from Raeburn (the painter), who told me he had come to London to look out for a house, and to see if there was any prospect of establishing himself.   I took him by desire to Sir William Beechey."

Another entry states that Wilkie took Raeburn to see several artists, "who happened to be from home or engaged."   On another occasion Sir David "went with Raeburn to the 'Crown and Anchor,' to meet the Gentlemen of the Royal Academy.   I introduced him to Flaxman; after dinner he was asked by Beechey to sit near the president (West) where his health was proposed by Flaxman; great attention was paid to him." Despite Wilkie's kindness and " great attention " Raeburn was persuaded to return to Edinburgh.   Sir Thos. Lawrence was the only painter who might have been affected by Raeburn's presence in London, and it has been hinted that the future president of the Royal Academy was responsible for the Scot's departure from the Metropolis.   Cunningham was told that Raeburn once dropped some words which clearly meant that "the President of the Royal Academy had been no loser by his absence from the field of competition."   If Raeburn ever suggested such an idea it must have been long after his visit to London in 1810 for Lawrence did not become President of the Academy until 1820.   W. E. Henley puts the case in this light.   Lawrence by advising Raeburn to leave London " secured himself in his position as the painter of fashionable and distinguished England.   He was wise in his generation, no doubt, but it is a matter for lasting regret that he prevailed ; for it is beyond question that Raeburn would soon have filled the larger stage, and it is reasonable to assume that his example might have passed into a tradition, so that his sane and vigorous opinion would thus have been felt as a force in English portraiture even to this day."

Raeburn's return to Edinburgh was "followed by a long period of brilliant work."   About this time were painted portraits like the "Lord Newton," "Mrs. James Campbell," "Lord Craig " and in 1814 came two pictures that produced several interesting Raeburn letters.   About the beginning of the Nineteenth century David Stewart Erskine, eleventh Earl of Buchan "that most absurd personage " discovered a portrait which he believed to represent George Buchanan the Scots scholar, by Titian.   The origin of the painting is doubted and some declare that the portrait is an effigy of Pierre Jeannin, Finance Minister to Henry IV. of France.   These doubts I cannot set aside, but there is proof that Raeburn made two copies of it, one for the Earl of Buchan, another for the Buchanan Society of Glasgow. On the 7th of February, 1814, Raeburn wrote a letter to the Earl of Buchan asking permission to make a copy of the picture for a representative of the family, who appears to have been Hector Macdonald, one of the principal clerks to the Court of Session. One of his colleagues was (Sir) Walter Scott who referred to him as "mine honest friend," and, according to Lockhart, visited almost every year at Macdonald's seat at Ross Priory, Loch Lomond. This gentleman had married Jean, a daughter of Robert Buchanan of Ross and Drummikill and added to his own name that of Buchanan.

Raeburn's letter, which Mr. C. Fairfax Murray kindly allows me to publish, reads:—

To THE RIGHT HONORABLE THE EARL OF BUCHAN,
DRYBURGH ABBEY, MELROSE.
EDINBURGH, 7th February, 1814.

MY LORD,

It would appear that you have deserted Edinburgh altogether—at least I am almost tempted to fear that you have forsaken me, for I do not know when I had the pleasure of seeing your Lordship.

Knowing your liberality and the friendship I have ever experienced from your Lordship, I venture to ask your permission to copy your portrait of Geo. Buchanan for the representative of that family. I need not say, if I am to copy it, that your Lordship may depend on my taking the greatest care of your picture, and I shall mark on the back of the copy that it is done from the original in your Lordship's possession.

I hope you will do me the honor to look in the first time you are in Edinburgh. I know you would think it an idle question to ask how you do, as there is never anything the matter with your Lordship.

I remain, with the highest respect, my Lord,
Your most obedient and faithful servant,
(Signed) HENRY RAEBURN.

Raeburn's letter is endorsed in the Earl's own handwriting:—

"1814. Feb. 7th. Fine arts. Henry Raeburn, Esqr., desires to copy the portrait of Buchanan for the family of Drummikill. The picture is now at Mrs. Fletcher's, in North Castle Street, and is to remain with Mr. Raeburn till I come to Edinburgh or send for it. (Initialed) B."

The portrait was painted in due time and there need be no uncertainty that this copy is the one still hanging at Ross Priory. The proposal that a copy should also be made for the Buchanan Society came from the Earl of Buchan as we see from the minutes of the society dated Oct. 18th, 1814:—

"A Letter from the Right Honorable the Earl of Buchan, addressed to the treasurer, was laid before the meeting, stating that his Lordship had an original painting of the celebrated George Buchanan, the Scottish historian, and politely offering to allow any artist to take a copy of it for the use of the society. The meeting is of opinion that the Letter should be communicated to the general meeting of the society, to be held on the eighth day of November next, and in the meantime they appointed Mr. Archibald Buchanan, of the Atlas Office, to enquire at Mr. Raeburn, artist in Edinburgh, as to the probable expense of a copy of the picture, and to communicate the result to the general meeting."

The general meeting considered the matter and its decision is recorded in the minutes thus:—

"The Letter from the Right Honorable the Earl of Buchan, mentioned in the minutes of last meeting of the directors, was communicated to the meeting, with the proceedings thereon, and Mr. Archibald Buchanan having read a letter from Mr. Raeburn stating that the expense of the copy of the picture of George Buchanan would be twenty-five guineas, exclusive of the frame: It was resolved unanimously that the picture should be obtained at the expense of the society, be kept under the charge of the treasurer to the society for the time being, and hung up in the room where the society's meetings are usually held during such meetings."

"The thanks of the society were then voted unanimously to the Right Honorable the Earl of Buchan for his politeness in allowing the society to take a copy of the picture, which they desire the preses, treasurer, and secretary to communicate by letter to his Lordship."

Raeburn's communications on the subject are preserved by the Buchanan Society, whose members and secretary, Mr. P. G. Keyden, kindly allow me to reproduce them from privately printed copies. The letter about the price is not included.

(1)

EDIN., 2 *Dec.*, 1814.

SIR,

In your letter of 9th November, you desired me to inform you when the Portrait of GEO. BUCHANAN should be finished, and I now beg leave to mention that it is done, and I shall be happy to receive your further orders.

I am, SIR,

Your mo. obedt. Servt.,

ARCH. BUCHANAN, Esq.   (Signed)   HENRY RAEBURN.

(2)

EDIN., 13 *Dec.*, 1814.

SIR,

I send you by the Carrier the Portrait of GEO. BUCHANAN, carefully packed, and I have no doubt but you will receive it safe. Lord BUCHAN is of opinion that the original was painted by TITIAN, I am not well enough acquainted with the history of GEO. BUCHANAN to be able to say whether he had an opportunity of being painted by that master, but it is not unlike his style, and at all events is an excellent Picture. I have been at great pains to make the copy like, and I hope the Society will be pleased with it. I would recommend that it should not be sent to a frame maker's shop for fear of accidents, 'tis enough that the measure of it be given.

You are pleased to bid me draw on you for the amount, which is 25 Guineas, but it will be easier managed if you will have the goodness to order that sum to be paid into the office of the Royal Bank at Glasgow on my account, and I receive it from the Bank here.

I remain, SIR,

Your most obedt. and faithful Servant,

ARCHD. BUCHANAN, Esq., Glasgow.   (Signed)   HENRY RAEBURN.

(3)

EDIN., 24 *Dec.*, 1814.

SIR,

I have this morning the honor of your letter of yesterday, covering a Dft. for £26 5s., being the payment for the copy of a Portrait of GEO. BUCHANAN, and for which I beg you will accept my best thanks. It gives me very great pleasure to believe from an expression of your letter that you are satisfied with what I have done, and I remain, with great respect, SIR,

Your most obedt. and faithful Servt.,

To ARCHD. BUCHANAN, Esq., Glasgow.   (Signed)   HENRY RAEBURN.

Two years before this Raeburn was elected an associate of the Royal Academy. His visit to London in 1810, and introduction to certain members of the Academy no doubt helped to bring this honour. Cunningham would make us believe that Raeburn was disappointed because of the apparent neglect of the English and other Academies, and in the Anderson collection of Royal Academy Catalogues, we find a note which states that Raeburn "had long sought for the honourable distinction of Royal Academician to be added to his name." This eagerness for Academic laurels is not borne out by the artist himself. In a letter written in 1814 to a friend in London :—

"I observe what you say respecting the election of R.A., but what am I to do here? they know I am on the list; if they choose to elect me without solicitation, it will be the more honorable to me, and I will think the more of it; but if it can only be obtained by means of solicitation and canvassing, I must give up all hope of it, for I would think it unfair to employ those means.. I am besides out of the way and have no opportunity. I rejoice in the worthy president's increasing reputation; it is pleasing and consolatory to see that additional powers come with the increase of years. Write and tell me what artists are about, and whether anything be indispensable for a person who desires to become a member of the Royal Academy. Were you in sufficient health to see Somerset House during last exhibition? I had some things there, but no artist of my acquaintance has been kind enough to write me one syllable on the subject, to say either what he thought himself, or what others thought."

Raeburn's pictures that year were " Sir David Baird," " Lord Seaforth," and two unnamed portraits, and they with the friendship Wilkie, may have secured Raeburn's election to full rank in the following year 1815. As his diploma picture, he sent the magnificent portrait of himself, now in the Scottish National Gallery, but it was refused because of the rule that self-portraits of the members were not accepted. Consequently he waited until 1821 before he•sent the beautiful " Boy and Rabbit," which is a portrait of his step-grandson who was deaf and dumb. Soon after his election he was made a member of the Imperial Academy of Florence; in 1817 the New York Academy of the fine arts elected him as an honorary member; in November a similar favour was bestowed by the Academy of arts, South Carolina, and he was admitted a fellow of the Royal Society of Edinburgh.

About 1815 he painted the splendid portrait of his wife, which now belongs to Sir Ernest Cassel, and it was succeeded by the portrait of Admiral " Sir David Milne." This work which was a commission from George Holme, of Paxton, was long delayed in the painting as will be seen by these letters. First I give a letter from Raeburn to Mr. Home about a copy of Lord President Blair's portrait, as this epistle precedes the others.

EDINBURGH, 12th May, 1814.

DEAR SIR,

Your copy of Lord President Blair's portrait was sent to me a few days ago. Have the goodness to inform me if it is to be sent out to you, and whether it is to be framed, and I shall give orders about it immediately.

I am with sincere respect, dear sir,
Your most obedient and faithful servant,
HENRY RAEBURN.

Then in a letter from Captain, afterwards Sir David, Milne to George Home, of Wedderburn, we read :—

"My father is just now very well. Yesterday he walked up and dined with me and walked home after. He has consented to go to Raeburn on Wednesday, which I am happy at."

From this extract it would appear that Raeburn painted a portrait of Sir David's father. If he did, there is no record of it.

Then follow three letters from Raeburn, all to Mr. Home.

xliv.

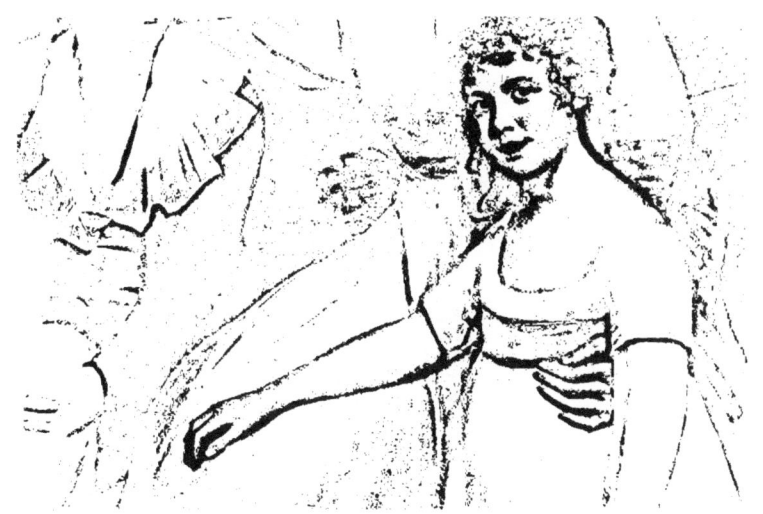

DEAR SIR,
I am t
of Sir De
possible.
it accompa
before
I am, w

Mr. Ho
portrait finis
year.

DEAR SI
I
finished,
wish, and
is upon t
picture i
the amou
insure th
loss of m
I rema

DEAR
I ha
quite
the very
I shall w
of a p
engraving
circumst

The sea
picture to it
know wheth
of Col. M
uniform, wi
The

DEAR
I
direct
its bein
possible
through
I am,

In refer
it was better
artists do

EDINBURGH, *28th November*, 1817.

DEAR SIR,

I am this moment favoured with yours, and am ashamed to say that your portrait of Sir David Milne still wants a good deal of being finished. It is my intention, if possible, to have it at the London Exhibition, and every exertion shall be made to get it accomplished; and the only apology I have to make for its not having been finished before now, and the true one, is just that I have really been oppressed with business.

I am, with great respect and esteem, dear sir,

Your most faithful servant,

HENRY RAEBURN.

Mr. Home's reply was to the effect that if Raeburn did not get the portrait finished for the next year's exhibition he could not wait another year.

(2)

EDINBURGH, *17th March*, 1818.

DEAR SIR,

I have the pleasure of telling you that the portrait of Sir David Milne, is not only finished, but shipped this morning for London for the Exhibition, according to your wish, and I flatter myself it is a picture that will do me some credit. As the weather is upon the whole boisterous, I presume you will think proper that I insure it. The picture itself is 140 gs., and the frame and case, although I do not yet know precisely the amount, yet I do not think they will be much under 30 gs., at which sum I will insure them, as I suppose you will, with me, think that it is not necessary to risk the loss of money.

I remain, with very great esteem, dear Sir,

Your most obedient and faithful servant,

HENRY RAEBURN.

(3)

EDINBURGH, *20th March*, 1818.

DEAR SIR,

I have the pleasure of your letter of the 18th. I know your name perfectly, and am quite ashamed of having written John, but I recollect some person came in upon me at the very time I was addressing the letter, which probably was the cause of the blunder. I shall write to London and endeavour to get you notice of what would be the expense of a print, but it will be necessary that you tell me the size, and also the nature of the engraving, whether a mezzotint or a stroke engraving, for much depends on these circumstances.

The rest of the letter deals with the insurance and sending of the picture to its owner at Paxton, at the close of the Exhibition. I do not know whether an engraving was made of the portrait, which is the property of Col. Milne Holme, and shows the Admiral standing at full length in naval uniform, with a view of Algiers in the background.

The last letter is dated Edinburgh, 9th July, 1818 :—

DEAR SIR,

I gave orders some time ago that Sir David Milne's portrait should be sent to you direct from London, and as the Exhibition is now closed, I expect to hear every day of its being sent off; but as these voyages are sometimes as expeditious as the post, it is possible that the picture may arrive at Berwick before the information can reach you, through me, of its being sent......I will write the moment I hear anything about it.

I am, with greatest esteem and respect, Dear Sir,

Your most obedient, faithful servant,

HENRY RAEBURN.

In referring to the 1818 Exhibition in the *Examiner*, R. B. Haydon said it was better than many past ones; for if many, or even the majority, of the artists do not advance, some have advanced greatly. Their thinking and executive powers have been nurtured by evident painstaking emulation. As proofs of this we refer to the greater part of the following works. Among the pictures mentioned are Raeburn's portrait of " Sir David Milne," and Constable's " Landscape, breaking of a shower." The story is told about the latter picture that Fuseli asked his housekeeper for an " ombrella, as he was goint to see Constable's ' Shower.' "

It has been said that Raeburn's later method was influenced by the work of Hoppner and Lawrence, the one an eclectic, the other, save in his best portraits of men, superficial and flimsy. The facts are against this assumption. Where and when did he find the opportunity to study their art ? He visited London on three occasions only, in 1795, 1810 and in 1815, after his election to the Royal Academy. He knew scarcely anything of what was going on in London Art circles as the following letter to Wilkie shows :—

EDINBURGH,
12th September, 1819.

MY DEAR SIR,

    I let you to wit that I am still here, and long much to hear from you, both as to how you are and what you are doing. I would not wish to impose on you any hardship upon you, but it would give me the greatest pleasure if you would take the trouble to write me at least once a year, if not oftener, and give me a little information of what is going on among the artists, for I do assure you I have as little communication with any of them and know almost as little about them as if I were living at the Cape of Good Hope.

    I send up generally a picture or two to the exhibition, which serve merely as an advertisement that I am still in the land of the living, but in other respects it does me no good, for I get no notice from anyone, nor have I the least conception how they'look beside others. I know not in what London papers any critiques of that kind are made, and our Edinburgh ones (at least those that I see) take no notice of these matters. At anyrate I would prefer a candid observation or two from an artist like you, conveying not only your own opinion but perhaps that of others, before any of them.

    Are the portrait painters as well employed as ever. Sir Thomas Lawrence, they tell me, has refused to commence any more pictures till he gets done with those that are on hand, and that he has raised his prices to some enormous sum. There came to me this morning two critical descriptions of Mr. Stothard's " Procession to Canterbury " and Mr. West's " Death on a Pale Horse," by Mr. Carey, but through what channel they have come I do not yet know. So far as I have looked into them they seem to me remarkably well written. Do you know is that true, and will you do me the favour to tell me what his prices really are, and what Sir W. Beechy, Mr. Philips, and Mr. Owen have for their pictures? It will be a particular favour if you will take the trouble to ascertain these for me precisely, for I am raising my prices, too, and it would be a guide to me—not that I intend to raise mine so high as your famous London artists.

    I was sorry to hear that Mr. West had been far from well. I hope he is now better. Accept my best wishes and believe me, with sincere esteem, yours faithfully,

(Signed) HENRY RAEBURN.

This is an extraordinary letter for a man of Raeburn's genius to have written. The unbounded modesty and childlike naiveté are rare even among men of outstanding talent. When one looks at his magnificent portraits and thinks of the huge sums they now realise at Christie's it is difficult to understand the lack of contemporary appreciation. Some years afterwards, in 1822, he wrote to William Paulet Carey, the painter and art critic mentioned in the epistle quoted, but only part of the former document has fallen into my hands.

The critic evidently had been in Edinburgh, and Raeburn's letter to him refers to a conversation of some art matter of interest to the artist who says he had not heard "A sylable upon the subject since you left this, nor have I ever to my recollection heard in what publication your thoughts are conveyed to the public. And having no correspondent in the metropolis but my friend Mr. Wilkie who generally writes me about once a year." The letter concludes thus —

"Now, my dear Sir, I know that all your countrymen are warm and very warm, but they are kind too, therefore, after cooling a little I will lay my account with an answer to this letter. Mrs. R. is seeing me employed in such an unwonted manner asks to know to whom I could be writing and requested I would send her best regards in which she was joined by her son and his wife. Before concluding, allow me to congratulate you on what I suppose must by this time have taken place, *viz.*, your having got your money from my Lord Strathmore."

After his visits to London in 1810 and 1815, his work certainly assumed a suaver aspect, a more delicate sense of colour, but the man who could paint a "Sir Nathaniel Spens," "Sir John Sinclair," "Mrs. James Campbell," "Lord Newton," "Mrs. Cruikshank," "Mrs. Campbell of Balliemore," had more to give Hoppner and Lawrence than they had to offer him. These works were followed by others that showed increasing power to the end of his career. In succession came splendid portraits of men like "Mr. James Byres, of Tonley"; the artist's own portrait; the magnificent "Lady Raeburn" (c 1815); the "Sir David Milne," 1818; the "Lord Craig," of the same year; "James Wardrop of Torbanehill"; "Andrew Wauchope"; the exquisite "Boy and Rabbit," 1821; and the masterly portrait of Scott, 1822-23. Then among portraits of women we have "Lady Maitland," 1817; the charming "Miss Margaret Suttie" and "Miss Janet Suttie"; the famous picture of "Mrs. Scott-Moncrieff"; "Miss Anne Cunningham-Grahame, of Gartmore" (c. 1821); "Lady Belhaven"; "Mrs. Gregory"; "Mrs. Simpson"; "Mrs. Hay, of Spot"; "Miss Ross"; "Mrs. Stewart, of Physgill"; "Mrs. Ferguson, of Trochraigne"; "Mrs. Grant, of Kilgraston"; "Mrs. Irvine Boswell"; "Mrs. de Vismes"; "Mrs. Vere, of Stonebyre," and "Mrs. Douglas"; "Lady Stewart, of Coltness"; all creations of great beauty.

A letter dated Edinburgh, the 17th July, 1816, is supposed to refer to a "Portrait of a Boy" exhibited at the Royal Academy in that year. The letter reads :—

DEAR SIR,

I had a letter from you—I am ashamed to say a long time ago—without my ever having the grace to reply to it, and I dare say you have long thought me unworthy of the trouble you gave yourself, and I must confess it to be all true, but trust to your goodness that you will forgive me.

Having a sketch of a young friend of mine lying by me for some time, I have taken it into my head to send it to you by the smack "King George," if you think it worth the having up in your own room, you may do so. I remain, with sincere esteem and best wishes, my dear sir,

Your most obedient and faithful servant,

HENRY RAEBURN.

CHAPTER VI.

RAEBURN PRICES.

RAEBURN, as we have seen, was a man of generous nature. In his busy life he found time to help his fellow artists in deed and word. We know how he encouraged David Roberts, R.A., whom he found when a boy sketching in the garden. He lent the showrooms of his studio in York Place to the Society of Artists when its members inaugurated a series of exhibitions in 1808; and in 1822 he used his influence on behalf of his fellow painters, who "partly in opposition to the Royal Institution," proposed to form an Academy. The letter written by Raeburn in support of this movement is fully transcribed in Mr. James L. Caw's excellent work, "Scottish Painting, Past and Present," and he kindly permits me to reproduce this interesting document, which gives an idea of the extent of his practice.

YORK PLACE, 24th December, 1822.

DEAR SIR,

I formerly mentioned to you that I had received several visits from some of the oldest and best established artists of this place, and also stated to you what had been the object of their visits.

It will probably be in your recollection that a few years ago the artists here had several Exhibitions, which were made by way of experiment, and which succeeded far beyond their expectations.

By these Exhibitions they had realised a fund amounting to between £500 and £600, and at that time it was the intention of those whose labours had, perhaps, contributed most to the success of the Exhibitions, to apply for a Charter and have themselves formed into a Corporate Body.

But unfortunately for their purpose, they had at the first outset been guilty of a great oversight. That they might not seem to act upon a system of exclusion, they had admitted too many into the Society whose works were of little importance to its success, but whose voice when a matter came to the vote was just as efficient as that of those by whom alone it may be said to have been sustained.

Before those members had matured their plan, the poorer and less efficient members threw their eyes upon the fund, a motion was made to divide it, and carried by a majority against the sense of the older and more efficient members; and thus what would otherwise have been a bond of union was dissolved.

This was to many a great disappointment, but there was no quarrel as the public supposed, for it was impossible to be displeased with them who voted for the division, as it was known that the fund, small as it was, had become an object to several, and that others to whom it was a matter of indifference had, from a knowledge of this circumstance, voted with them.

It had been found at the same time from experience, that an annual Exhibition was too great an undertaking for this place, and more than they were able to sustain. The idea of continuing it was, therefore, laid aside for the present, and it was just beginning to be taken up again when the Institution for the encouragement of the fine Arts was established.

The purpose of instituting a Society having again been resumed by those who first projected it, they now propose to admit only a limited number, and to make it a *sine qua non* of admission, that the funds shall never be divided, but shall be applied to the purposes after mentioned.

When these gentlemen came to inform me of their intention, I begged to know if they were influenced by any motives or views that were hostile to the Institution. They replied that it was quite the reverse. They had the highest esteem and respect for the gentlemen of the Institution, and both their motives and their conduct met with their most unqualified approbation. But as it was their own fixed purpose that their

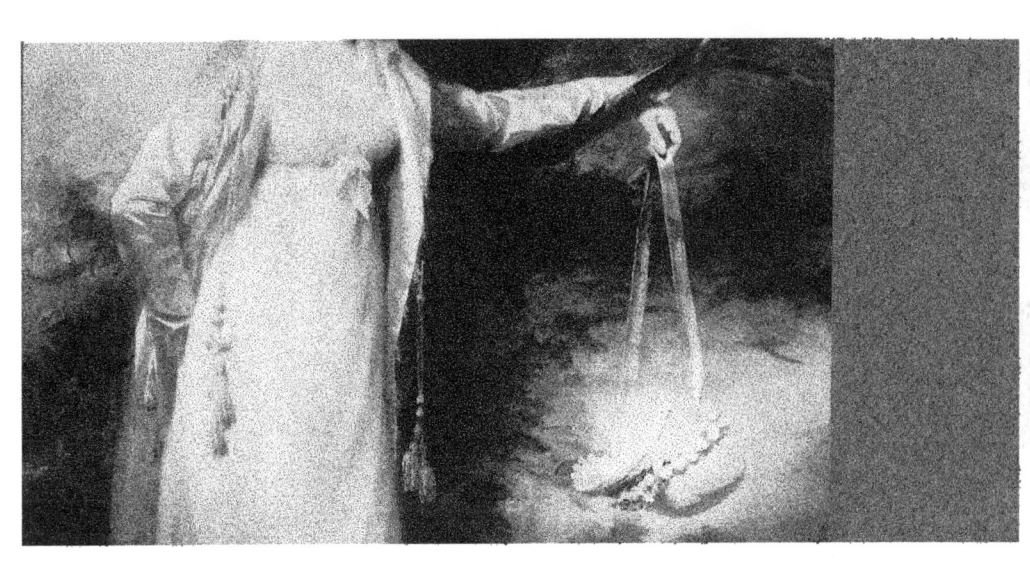

funds, as ▮
other articl
artist, they
therefore,
approbatic
   Upon m
the funds
might be :
necessary
   1st. B
Institutio
every and
Committee
and that c
thus take
   2nd. T
and a ▮
their ▮
for subject
   3rd. T
little circu
would req
the use ▮
condescen
   4th. A
abroad th:
necessary
   Now, m
I thought :
you comm
   As for a
as many of
though it :
personally :
place, whic
Artists ▮
profession, a
I cannot ▮
   The ▮
I have of i
considered :
   I am, wi

To James

Raeburn'
of artists on
Academy wa
artists was s
In this epist
secretary of
to enter the :
admiration ex
of a visit of (
Scotland, th
August 29th, :
Nasmyth and

funds, as they came in, should be laid out in the purchase of Books, Prints, and such other articles connected with Art, as would be useful both to the student and advanced artist, they considered themselves co-operating in the views of the Institution, and, therefore, had no doubt but that they would meet with their countenance and approbation.

Upon my stating that, in all probability the Institution, in as far as the application of the funds was concerned, had the same things in contemplation, they replied that it might be so, but even in that case that a separate Society and distinct funds would be necessary for the following reasons :—

1st. Because they could in no instance derive benefit from the good intentions of the Institution without previous or perhaps frequent applications to that Society, that every such application would of course be delayed till there should be a meeting of the Committee, and probably a reference made by the Committee to the general meeting, and that delays even with the kindest intentions on the part of the Institution might thus take place, till the very purpose for which the application was made had gone by.

2nd. That every application necessarily implied a power of control on the one side and a state of dependence on the other, to which, in so far at least as concerns the use their own property arising from the fruit of their own labours, there was no necessity for subjecting themselves.

3rd. That in the management of their own affairs, it was easy to foresee a variety of little circumstances which would require to be attended to, and arrangements that would require to be made, in order to afford conveniences and facilities to themselves in the use of their property, which it could not be expected that the Institution would condescend to be troubled with.

4th. And beside all this, there was something degrading in the idea which had gone abroad that they were unfit to conduct their own affairs, and, therefore, it had become necessary to take the management into their own hands.

Now, my dear Sir, I confess to you that there were several of these arguments which I thought unanswerable, but I shall be glad to have your opinion upon the subject, before you communicate these views of the artists to any members of the Institution.

As for myself, I have nothing to gain by the measure. I have in my own possession as many of the means of improvement as I have time to attend to, and my business, though it may fall off, cannot admit of enlargement. In so far, therefore, as I am personally con—, I am quite indifferent about it, but I wish well to the Arts of this place, which I think this measure would rather tend to improve, and I wish well to the Artists because I believe them to be as worthy a set of men as can be found in any profession, and I have uniformly received so much kindness and regard from them, that I cannot refuse to go along with them in any matter that appears reasonable.

The present proposal I consider to be of this kind, at least according to the view that I have of it, but as I am anxious to be concerned in nothing but what shall be considered just and reasonable, I shall be glad to receive your opinion upon the subject.

I am, with great esteem and regard, my dear Sir,
Your most obedient and faithful servant,
HENRY RAEBURN.

To James Skene, Esq.

Raeburn's death in 1823 evidently deferred the formation of a society of artists on the basis proposed, for it was not until 1826 that a Scottish Academy was founded. Another instance of his readiness to befriend young artists was seen in a short letter which was sold at Sotheby's last year. In this epistle written a few months before his death, he wrote to the secretary of the Edinburgh Trustees Academy, about a youth who wished to enter the schools. Raeburn's popularity as a man was as great as the admiration expressed for his paintings. This was shown when on the occasion of a visit of George IV., to Edinburgh, in 1822—the first visit of a king to Scotland, since the Union of Parliaments—Raeburn was knighted on August 29th, his fellow artists entertained him to a public dinner, Alexander Nasmyth and the painter as chairman. Sir William Beechey sent his congratulations, and the following letter was Raeburn's response.

MY DEAR SIR,
  Yesterday I had the pleasure of your kind letter, and do assume now that the hearty congratulations of my friends, among whom I have much reason to rank Sir W. Beechey, have not been less acceptable to me than the honour which His Majesty has been pleased to confer upon me. Accept my best thanks for your kind wishes, and allow me to add that I have never forgotten the liberal manner in which you were pleased to take of any little merit I possess, even long before I had the pleasure of knowing you—and also since has reached my ears from different quarters. But this is just what I would expect from Sir W. B.—an able artist himself, and far above that little jealousy which sometimes enters into the feelings of artists of inferior note. I need not say that you have always had my best word, and my best wishes in the fullest sense of the word. Our friend Wilkie is here—to whom I have sent your letter; he leaves this (place) to-day, and by him I send this letter.

Ever yours,
HENRY RAEBURN.

  In May, of the next year, the king appointed him his " Limner and painter in Scotland, with all fees, profits, salaries, rights, privileges, and advantages thereto belonging."
  In an entry under Raeburn's name in the second volume of " Engraved British Portraits." It reads thus: "George IV., nearly whole length, to right, seated in armchair, looking to right; in private dress, book in right hand; mezzotint; T. Hodgetts. Published by D. Hatton, Edinburgh." As a matter of fact Raeburn never painted a portrait of George IV. Sir Henry was commanded to do so, but he died before he could undertake the work. Here is the history of the portrait which has misled the British Museum authorities. The story was told by James Drummond, R.S.A., to Dr. John Brown, who relates it in his delightful " Horae Subsecivæ." Hatton, the print-seller, had a fine plate of Raeburn's portrait of Dr. Thomas Hope, professor of chemistry at Edinburgh University, and when George IV. came to Scotland, "we were all mad about him from Sir Walter (Scott) downwards." The print-seller, having made "his utmost out of the plate as 'Dr. Hope,' scraped his head out and put in that of the bewigged and becurled ' First Gentleman in Europe '. The rest of the plate remains unchanged, except the Royal Arms on the book and the Star of the Garter on the doctor's breast . . . It is altogether the best of jokes." The British Museum cataloguer in the volume referred to also records the Hope engraving somewhat as follows : " Hope, Charles Thomas ; whole length ; to right, seated in easy chair, book in right hand. T. Hodgetts. Mezzotint."
  As it proved these honours came at the very end of his life. In July he joined an excursion to Fifeshire. Among the company were Sir Walter Scott, Miss Edgworth, Sir Adam Ferguson, and Lord chief Commissioner Adam. A delightful time was spent and Raeburn "contributed largely to the enjoyment of the party." But on the day after his return Sir Henry went to his gallery in York Place, " and began to touch the portrait of a Mrs. Dennistoun, but was unable to proceed. He walked home, and with considerable headache, went to bed whence he never rose." This account differs from that of Sir Walter Scott who believed that his (Scott's) own portrait was the last one touched by Raeburn. There is no other record of the Dennistoun picture. Morrison hearing of his illness called late in the evening to see Raeburn and was told that there was no hope of his recovery. " This was twenty-four hours before his death. He was lying with his eyes

shut, but not asleep. I touched softly the hand which was lying across his breast—the hand which had been so often outstretched to welcome me." Raeburn died on the 8th July, 1823, and was buried in St. John's Church at the West End of Princes Street. A few years ago an anonymous admirer placed a tablet in the wall to show the spot where the painter's grave lay undistinguished, and a life-size statue of him by Mr. Pittendrigh Macgillivray stands in one of the niches in the Scottish Portrait Gallery, in Queen Street, Edinburgh. Lady Raeburn, who on no account would allow herself to be called "My lady," died ten years after her husband. They had two sons, Peter who died young, and Henry. The latter had three sons and five daughters; the second daughter married Sir Wm. Andrew and one of their sons William Raeburn Andrew wrote a life of Sir Henry.

If Raeburn kept no diaries, the under-noted letters to the Earl of Hardwicke prove that he kept Account books which if they were discovered would furnish much information about the names of sitters and the prices paid for his pictures.

ED., 13 BANK ST.,
3d Oct., 1823.

MY LORD,
Mr. Raeburn has put into my hands the books of the late Sir Henry Raeburn in order to ascertain the sums due to him. There appears to be due by you 100gs. for a portrait of your Lordship which Mr. Raeburn will be obliged by your ordering payment of to me who am authorised to receive and discharge the debts due to his father.
H. D. DICKIE.

30 *June*, 1824.
I have now the honor of informing your lordship that your portrait was yesterday shipped on board the "Forth," George Stewart master, conform to receipt enclosed. The case is addressed to your lordship " London," not knowing your particular residence so that it may be necessary for your Lordship to cause directions to be sent to the Leith and Glasgow Wharf, London.

The following docket is then presented :

	Price £105		
when if your Lordship has already remitted	50		
	55		
Frame	15	15	
Packing case and packing	2	12	6
Carriage to Leith		5	
	£73	12	6

H. D. Dickie was a writer to the *Signet* and legal adviser to Raeburn, He died in 1839, but I have failed to trace his successors. If there were any they no doubt preserved Raeburn's books which may be in existence to-day. His name appears on a feu charter for 16 Ann Street, Edinburgh, by Henry Raeburn granted on the 7th May, 1820, to James Mackenzie, W.S., who was a son of Henry Mackenzie, the "Man of feeling," and the original of one of Raeburn's finest canvases. Ann Street which was named after Raeburn's wife, formed part of the land purchased by Raeburn in 1798, at a public sale from the trustees of Mrs. Ross, widow of Walter Ross, W.S., with the barony of Dean, which belonged to Sir John Nisbet. Mr. John Geddie, author of " Romantic Edinburgh," and present occupier of No. 16

Ann Street, says in an account of "Sculptured Stones of Old Edinburgh" that "strict rules were laid down in the feu charters for the preservation of the amenity of the district, as well as the rights of the superior . . . . . Feuars were bound to take their ale or beer from any brewer within the barony of Dean that Sir John Nisbet and his successors should nominate." In Mr. Geddie's charter this rule is set forth and I suppose it could be put in force to-day.

A word may be said about the prices Raeburn received for his portraits. In 1787 he was paid £18 for a three-quarter length; he had sixty guineas for "Sir John and Lady Clerk," which now belongs to Mr. Otto Beit. About 1804 his price for a head was twenty guineas; by 1810 it rose to twenty-five guineas. In 1818 he received £147 for portraits of Mr. and Mrs. Gordon Aitkenhead, measuring 50 by 40. We gather this in the following extract from a letter by Raeburn :—

"To say that the Gentlemen of Glasgow pay like princes would be doing them the highest injustice, for they pay better than any of your great folks that ever I had anything to do with. I have just had the pleasure of your letter a bill on Messrs. Kinnear and Sons for £147, for which I beg you will accept my best thanks. With much esteem and many good wishes for yourself and family."

We have seen that in the same year his portrait of "Sir David Milne" was insured for £140, but that may not have been the actual cost of the picture. It is known, however, that in 1820 his price for a bust was fifty guineas, and in 1822 the W.S. Society gave him a hundred guineas for the portrait of "Lord Hume" (50 by 40), and a similar sum was paid to his trustees by Lord Hardwicke for a portrait. Of late years some of his finest portraits have changed hands at sums amounting to five figures.

But it was not until last May and July that his art triumphed at Christie's. On the 19th of the former month all auction records for a picture of any school were broken by the 22,300 guineas paid for a portrait of "Mrs. Robertson Williamson" (94 by 58½), which was painted about 1823. This enormous sum exceeds the £22,000 realised in the Secretan Sale in Paris in 1889 for Millet's "Angelus," and passes by 8,250 guineas the 14,050 guineas which Messrs. Duveen gave for Hoppner's "Lady Louisa Manners" in 1901. Raeburn's own former maximum of 8,700 guineas, the price of his splendid portrait of his wife, now the property of Sir Ernest Cassel, is a trifle compared with the figure of yesterday. Yet for many years after his death Raeburn's art met with no appreciation. He was classed as of the school of Lawrence; in 1877 forty-nine of his portraits fetched only £6,000, one of that number being his likeness of "Lady Raeburn" just mentioned. I am not forgetting the £14,700 at which his "Sir John Sinclair" was "hammered" in 1903, but that sale does not count as the picture was "bought in." Though the 22,300 guineas establishes a British record, America still leads in auction values. In the Yerkes Sale, in New York last year "A Woman," by Franz Hals, realised £27,400, and Turner's "Rockets and Bluelights" brought £25,800. Mrs. Williamson, whose maiden name was W. Boyd Robertson, was the daughter of William Boyd Robertson, who inherited Trochrig, Dumfriesshire, as a descendant of Zachary Boyd, the famous minister of the Barony Church in Cromwell's time, founder of Glasgow College, author of the "Battle of the Soul," 1619, and the "Garden of Zion," 1644. In 1814 she married her cousin Davidson

Robertson Williamson, of Balgray, who afterwards became a Judge of the Court of Session under the title of Lord Balgray. On the death of her uncle, General Archibald Robertson, she succeeded to the estate of Lawers, in Perthshire, it afterwards passing to Mr. Charles Williamson and to his son, Colonel David Robertson Williamson, who was the owner of the now famous picture of his grandaunt, which was painted by Raeburn shortly before he died in 1823. This portrait had never previously been offered for sale, and had been housed either in the family residence in George's Square, Edinburgh, or at Lawers.

In the picture she is seen in a white dress, cut low at the neck, and fastened at the waist with a white satin bow. Over her gown she wears a pink satin coat with long sleeves and tassels, and she stands in easy, graceful fashion in front of a tree. Her left arm rests on a branch, and in her hand she holds a grey ribbon from which dangles a dainty poke bonnet trimmed with roses. The figure, which is set in a landscape, has great beauty, and is painted with the supreme mastery that characterised his art at the end of his life. It is the most decorative of all his paintings known to me, and it is almost similar in dress and arrangement to the lovely " Mrs. Stewart of Physgill," painted about 1823, which Messrs. Duveen sold last year to Sir George Cooper. The chief difference is that the figure, instead of standing to the left as in the latter, is turned to the spectator's right. The face is not of the accepted type of feminine beauty. Here is no compromise to fashion, no exquisite mask that merely makes an attractive patch of colour in a design. The features not only express individuality but national character. The broad cheek bones, the large, lustrous, brown eyes, and the parted lips are symbols of the force that made and keeps Scotland great.

During the week of the sale this superb portrait commanded the admiration of all. The public and the expert were loud in its praise, and the general belief was that it would realise a vast sum. But the most perfervid Scot never dreamed that it would establish a British record. Immediately before the sale a well-known dealer said he thought it would at least exceed the former Raeburn maximum of 8,700 guineas. But that same gentleman was the under-bidder at 22,000 guineas. A burst of applause rang through the room when the green-baize draping was removed from the picture, and in three bids the figures rose to 5,000 guineas. Everyone then felt that it would reach 10,000 guineas. Messrs. Agnew and Duveen found a determined opponent in Mr. Smith, the auctioneer's clerk, and the thousands accumulated until the Hoppner record of 14,050 guineas was broken. Still there was no sign of slackening. In a three-cornered fight hundreds of pounds were exchanged; 17,000 guineas, 18,000 guineas, and amid applause 20,000 guineas was reached. But the end of the contest had not yet come. Mr. Smith was receiving mysterious toe-telegraphic messages, and Mr. Louis Duveen wondered who was his real opponent. But, like James FitzJames, he seemed to say :

Come one, come all, this rock shall fly,
From its firm base as soon as I.

Again to quote from Raeburn's countryman, Sir Walter Scott, Mr. Duveen and Mr. Smith suggested :

Two dogs of black St. Hubert's breed,
Unmatched for courage, breath, and speed.

Someone, however, had to win, and the "holiest draught of power" fell to Mr. Duveen at 22,300 guineas amid great applause. Mr. Gutekunst, of Messrs. Colnaghi and Co., was the *deus machina* who moved Mr. Smith. This triumph for the art of Sir Henry Raeburn for the moment made all forget that it also meant a defeat and loss to Britain of a great picture. Though Mr. Duveen bought for his own firm there can be little doubt that the portrait will eventually add to the parade of wealth on the other side of the Atlantic.

After the sale I called at Messrs. Duveen's premises and saw the picture in a better light than that at Christie's. Its qualities were more apparant, its suave force was more impelling. On examining the back of the canvas there appeared the inscription "Middleton, St. Martin's-lane, London," which was the name and address of the artist's colourman, who supplied Raeburn with all his canvas, paint, and brushes. A letter in Sir Henry's handwriting in proof of this statement is reproduced on page 37.

This extraordinary sum was the means of bringing to Christie's a great number of portraits ascribed to Raeburn. Several of those offered on the 14th of July were beneath consideration, the work, no doubt, of some contemporary or more recent *Amico di* Raeburn. Those that might with reason be accepted as by Sir Henry were of varied quality, not one in my opinion representing the Scotman's art in its greatest phase of expression. None of them as a whole had the mastery qualities of, say, the "Mrs. James Campbell," shown at the Japan-British Exhibition last year at Shepherd's Bush, nor of the "MacNab" now in the International Exhibition at Rome. From the head to the waist the portrait of "Lady Janet Traill" (49½ by 39½), which, after an opening bid of 3,000 guineas, went to Messrs. Duveen at 14,000 guineas, is of great charm, but the painting of the dress has not the distinction which characterised the gown of the "Mrs. Robertson Williamson" also acquired by the same firm. Lady Janet is shown, seated in a typical Raeburn landscape, in a yellow dress, cut low at the neck, and relieved by white. Powder pales her light brown hair, bound by a blue ribbon, which forms a lovely note of colour. This portrait resembles in style the splendid "Lady Alicia Stewart," which belongs to Mrs. F. C. K. Fleishmann. The original, who was the daughter of the tenth Earl of Caithness, was very popular in the Edinburgh society of her day. In 1784 she married James Traill, of Hobbister and Rattar, and died in Edinburgh, in 1806, about six years after the date of her portrait, and was buried at Rosslyn Chapel.

Lady Janet's husband, James Traill, was an advocate and Sheriff of the Counties of Caithness and Orkney. His portrait, which is one of the most sensitive images of men ever painted by Raeburn, fetched 3,500 guineas (Colnaghi and Obach). These two canvases were the property of Mr. James Christie Traill, and came from Castlehill House, Caithness.

Few artists were more favoured by nature, environment and circumstance than was Henry Raeburn. He was born with great gifts. In mind, temperament and person he had all the elements that bring success. His energy, mental and physical, was untiring; his interests were numerous, and splendid spirits and bodily strength enabled him to attend to each and at the same time to the development of his art. If he went sketching he took his fishing rod with him, for he was an "honest" and enthusiastic

aliest draught of power" fell to
t applause. Mr. Gutekunst, of
machine who moved Mr. Smith.
eburn for the moment made all
ss to Britain of a great picture.
irm there can be little doubt that
ide of wealth on the other side of

Duveen's premises and saw the
ristie's. Its qualities were more
elling. On examining the back of
m "Middleton, St. Martin's-lane,
ess of the artist's colourman, who
int, and brushes. A letter in Sir
ment is reproduced on page 37.
os of bringing to Christie's a great
 Several of those offered on the
a, the work, no doubt, of some
Raeburn. Those that might with
 of varied quality, not one in my
in its greatest phase of expression.
stery qualities of, say, the "Mrs.
 -British Exhibition last year at
now in the International Exhibition
ce portrait of "Lady Janet Traill"
g bid of 3,000 guineas, went to
I great charm, but the painting of
aracterised the gown of the "Mrs.
g the same firm. Lady Janet is
spe, in a yellow dress, cut low at
 pales her light brown hair, bound
g note of colour. This portrait
licia Stewart," which belongs to
al. who was the daughter of the
lar in the Edinburgh society of
Traill, of Hobbister and Rattar,
t six years after the date of her
ged.
al, was an advocate and Sheriff of
 His portrait, which is one of the
painted by Raeburn, fetched 3,500
a two canvases were the property
from Castlehill House, Caithness.
by nature, environment and circum-
was born with great gifts. In mind,
elements that bring success. His
ming; his interests were numerous,
 enabled him to attend to each
t of his art. If he went sketching
 was an "honest" and enthusiastic

follower of Isaac Walton. When tired after a d:
archery took him out to the fields and woodl
mechanics occupied his thoughts, the mystery of per
him; or he made three-foot models of naval archite
of abstract love for the subtle science of law"; ti
intimate with flowers. His knowledge of the plannin
was also practical, for in later years he laid out the
designed the houses that formed most of its streets
man of action but not infrequently the Jack-of-all-tn
was otherwise with Raeburn, as it was with some
Renaissance for example, Giotto, Leonardo, and Mi
not painting pictures, were raising a campanile, a cb
producing great statues or noble poetry. The youn;
were pulsing with the blood which in earlier days fo
or tribal feud or religious frenzy. It had to find
action. If little drops now and again led hin
matters, the main flood stirred his artistic impulse
the finest types of his country men and women—a I
a Macnab, a Sinclair, a Wardrop, of Torbanehill.

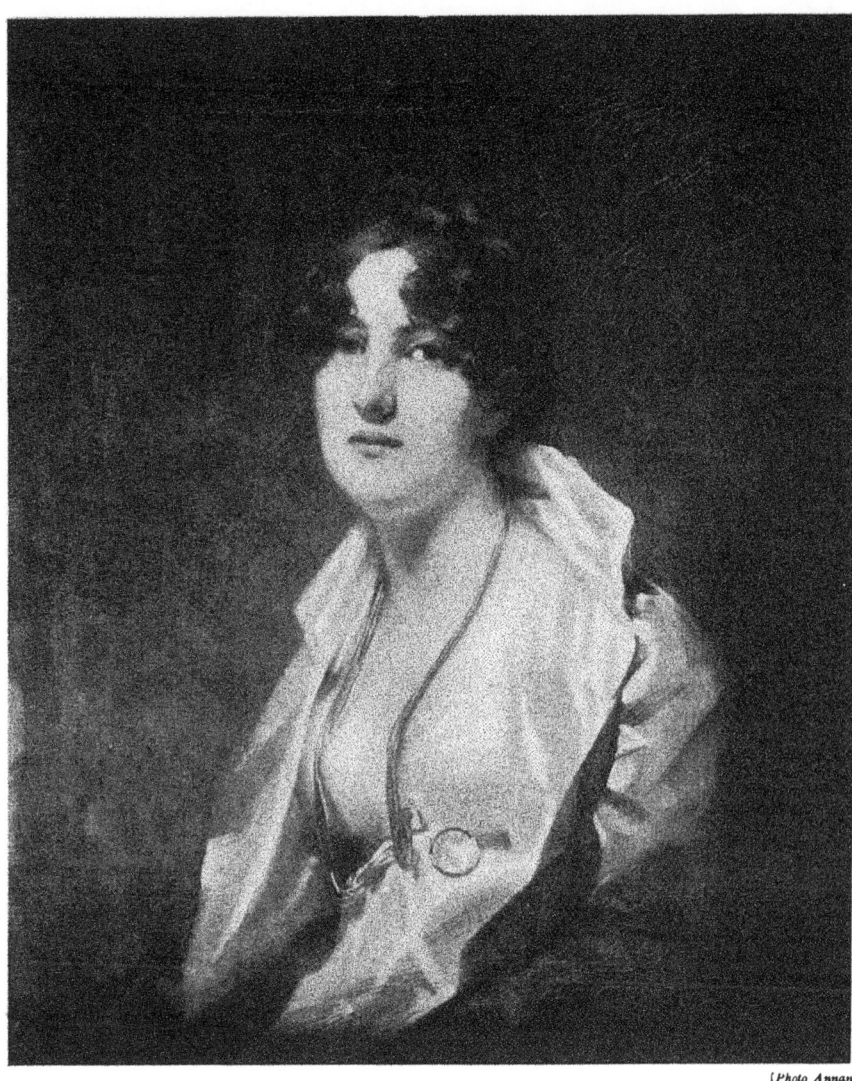

MRS. CAMPBELL OF POSSIL

[Photo Annan

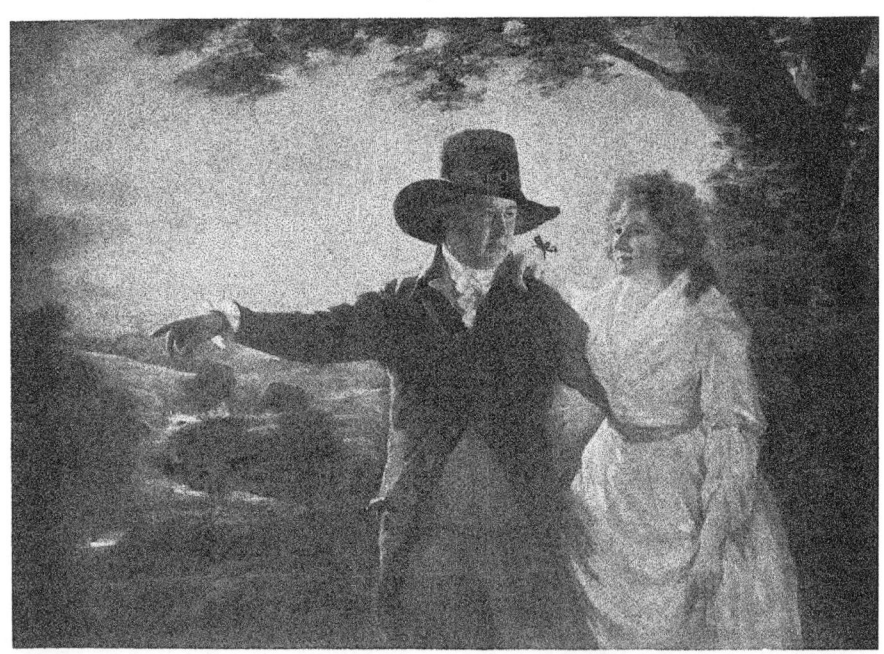

SIR JOHN AND LADY CLERK

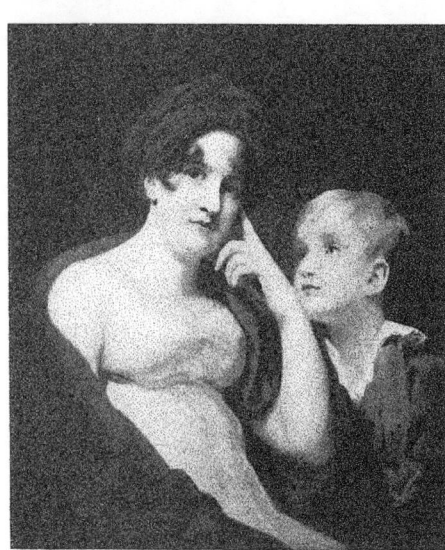

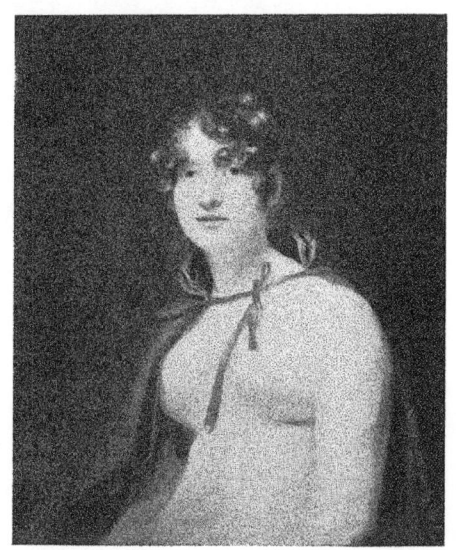

MRS. CAMPBELL AND SON   MRS. MUNRO

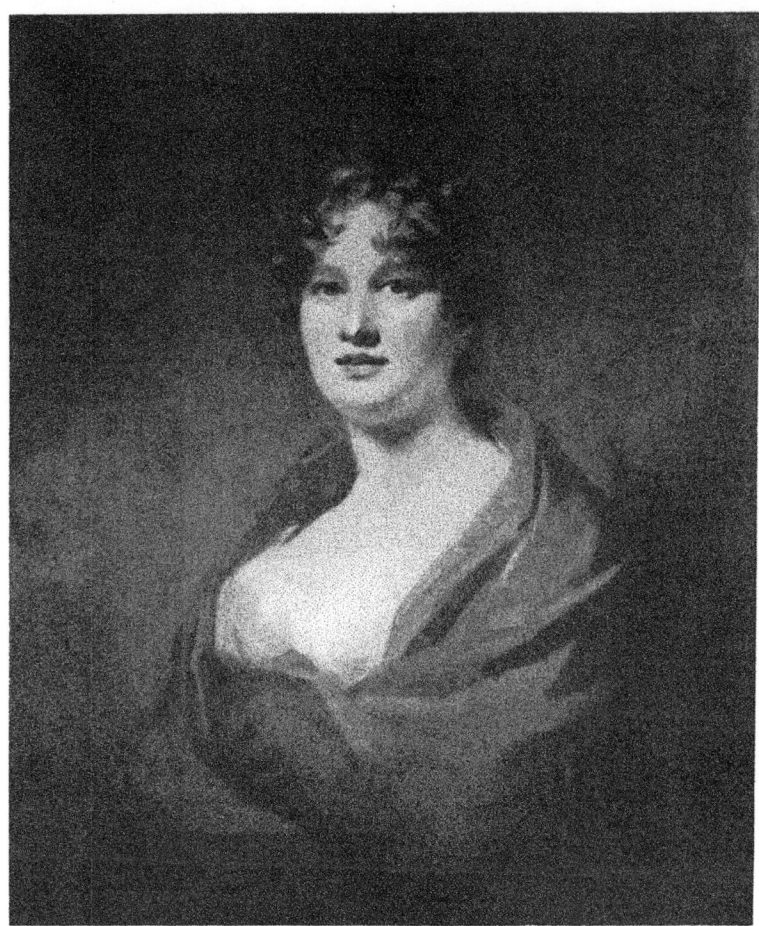

LADY CARMICHALL

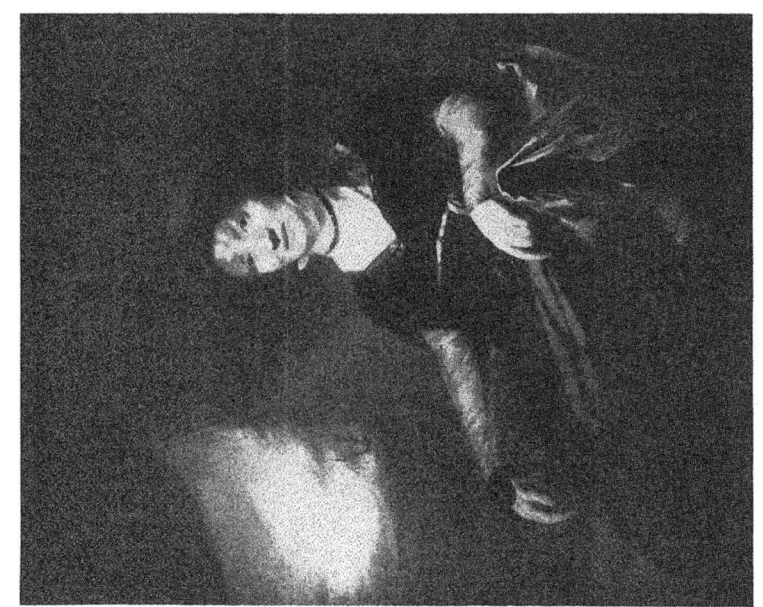

MRS. ADAM

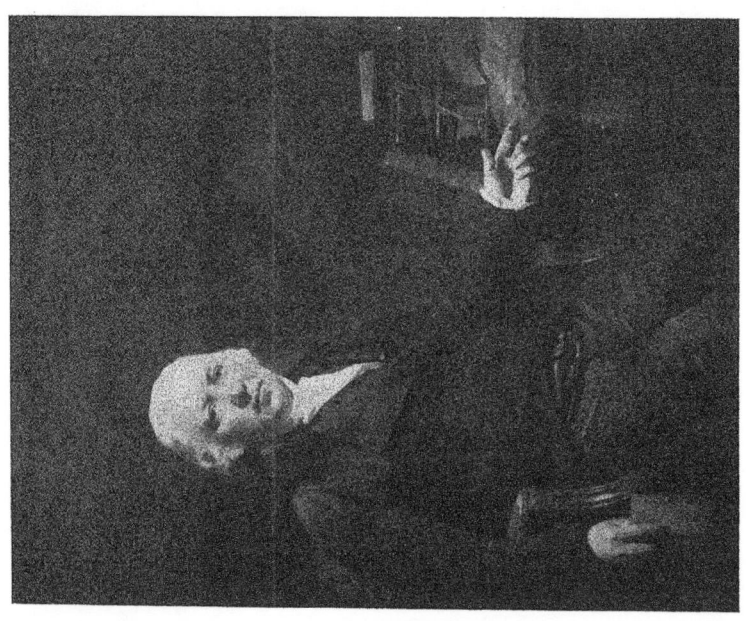

MR. ADAM

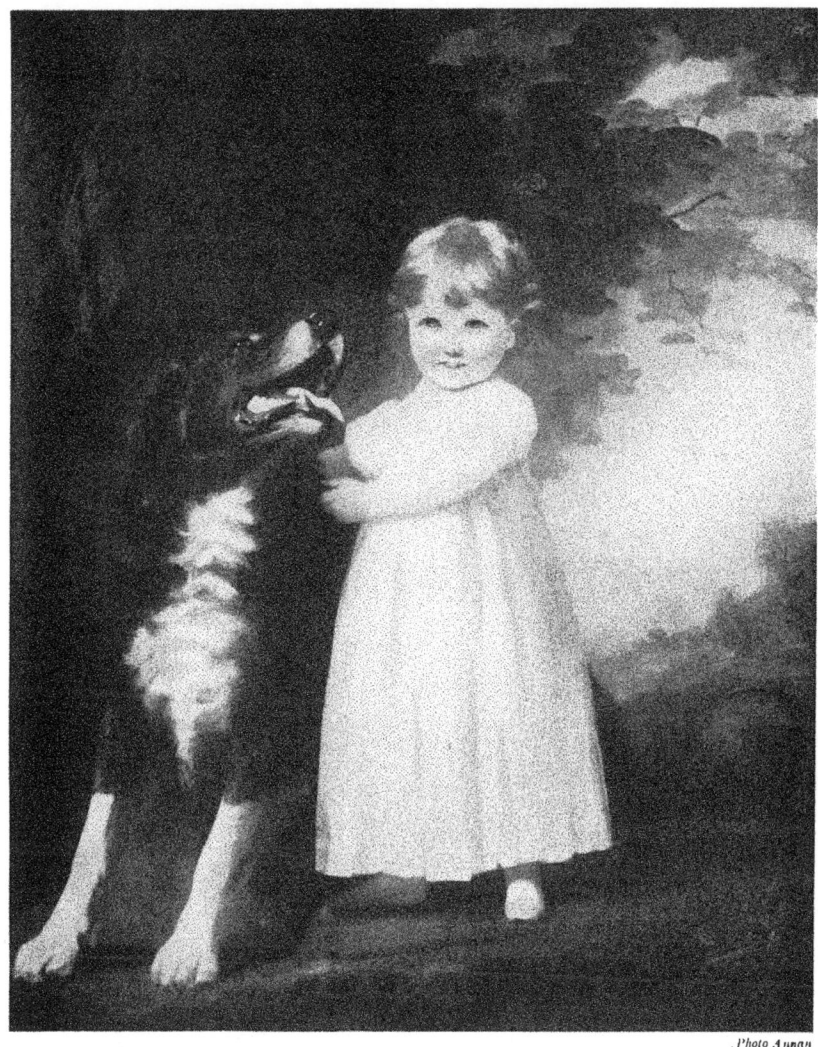

MISS E. M. GIBSON CARMICHAEL

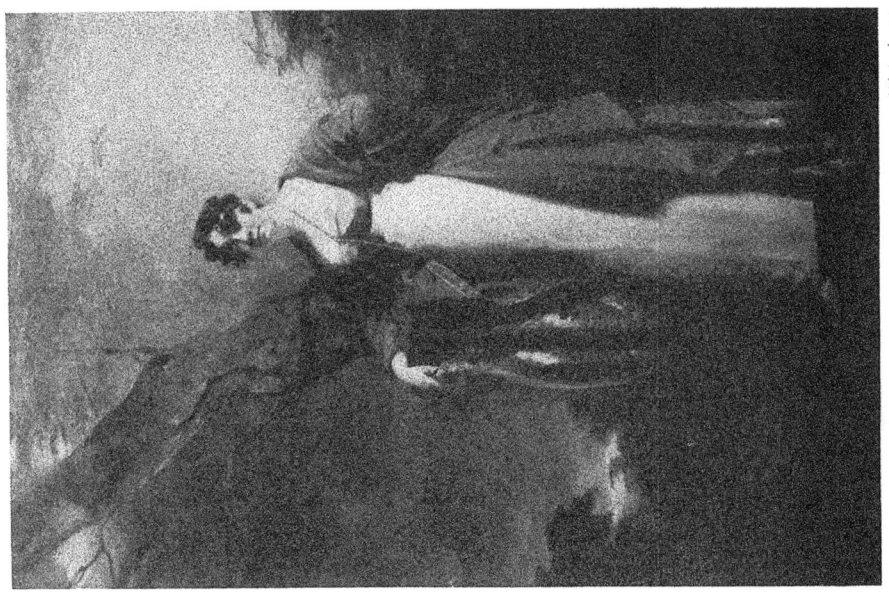

[Photo Annan

MRS. HAMILTON OF KAMES

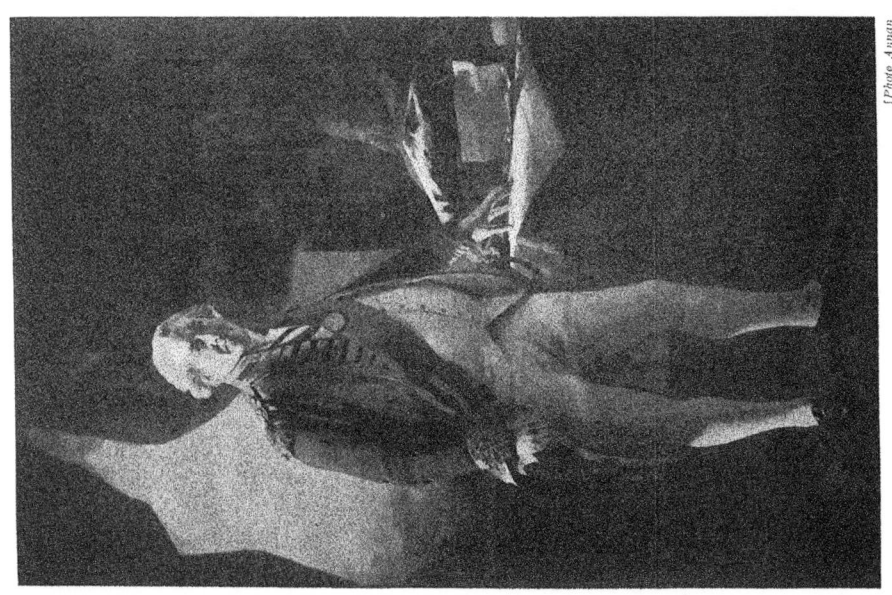

[Photo Annan

ADMIRAL LORD DUNCAN

6

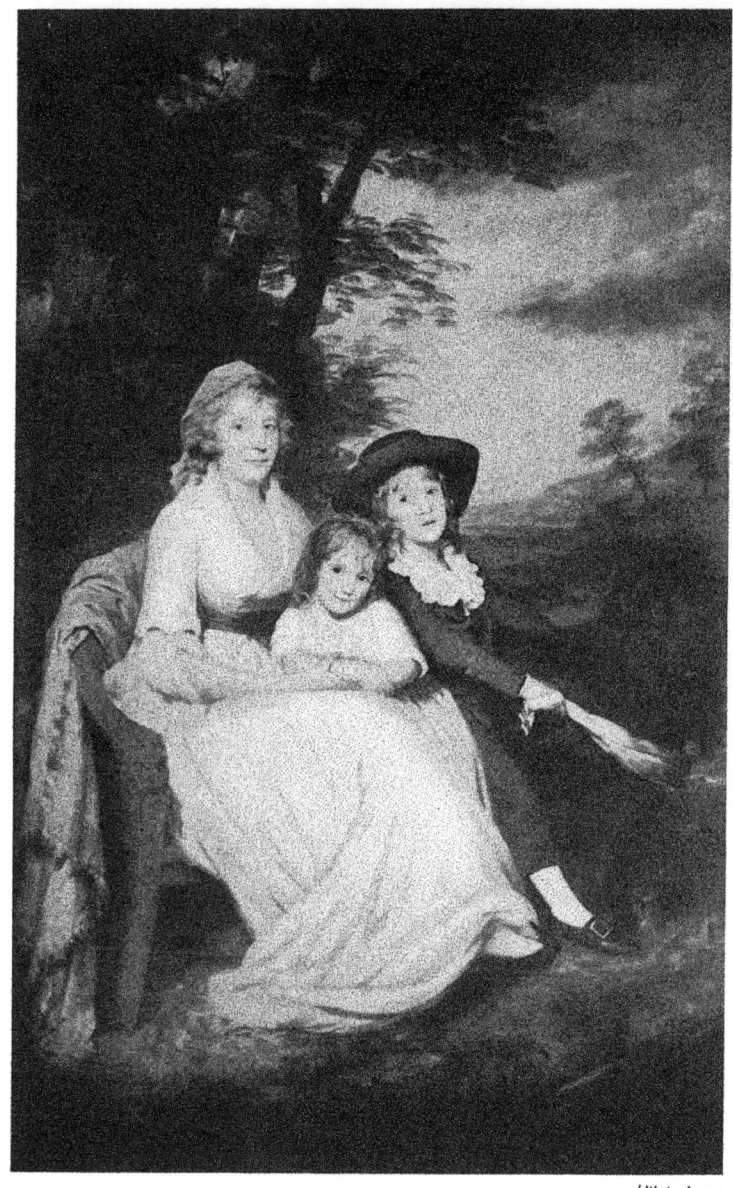

MRS. FERGUSON OF RAITH AND HER CHILDREN

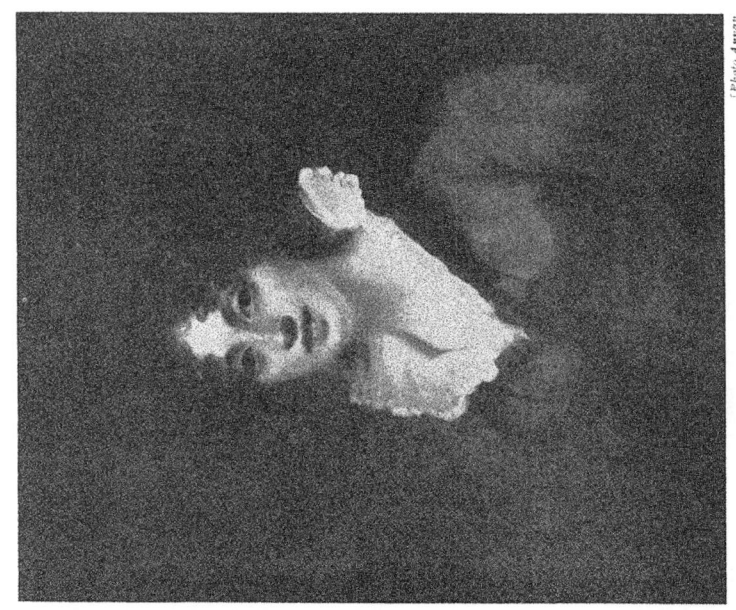

MRS. JANE ANNE CATHERINE FRASER, OF REELIG

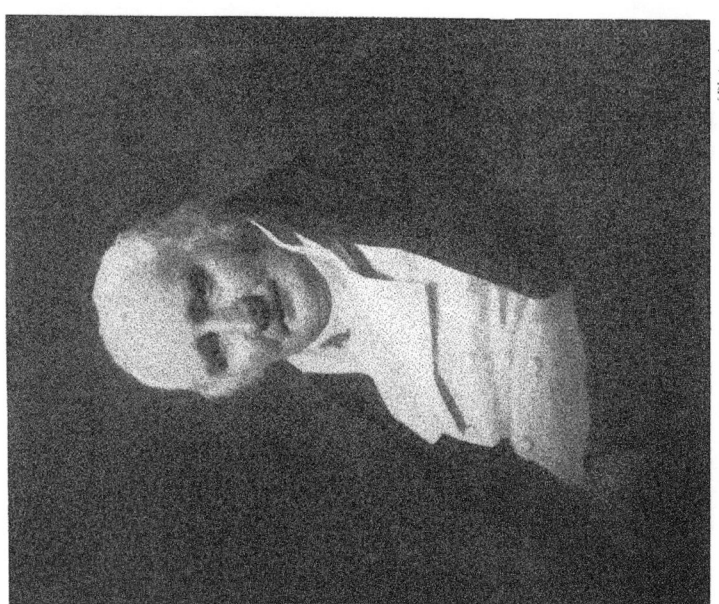

JOHN WAUCHOPE, W.S.

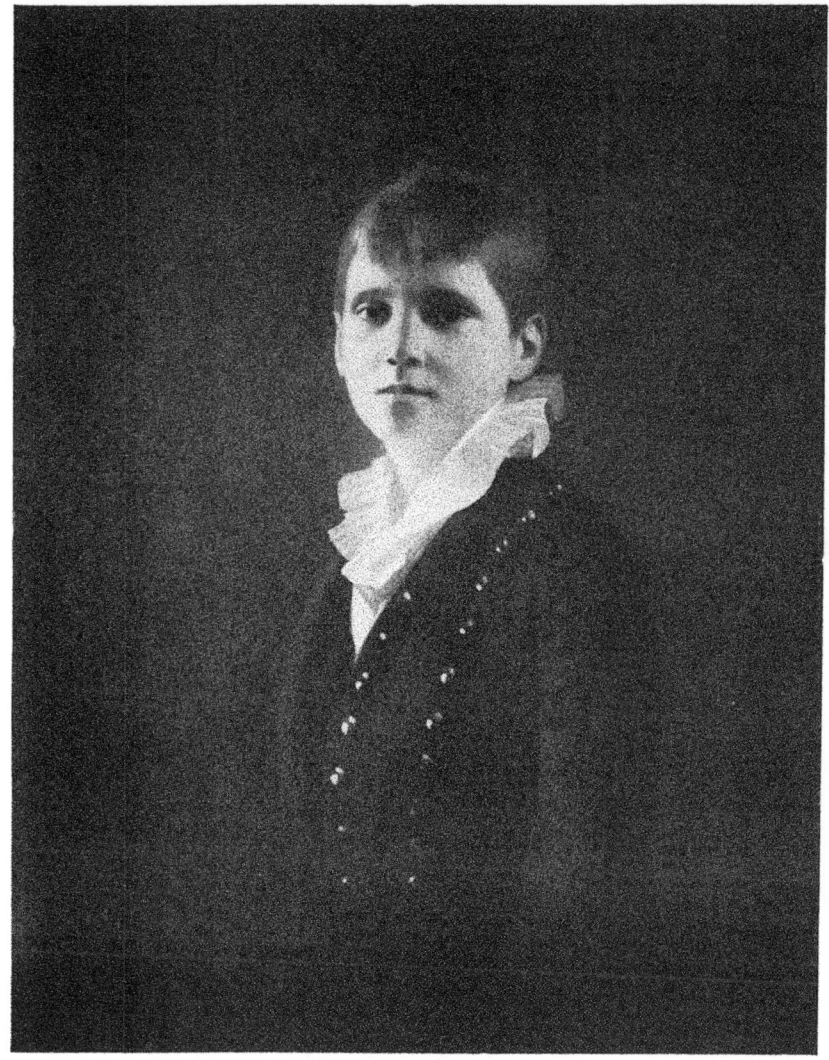

[Photo Annan

MASTER HAY

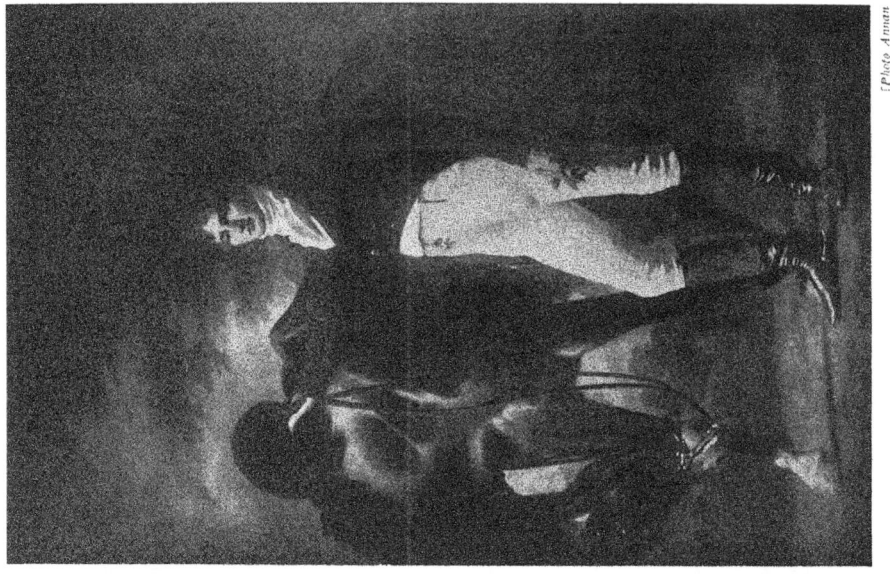

PROFESSOR JOHN WILSON

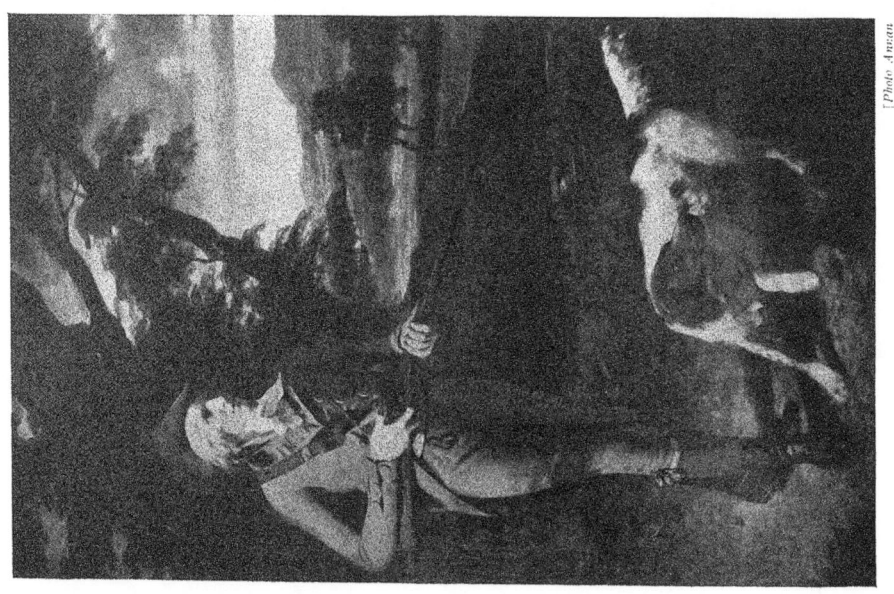

GENERAL SIR RONALD FERGUSON, G.C.B.

10

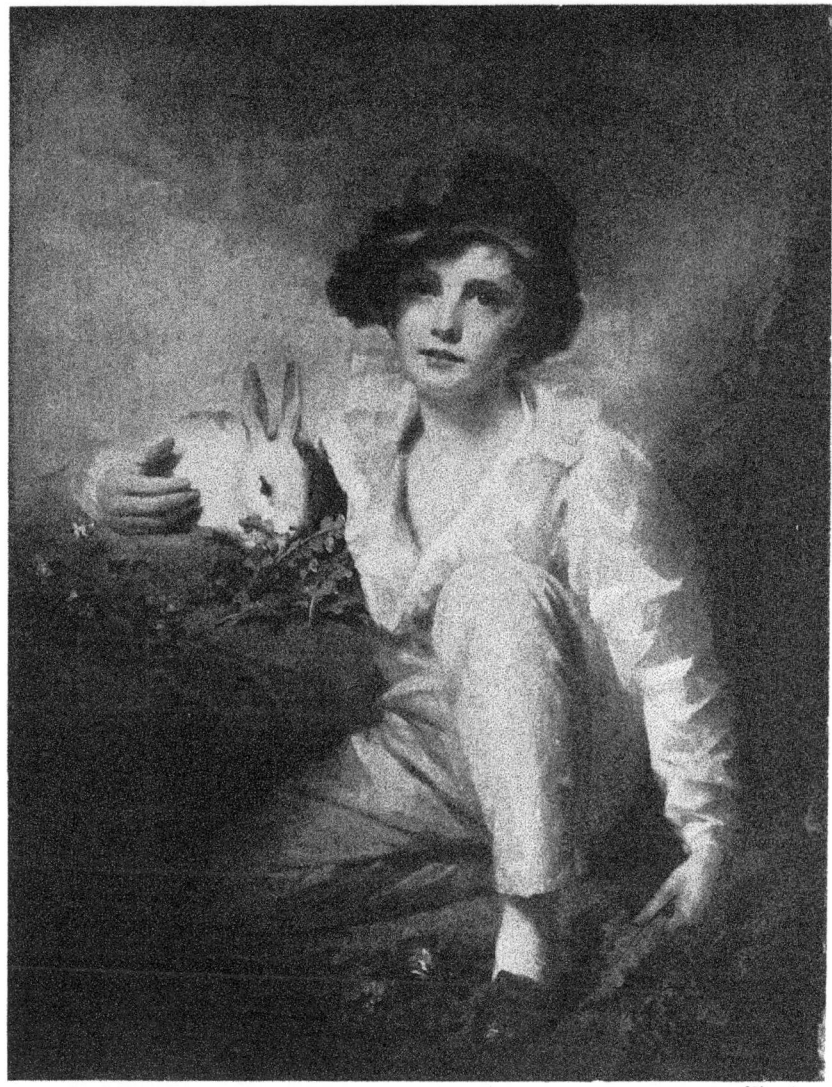

BOY WITH RABBIT

11

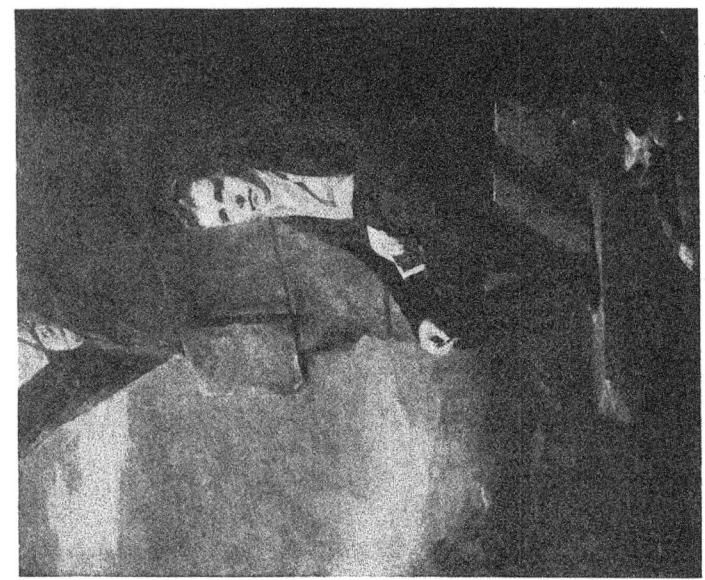

SIR WALTER SCOTT

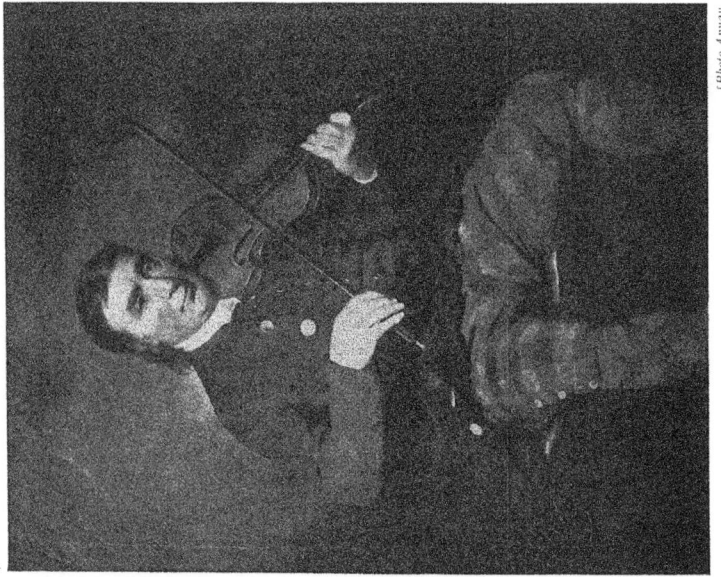

NEIL GOW

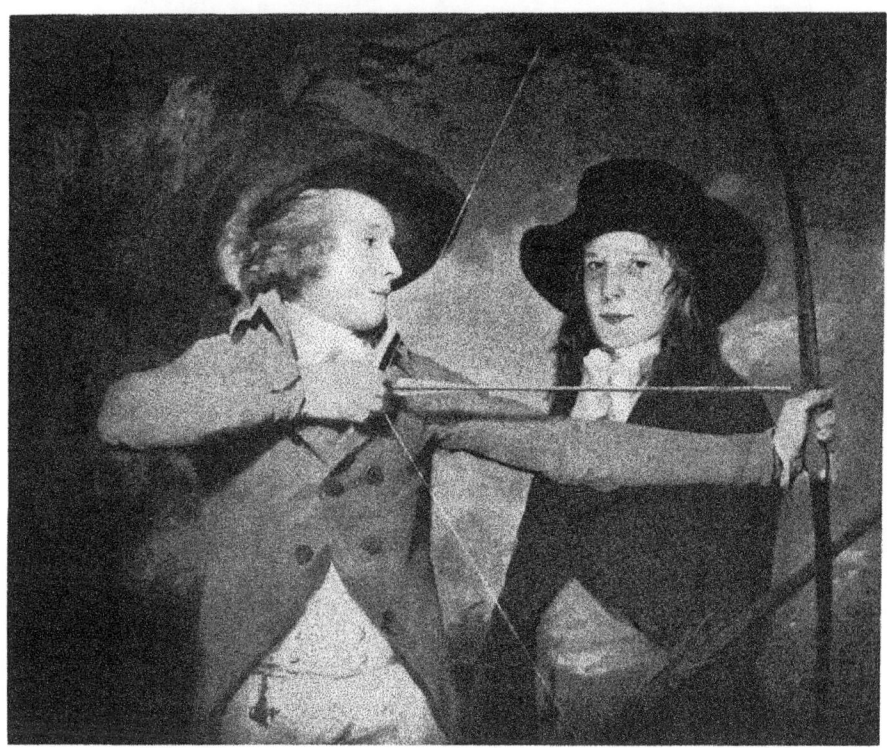
[Photo Annan

SIR RONALD AND ROBERT FERGUSON, OF RAITH

13

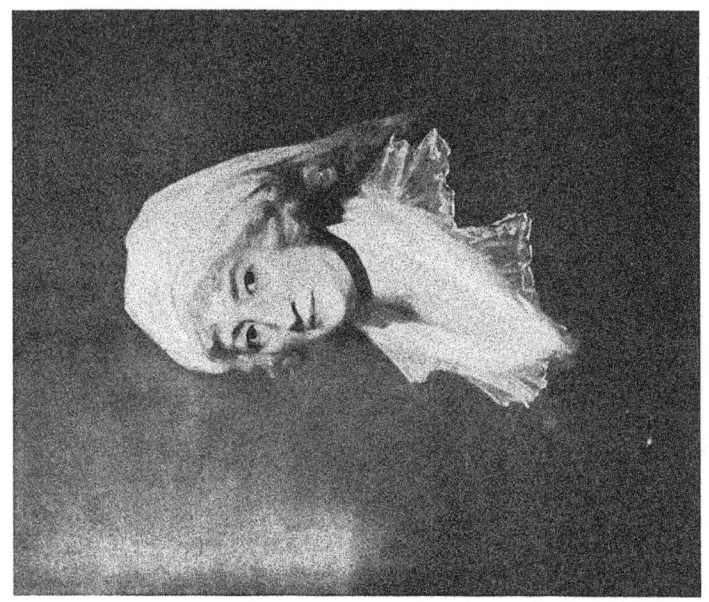

LADY MILLER, OF GLENLEE

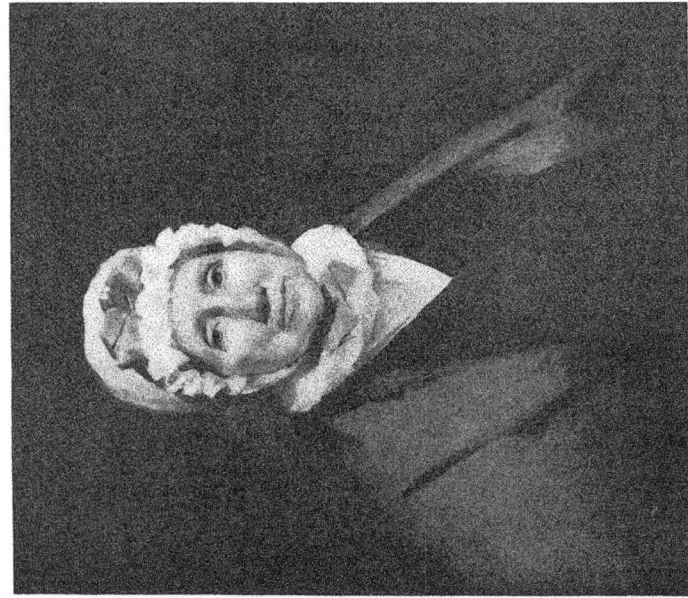

MRS. ADAMS

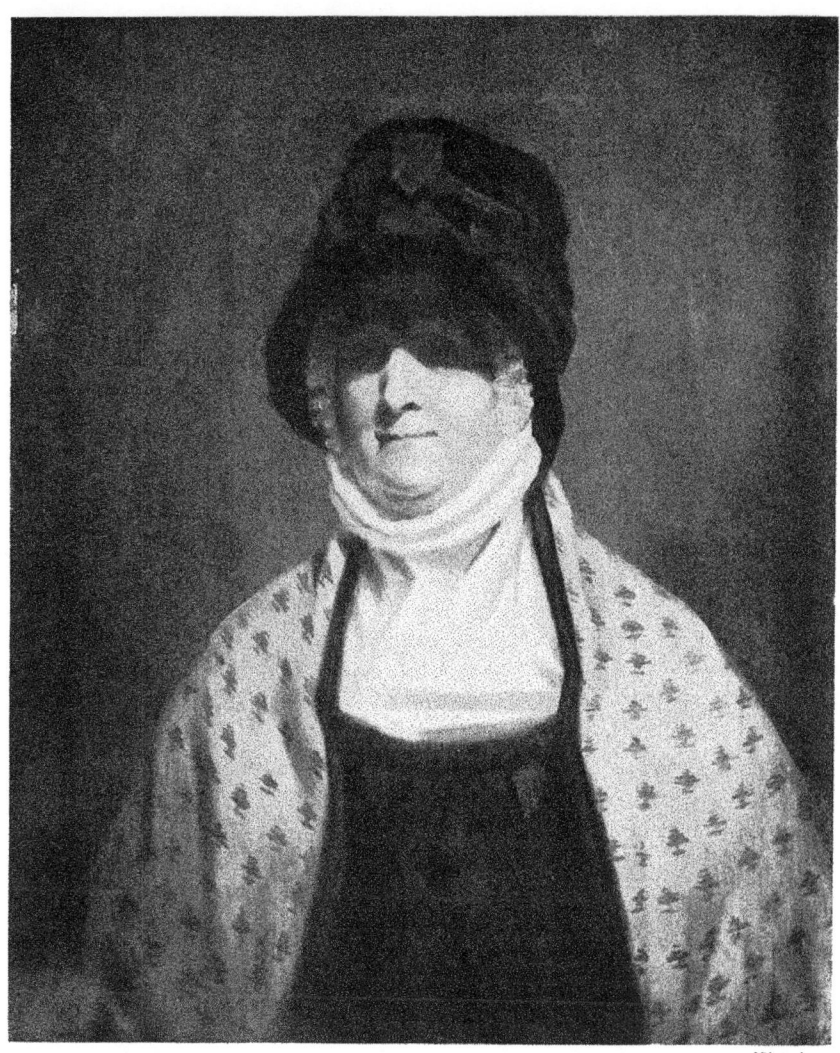

[Photo Annan

MRS. CAMPBELL, OF PARK

15

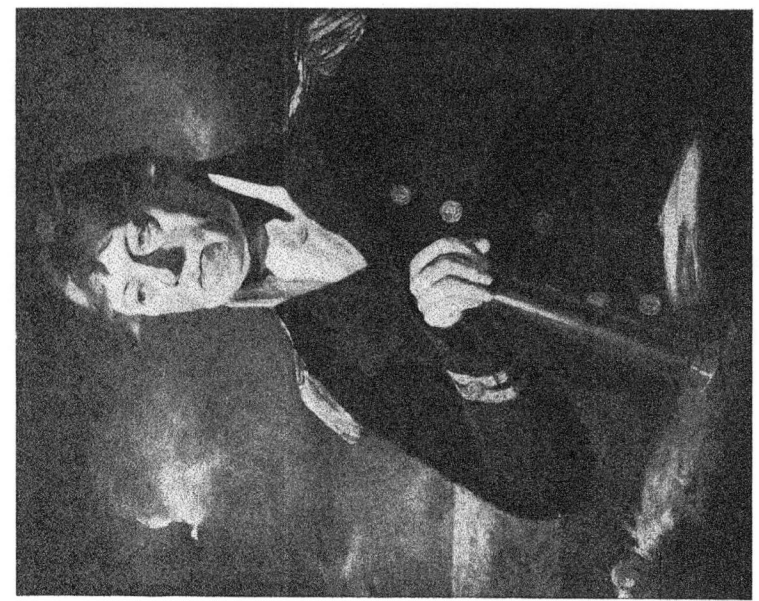

ADMIRAL RICHARD DEANS
National Gallery, Melbourne

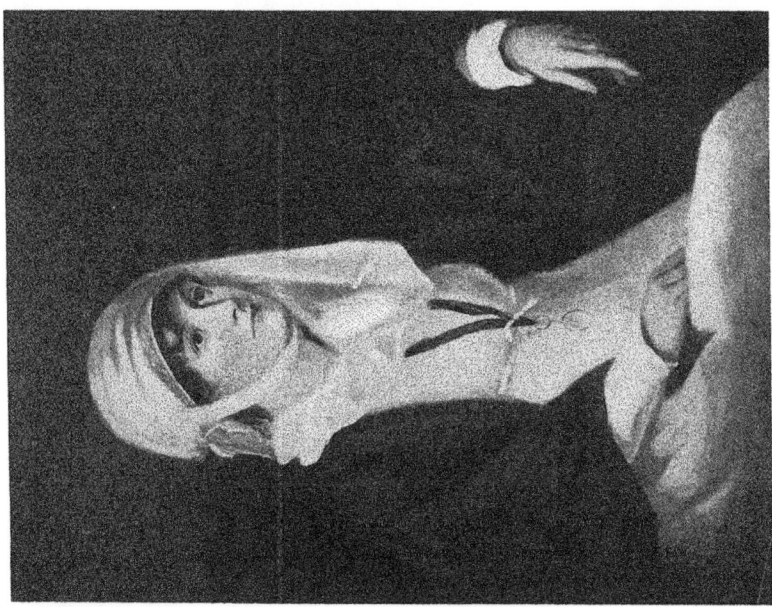

MRS. DEANS

16

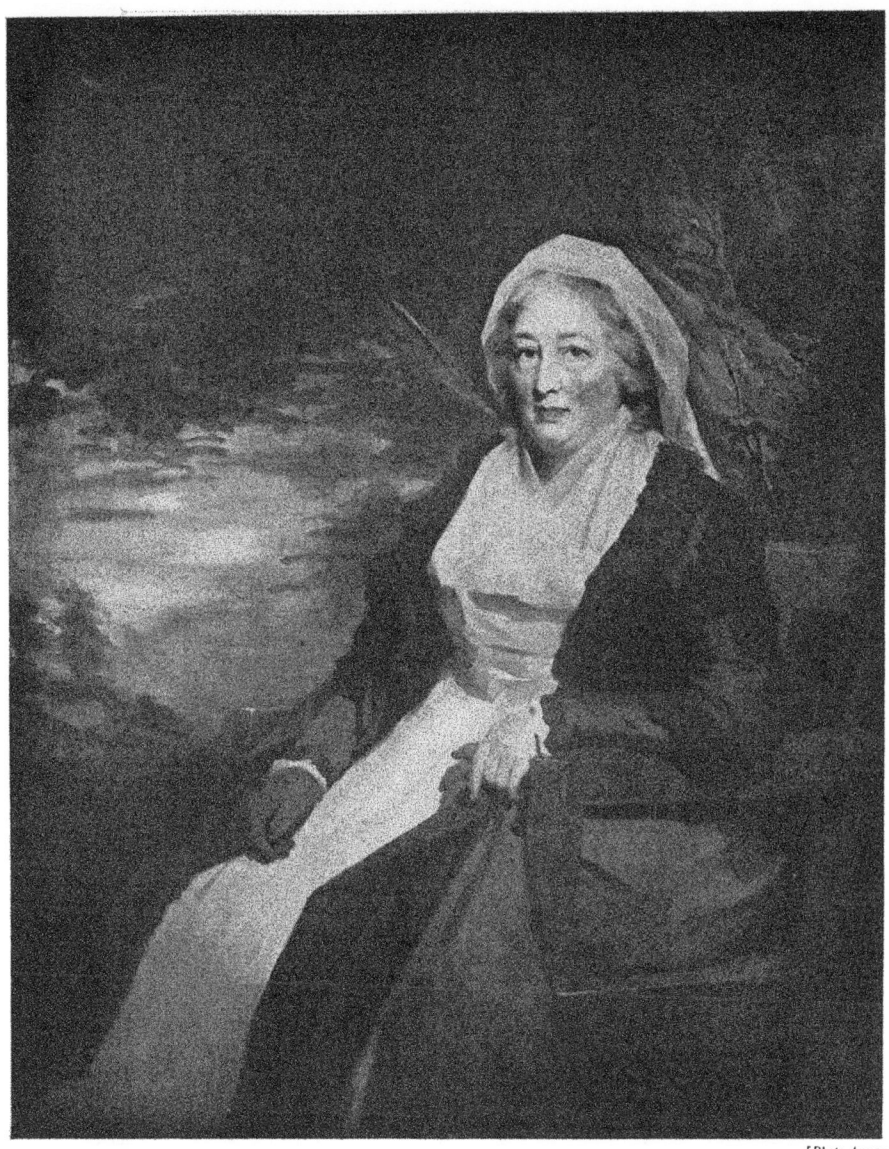

MRS. CAMPBELL, OF BALLIMORE

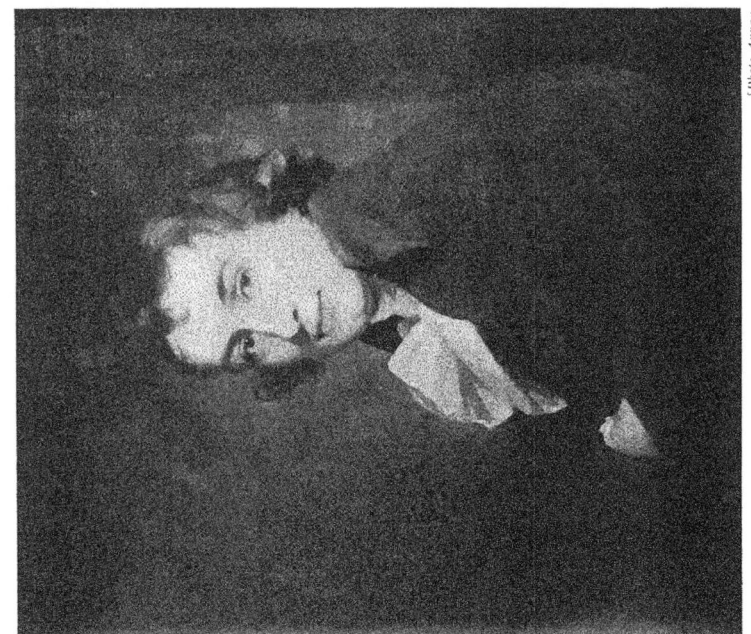

LORD ABERCROMBY

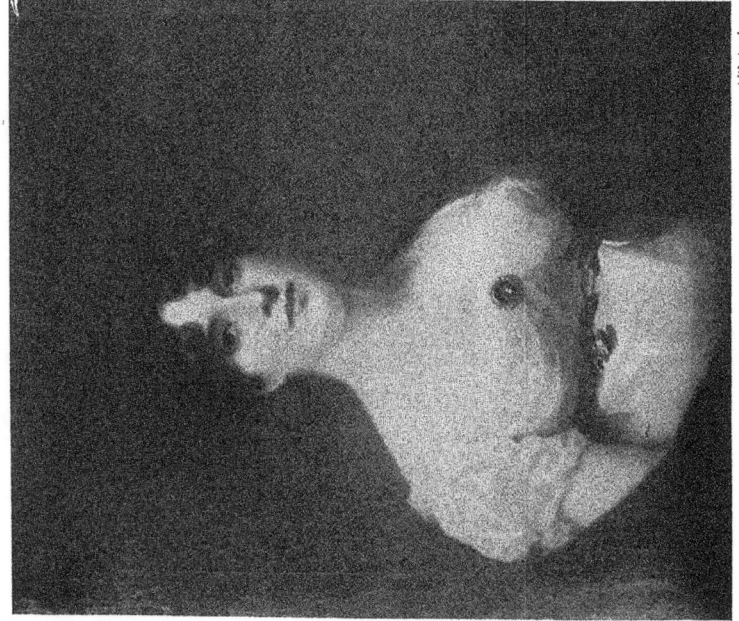

PORTRAIT OF A LADY

18

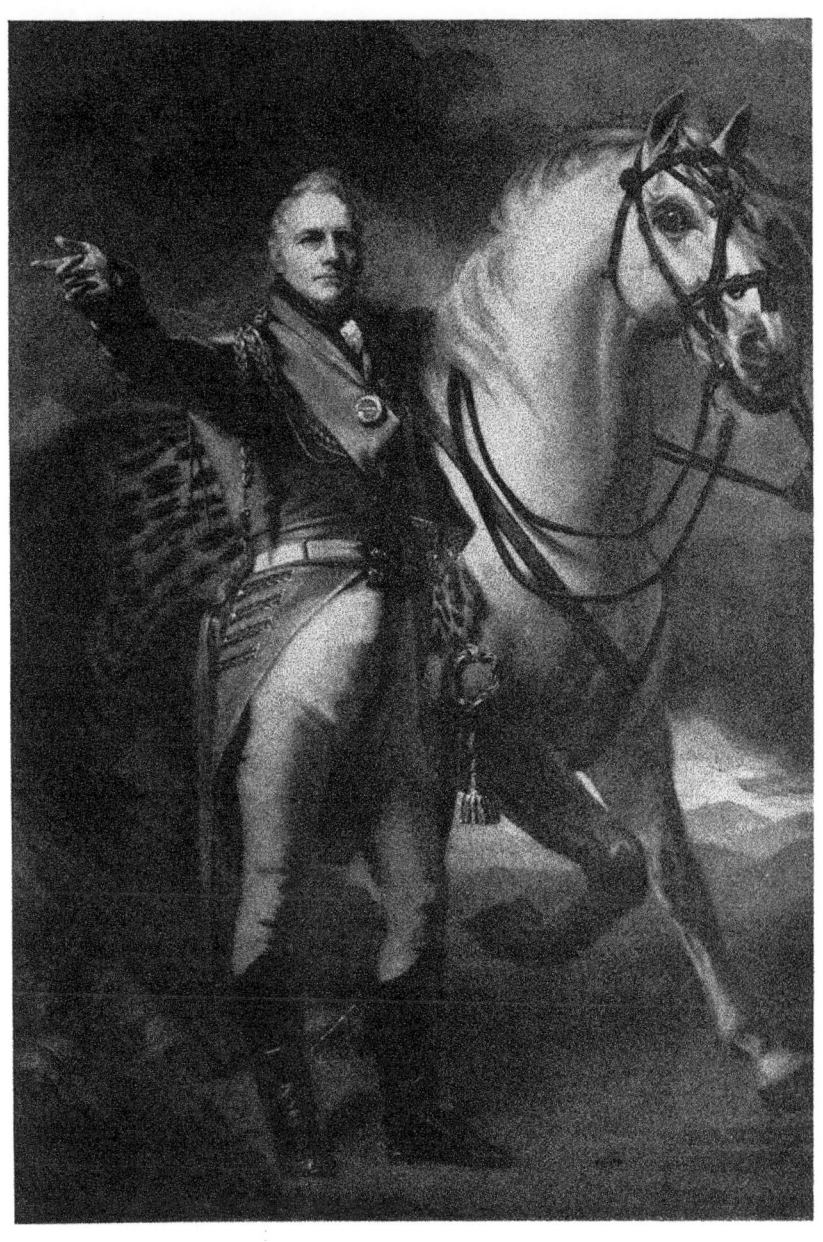

GENERAL SIR DAVID BAIRD

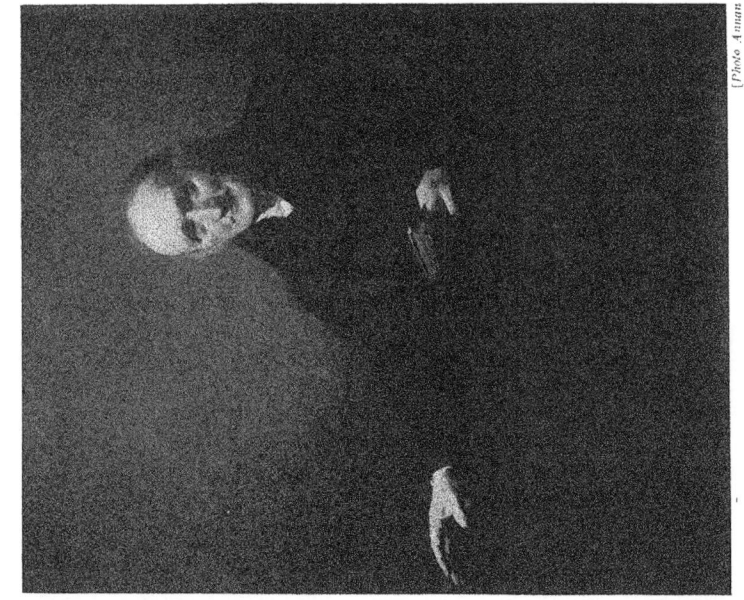

[Photo Annan

DR. ADAM

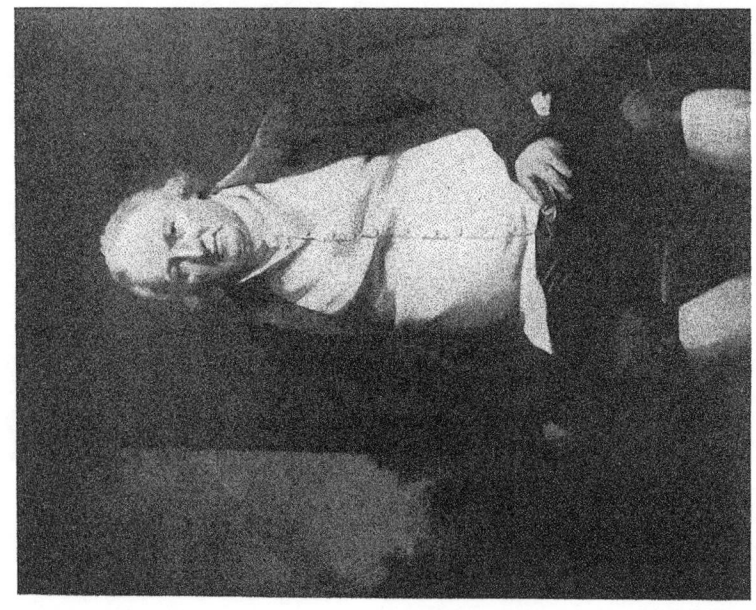

[Photo Annan

JOHN GRAY, OF NEWHOLM, W.S.

20

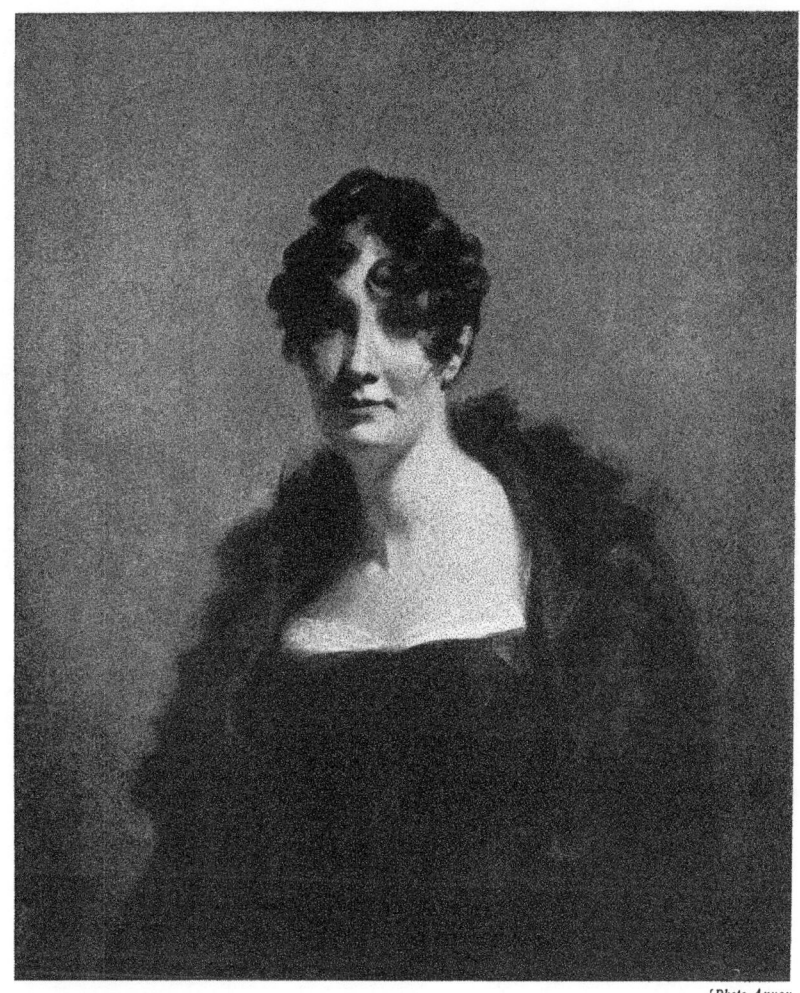

LADY CHARLOTTE HOPE

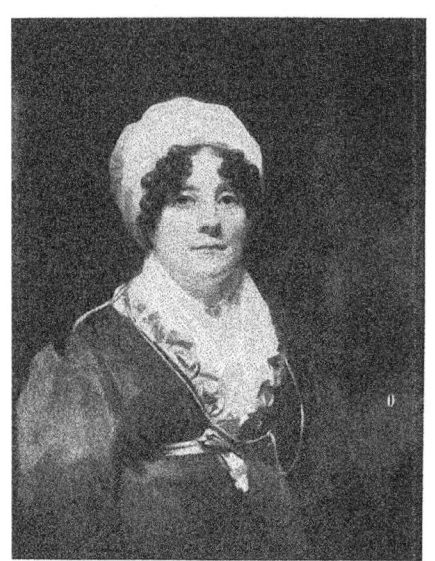

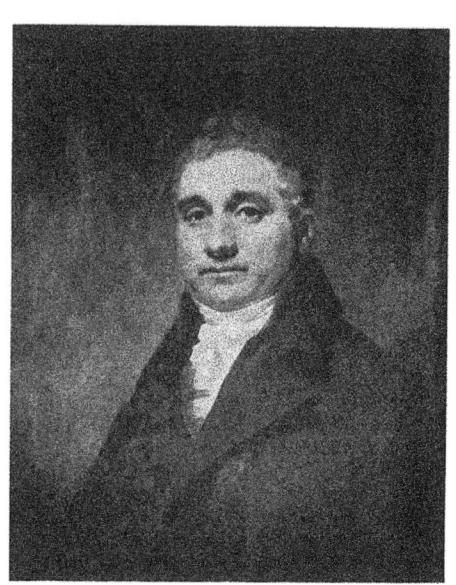

RS. ALEXANDER HENDERSON

MR. ALEXANDER HENDERSON

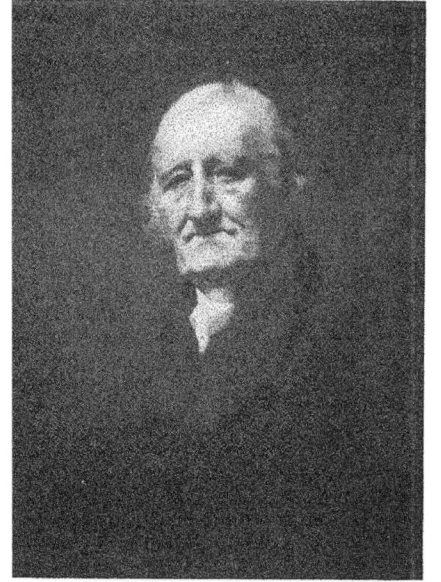

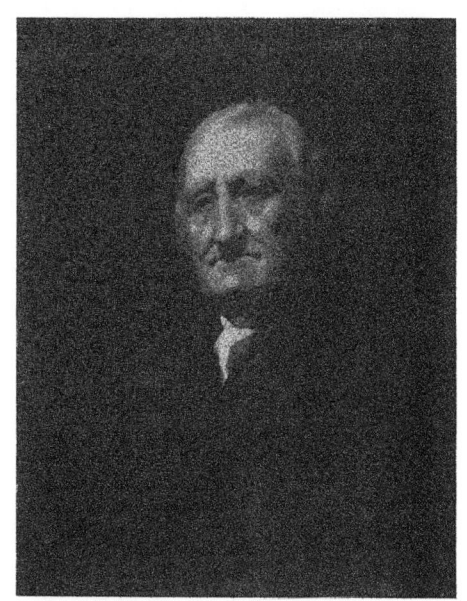

[Photo Annan

MES. WARDROP, OF TORBANEHILL
C. Wardrop, Esq.

JAMES WARDROP, OF TORBANEHILL
Replica the property of G. S. Davidson, Esq.

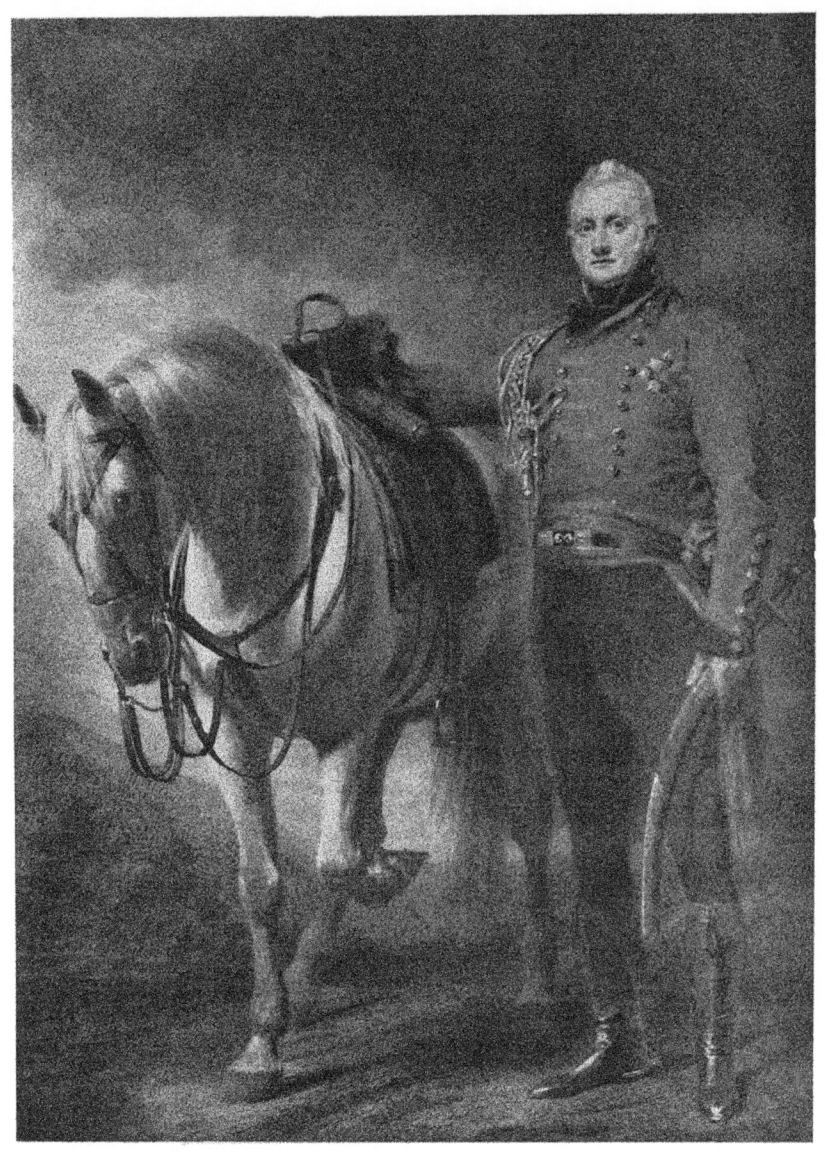

JOHN, EARL OF HOPETOUN

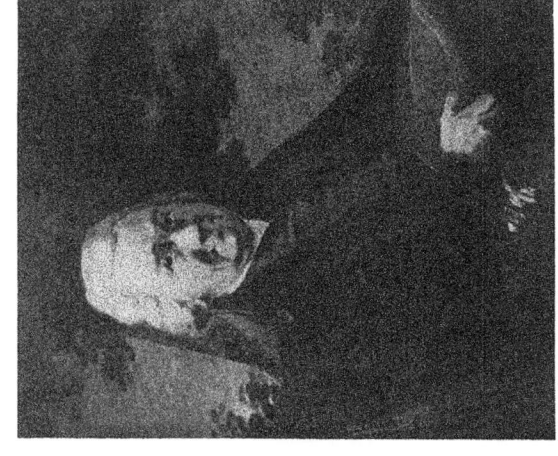

JOHN TAIT, ESQ.
By Andrew Robertson
After Sir Henry Raeburn

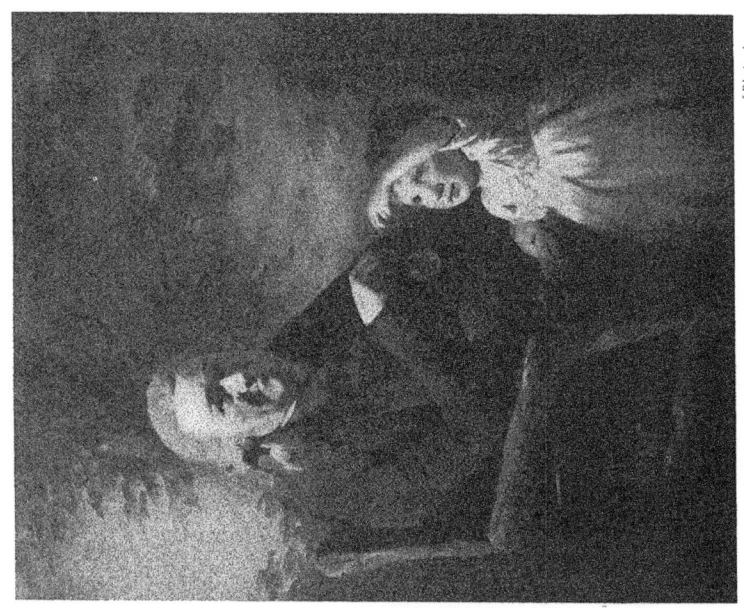

JOHN TAIT, OF HARVIESTON, AND HIS GRANDSON

[*Photo Annan*

24

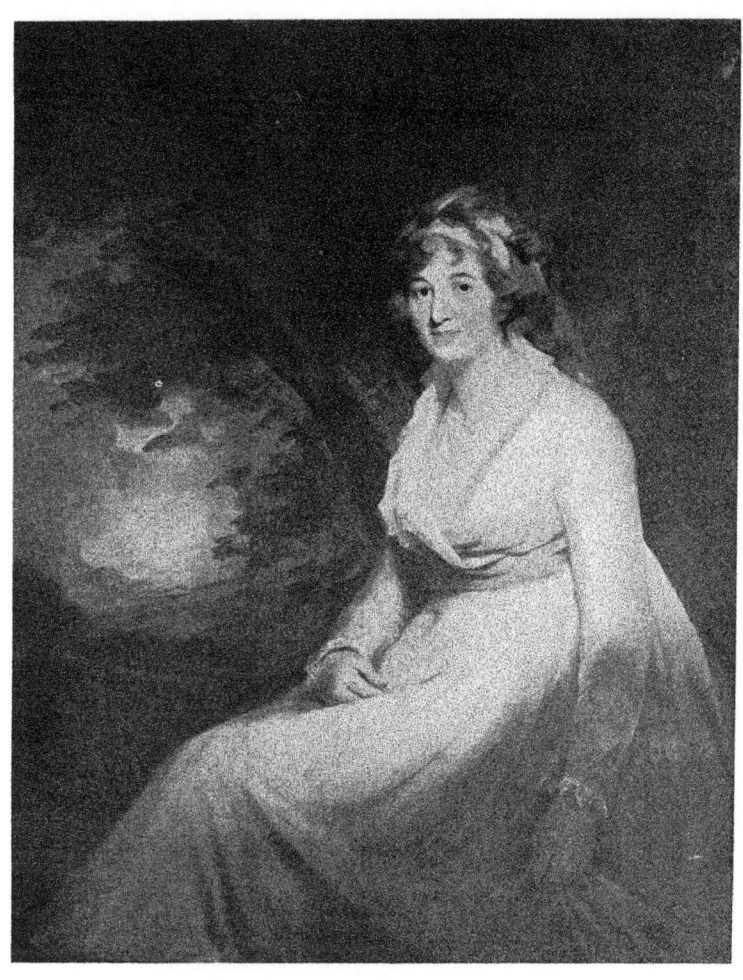

LADY JANET TRAILL
Reproduced by permission of Messrs. J. & J. Duveen

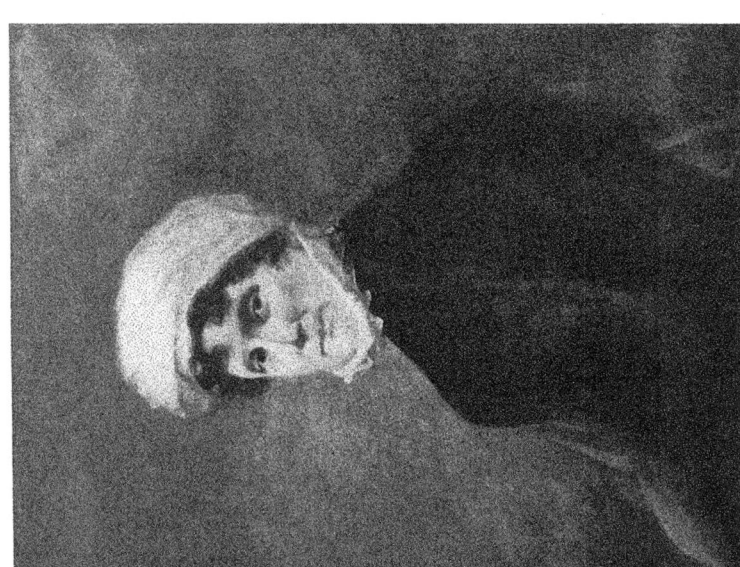

MRS. SIDDONS (PROBABLY)

[Photo Annan

W. MACDONALD, OF ST. MARTIN'S, W.S.

[Photo Annan

26

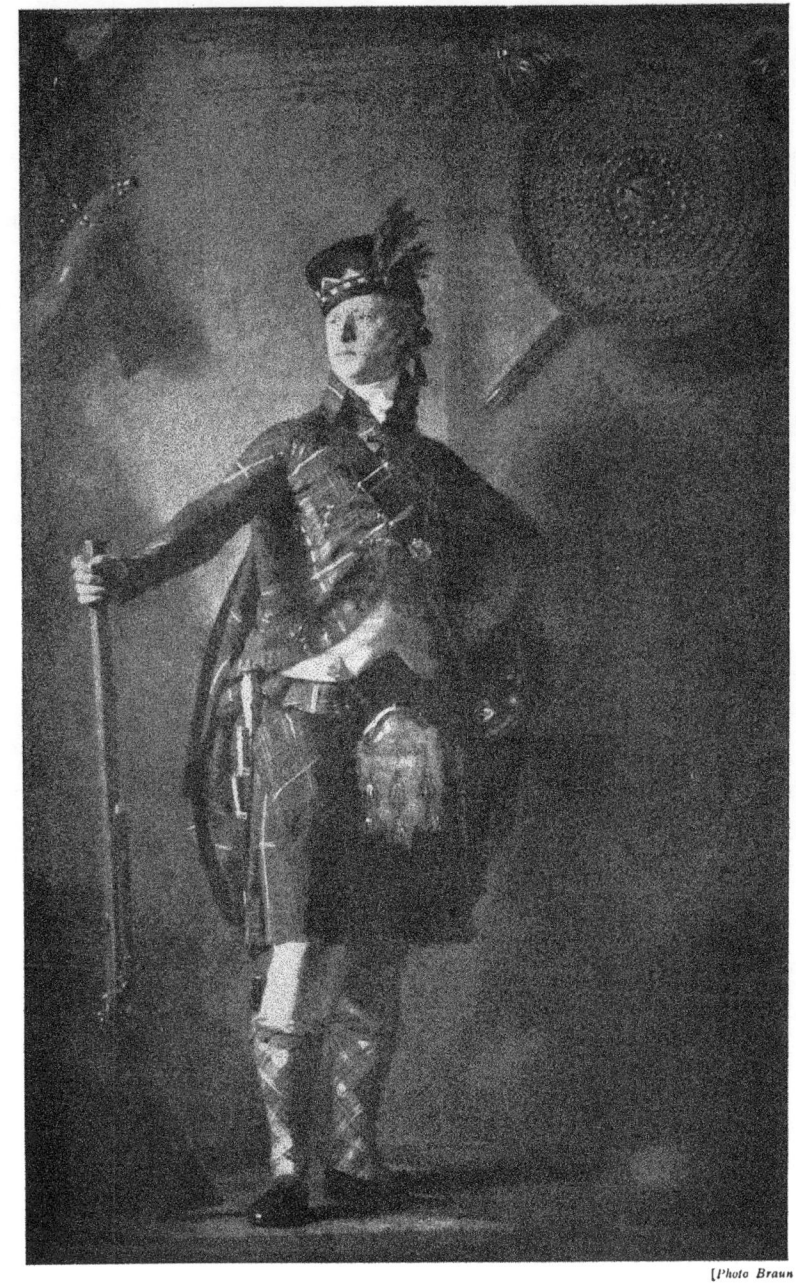

COLONEL ALASTAIR MACDONELL, OF GLENGARRY

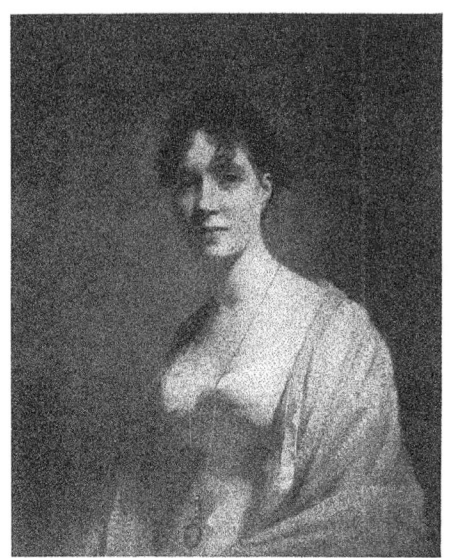

MRS. G. J. BELL

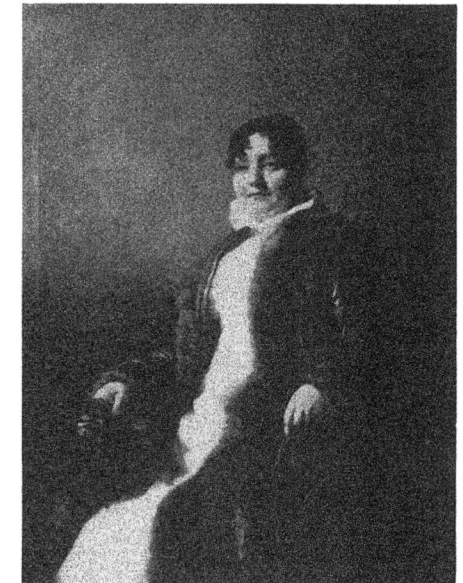

MRS. CRUIKSHANK

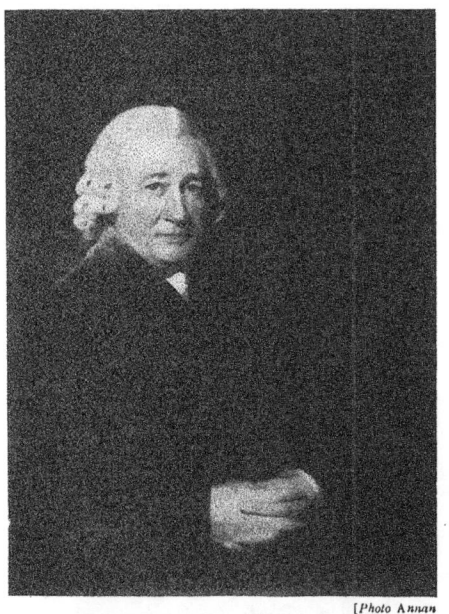

LORD BRAXFIELD—FACULTY OF ADVOCATES

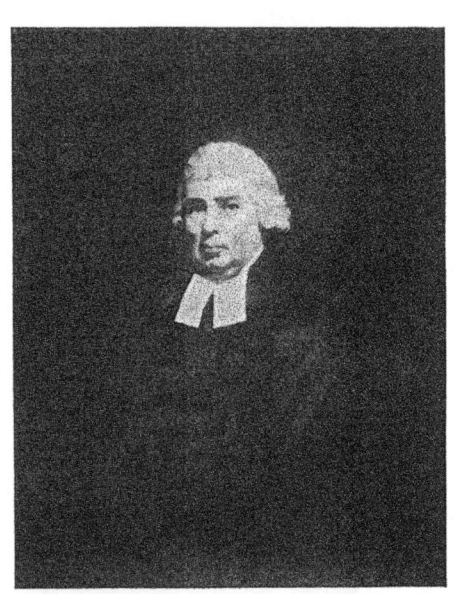

PROFESSOR ANDREW HUNTER, D.D., F.R.S.E.

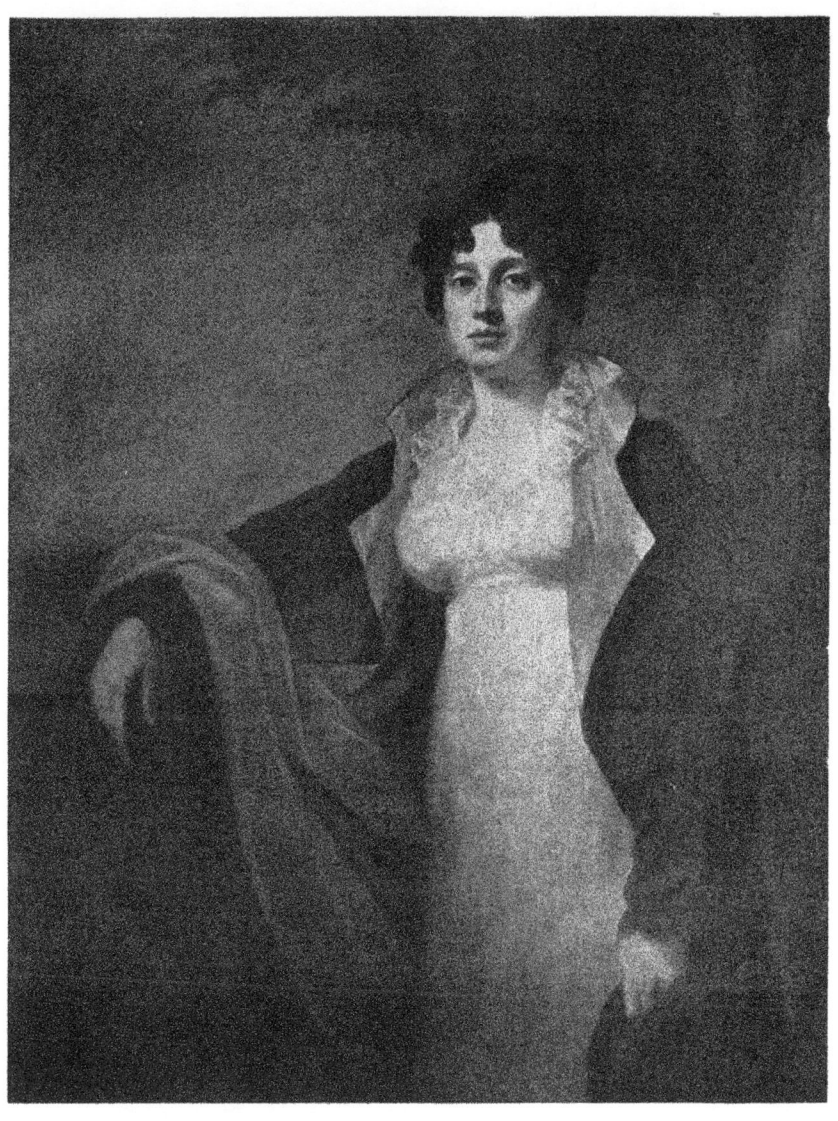

LADY SETON-STUART

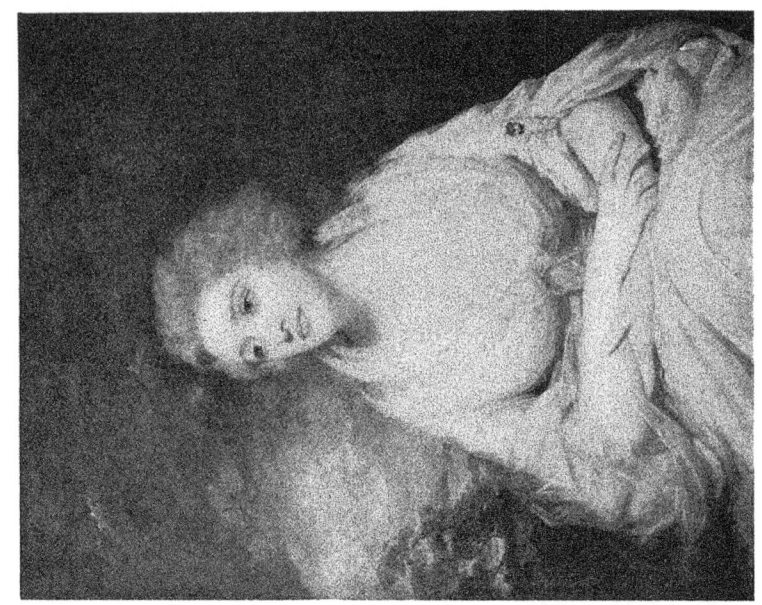

LADY BELHAVEN

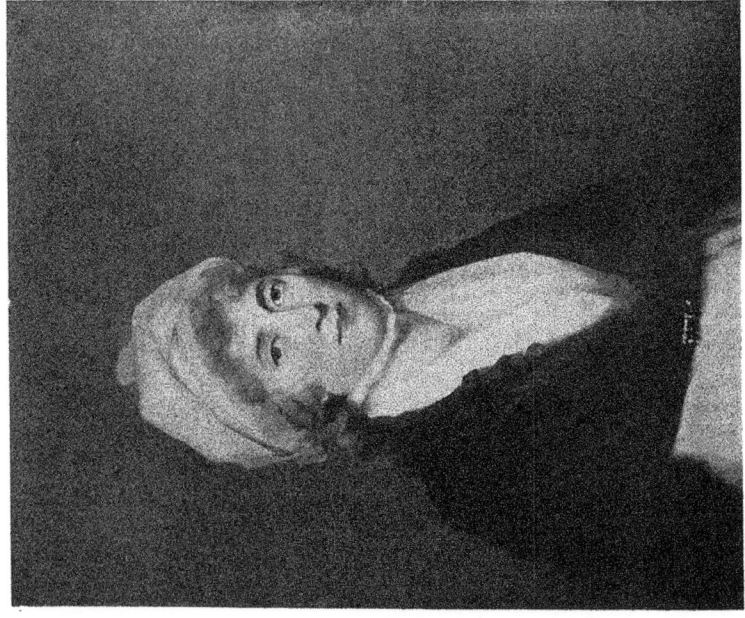

LADY DALRYMPLE

·30·

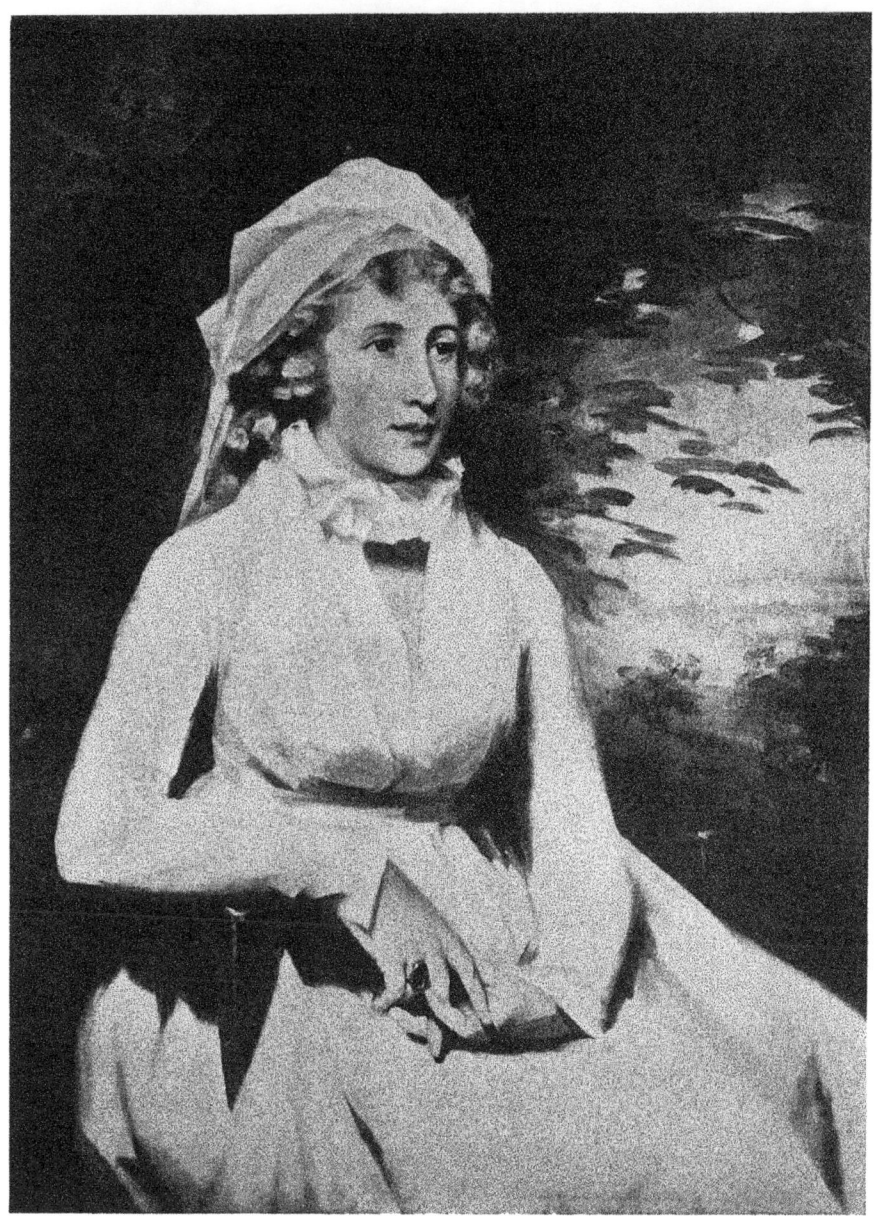

MRS. DOUGLAS, OF BRIGTON

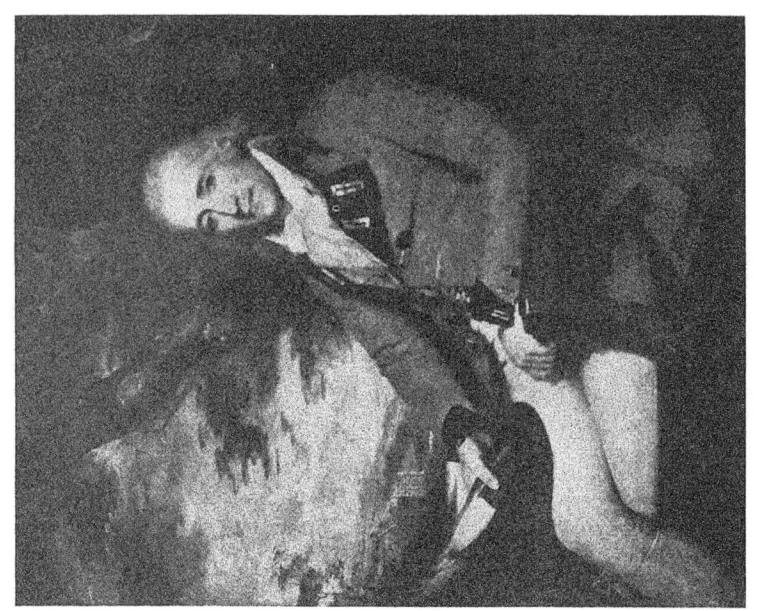

THE EARL OF HYNDFORD

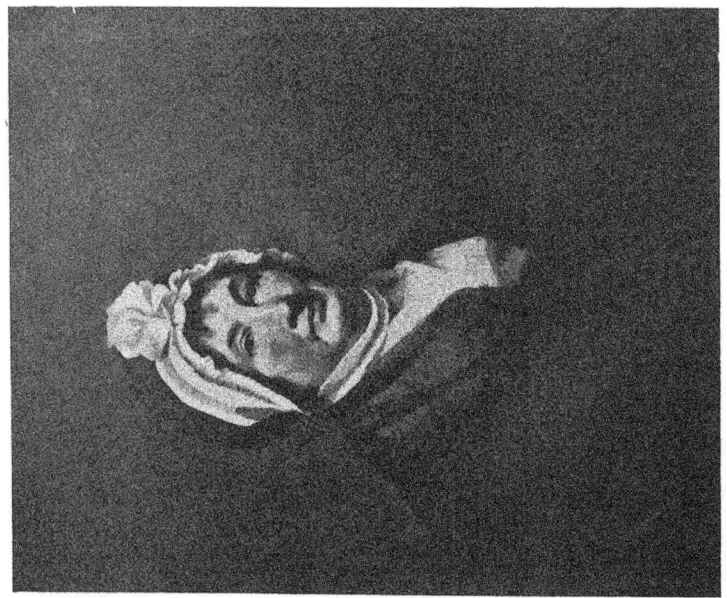

MRS. TOD, OF DRYGRANGE

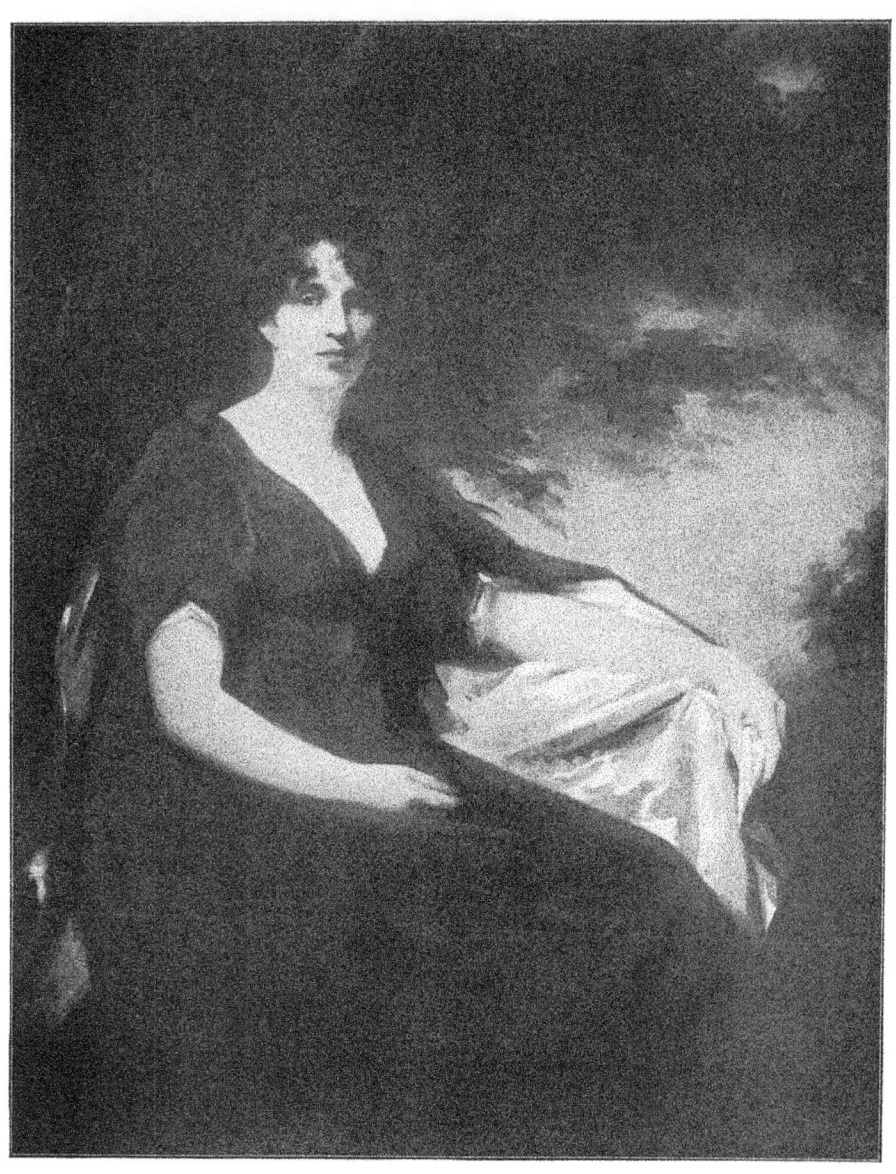

PORTRAIT OF MRS. HAY

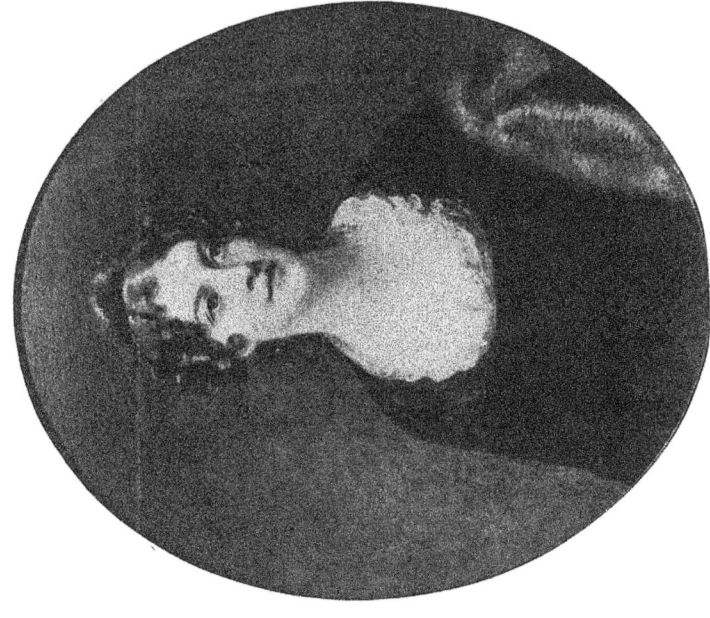

MISS ANNE CUNNINGHAM GRAHAM OF GARTMORE

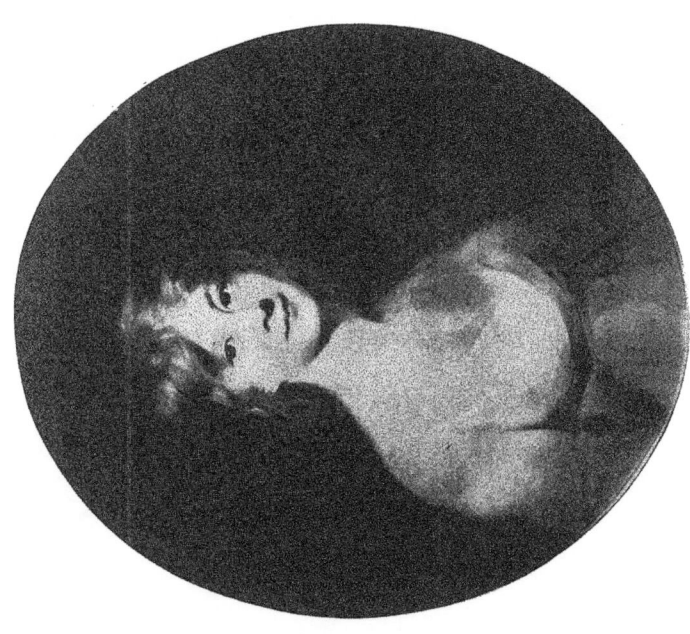

MISS JANE NISBET

34

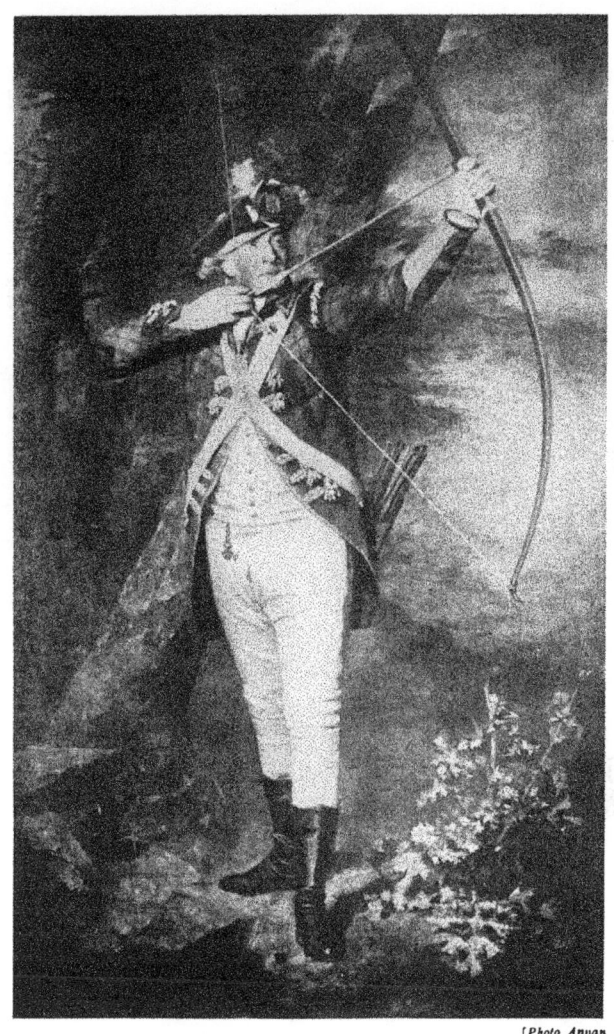

DR. NATHANIEL SPENS

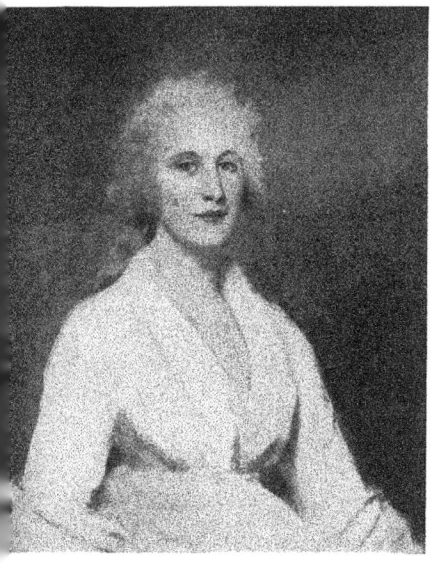

ADY SETON

THE HON. HENRY ERSKINE

[Photo Annan

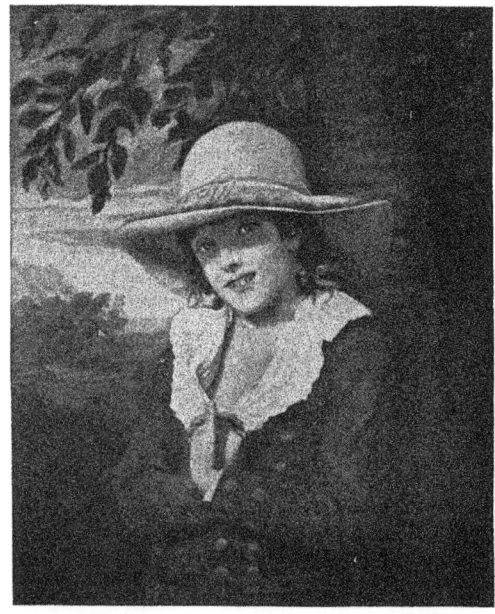

THE LESLIE BOY

36

List of Pictures by Sir Henry Raeburn, R.A.

[In the following List the initials R.A. stand for Royal Academy; R.S.A., Royal Scottish Academy; N.G., National Gallery; N.P.G., National Portrait Gallery; S.N.G., Scottish National Gallery; S.N.P.G., Scottish National Portrait Gallery; C., Christie's; R. & F., Robinson & Fisher.]

Abercrombie, Dr. John (1780-1844). Physician and Author. Miss Abercrombie.

Abercromby, Alexander, son of George Abercromby, and brother of Sir Ralph Abercromby. Admitted to the Faculty of Advocates in 1766; Sheriff of Stirlingshire and Senator of the College of Justice; sat on Court of Session bench as Lord Abercromby, 1792. In grey coat, with white vest and frill; figure turned to the right with arms folded; head nearly full face. 29 × 24. Lord Abercromby. Agnew (c) 1911.

Abercromby, Alexander of Tullibody, Lord of Sessions; 29¼ × 23¾. The property of the Faculty of Advocates, in Parliament House, Edinburgh. Painted 1789; engraved by J. Dawe. Seated, arms folded; head turned to right.

Abercromby, George, of Tullibody. "Old Tullibody," grandson of Alexander Abercromby, of Birkenbog, and father of the celebrated Sir Ralph Abercromby. In green coat, red tartan vest, black breeches, and high boots, grey wig; seated in an armchair, with his hands clasped before him. 48½ × 39. Lord Abercromby, Mason (c) 1911.

Abercromby, Sir George, fourth Baronet of Birkenbog (1750-1831); 30 × 25. Engraved by T. Lupton. Lady Abercromby.

Abercromby, Lady. 30 × 25. Lady Abercromby.

Abercromby, General Sir Robert, G.C.B. Son of George Abercromby, and brother of Sir Ralph Abercromby; served throughout the American War; Governor and Commander-in-Chief at Bombay, 1790, Commander of the Indian forces, and reduced Tippoo Sultan, 1792; Governor of Edinburgh Castle, 1801. In scarlet military uniform; wearing the Star of the Bath. 29 × 24½. Lord Abercromby, Cremetti (c) 1911.

Abercromby, Sir Robert, fifth Baronet (1784-1855). 30 × 25. Lady Abercromby.

Abinger, Lord. Engraved by William Walker.

Aboyne, Charles Gordon, Fourth Earl of. See Charles Gordon.

Aboyne, the Countess of. Lady Mary Douglas, daughter of James, fourteenth Earl of Morton, second wife of the fourth Earl of Aboyne; 40 × 50. Wallis & Son, 1910.

Adam, Dr. Alexander. Painted for fourteen of Dr. Adam's pupils of High School, Edinburgh, where it hung until 1860, when it was presented to the National Gallery of Scotland by the survivors; 49 × 39. Engraved in mezzotint by C. Turner, 1809, and by S. Freeman.

Adam, Robert, architect. Seated, three-quarter length. Scottish National Exhibition, 1908. W. A. Coats, Esq.

Adam, Mrs. Three-quarter length, seated. Scottish National Exhibition, 1908. W. A. Coats, Esq.

Adam, Mrs. Robert. Forbes & Paterson's Exhibition, 1901.

Adam, Right Hon. William, of Blair Adam. A friend of Sir Walter Scott, and founder of the Blair Adam Club. Seated, in black coat with white neck cloth, resting his left hand on arm of chair; 41 × 50. Mrs. Mary Antrobus (R. & F., 1901). Wallis & Son.

Adams, Mrs. Bust, white cap and collar, red shawl; 30 × 25. Mrs. Keddie; Shepherd, 1908. Sir Hickman B. Bacon.

Agnew, Andrew. Sir Andrew N. Agnew, Bart. Painted about 1791. 30 × 25.

Agnew, Sir Andrew, 7th Baronet, of Lochaw. Sir Andrew N. Agnew, Bart. Painted about 1816 30 × 25.

Alexander, Colonel, of Ballochmyle (1789-1845). Sir Claude Alexander, Bart.

Alison, Rev. Archibald, LL.B., F.R.S., L. & E., Prebendary of Sarum, Rector of Roddington, etc., and Senior Minister of St. Paul's Chapel, Edinburgh. Father of Sir Archibald Alison, the eminent historian and lawyer. Three-quarter length; engraved by Wm. Walker. Raeburn Exhibition, 1876. Raeburn family. Lent to Glasgow International Exhibition by Sir John Stirling Maxwell, M.P.

Allan, Alexander, Esq., of Hillside, Edinburgh; banker. In dark dress with white stock, holding a paper in his left hand, seated at a table on which are some books; 81 × 57½. Raeburn Exhibition, 1824. Raeburn Exhibition, 1876. Major-Gen. Allan, of Hillside, Bidborough; Sully (c) 1908. Colonel Allan, R.S.A., 1863. Alex. Allan, Esq.

Allan, Col. R.S.A., 1863. Alex. Allan, Esq.

Allan, Mrs., and child. Mrs. Allan (*née* Ann Losh), wife of Alexander Allan, Esq., in crimson dress, and crimson and white turban; seated on a couch with her young daughter, Matilda, who is dressed in white and holds a book; 81 × 57½. R. S. A., 1863. Raeburn Exhibition, 1876. Lieut.-Col. William Allan. Major-Gen. Allan, White (c) 1908.

Allan, Robert, banker (1740-1818). Seated in armchair, in dark blue coat and breeches, holding a paper in his hand. 50 × 38. Painted in 1800. On loan to Glasgow Art Gallery, 1908. Captain Percy S. Allan.

Allen of Errol (?). See "Two Boys."

Anderson, David (1750-1825), of St. Germains. 56 × 45. Captain D. M. Anderson, Dott & Co., Colnaghi & Co., Dr. Eissler.

Anderson, John, of Inchyra. Lent by Mrs. Anderson, of Dalhousie Grange, to Raeburn Exhibition, 1876.

Anderson, Mrs., of Inchyra (*née* Mary Mitchelson); 35¼ × 26¾. Half figure, seated to right in a crimson chair, head turned and looking at spectator, arms crossed in front; white gown, yellow background. Sir George Donaldson, R.A., 1907. Engraved by J. Cother Webb, and published by Messrs. Gooden and Fox.

Arbuthnot, Mrs. Engraved as "Isabel," by T. G. Appleton.

Argyll, John, 7th Duke of (1777-1847). 93 × 59. International Exhibition, Glasgow, 1901. Duke of Argyll, K.T.

Armadale, Sir William Honyman, of Armadale, Lord of Session (1756-1825). Senator of the College of Justice. Married, in 1777, Mary, eldest daughter of Robert Macqueen, Lord Braxfield. Painted about 1800. Lent to Raeburn Exhibition, 1876, by Mrs. Catherine Dallas.

Austin, Hon. Mrs. (Hon. Anne Sempill). Seated in a green garden chair; white cap, black shawl and dress, showing white fichu at neck; 48 × 39. R.S.A., 1863. The Baroness Sempill. Agnews, 1910.

Baillie, John. Half length, seated, pen in hand; 35 × 27½. Rev. W. Gordon Baillie.

Baillie, William, of Polkemmet, Lord of Session. In crimson robes with white bands; powdered wig. 29½ × 24½. Sir Andrew Agnew, Bart. Colnaghi & Co. (c) 1911.

Baillie, William, Lord Polkemmet. In red gown, white bands and white wig; seated, holding a scroll in his right hand; red curtain background. 51 × 39½. Lady Baillie, of Polkemmet. Agnew (c) 1911.

Baillie, Mrs., second wife of Lord Polkemmet, and sister of Sir John Sinclair of Ulbster. In white dress, with blue striped sleeves; pale green spotted shawl over her arms; powdered hair, with white ribbon; seated on a bank, with her hands resting on her lap; landscape background. 51 × 39½. Lady Baillie, of Polkemmet. Tooth (c) 1911.

Baird, General Sir David (1757-1829). Engraved by T. Hodgetts. Lord Ronald Gower in his "Reminiscences" says there is no portrait of Sir David at Newburgh, the family seat, only prints after Raeburn's fine full length portrait of him belonging to Lord Abercromby. Lord Abercromby, Crieff. Lenygon (c) 1911.

Baird, Lady. Miss Preston Campbell, of Fern Tower and Lochlane, Perthshire, wife of General Sir David Baird, Bart. In deep red dress, cut low at the neck and with short sleeves; wearing a cloak of the same colour, edged with brown fur, which she draws round her and holds together at her waist; standing to the right before a pillar and curtain background; on the right her large black retriever dog is springing up to welcome her; trees in the distance. 93½ × 59. Lord Abercromby. Fielding (c) 1911.

Balfour, James (Jamie singing "Toddlin' Hame"), a well-known Jacobite who fought in the Rebellion of 1745. Three-quarter length. Painted for the Leith Golfers' Hall; and engraved by J. Jones. Raeburn Exhibition, 1876. Colonel Babington.

Balfour, John. Publisher and bookseller in Edinburgh, son of James Balfour, Esq., of Pilrig. In blue coat and vest with brass buttons; white stock; powdered wig. 29¾ × 24½. Mrs. Beith. Balfour (c) 1911.

Balfour, Mrs. John. Catherine, daughter of Mr. Cant, of Thurston and Giles Grange. In white dress and flowered shawl, with a black scarf over her arms; large mob cap; powdered hair. 29½ × 24¾. Exhibited at the Grafton Gallery, 1895. Mrs. Beith. Balfour (c) 1911.

Balfour, John, of Trenabil, Orkney. Brown coat and white stock; about 30 × 25 . R. and F. 1903.

Balfour, Mrs. Jane Elliot, of Wolflee, branch of family of Earl of Minto; M. in 1765 Major Henry Balfour of the Lothian Regiment (the Royal Scots). Painted in 1810; 25 × 30. Wallis & Sons. W. D. Matthews, Esq , Toronto, 1809.

Balfour, Mrs.; 29 × 33. Japan-British Exhibition. Sir Julius C. Wernher, Bt.

Balfour, Mrs. 34 × 26. Sanderson. Colnaghi & Co. 1911.

Balfour, Miss, of Pilrig.

Bannatyne, Sir William Macleod, Lord of Session (1743-1833). 35 × 28. Lent to Raeburn Exhibition, 1876, by Sir Daniel Macnee, P.R S.A. W. McEwen, Esq.

Barclay of Urie. Engraved by Bengo.

Barns, Sir James Stevenson. 30 × 25. James Hope, Esq.

Bedford, John, Sixth Duke of, three-quarter length. 50 × 40. Raeburn Exhibition, 1876. W. P. Adam, of Blair Adam; Paul Levoi sale (*dit* Leon Gauchez), Paris, 1907; lot 33. Photograph in catalogue.

Begbie, Mrs., when a child (*née* Miss Eleanor Margaret Gibson Carmichael). Sir T. D. Gibson Carmichael.

Belhaven, Penelope, The Lady, wife of the seventh Baron of Belhaven, and daughter of Ronald Macdonald, of Clanranald, died 1816; 35 × 27. Half figure seated, head turned slightly to left, arms crossed on her lap, white dress open in front, short sleeves, the left looped up with pearl ornament; landscape background. J. H. McFadden Esq., R.A., 1896. French Gallery, Edinburgh, 1909. Wallis & Son, 1910.

Bell, Dr. Benjamin (1749-1806). Author of "A System of Surgery." Engraved by Bengo and Wm. Walker.

Bell, Mrs. Catherine; unfinished. Sir E. Vincent, K.C.M.G.

Bell, G. J. (1770-1843), Scots Professor, Edinburgh University. 35 × 25. Author of Commentaries on Scots Law. Glasgow International Exhibition, 1901. Wallis & Son, 1910. Hon. E. Charteris.

Bell, G. J. 49½ × 39. Raeburn Exhibition, 1876; Faculty of Advocates, Edinburgh.

Bell, Mrs. (*née* Barbara Shaw), wife of Prof. Bell; 30 × 35. Lent to Glasgow International Exhibition, 1901, by T. Jeffrey Bell, Esq.

Bell, Mrs. (*née* Eleanore Jane Ross), wife of Robert Bell. Painted in 1801-2; 50 × 40. Agnew, 1906 (c).

Bell, Mrs., sister of Dr. Hamilton. R.S.A., 1880.

Bell, Robert (1782-1861), Advocate, Sheriff of Berwickshire. 30 × 25. Lent to Raeburn Exhibition, 1876, by Lord Moncrieff, of Tullibole. Trustees of late Lord Moncrieff.

Bell, Mrs. Robert. 30 × 25. Trustees of late Lord Moncrieff.

Berkeley, Miss; 25 × 25 Heyman, New Bond Street.

Bethune, Mrs., in black dress. Lesser, 1890 (c).

Binning, Portrait of the two sons of David Monro Binning, Esq., in plum brown dresses with white ruffs and stockings, seated in a landscape; 50 × 40. (c) 1811. Agnew, 1902 (c).

Bisland, Master Thomas, afterwards Rector of Hartley Maudit; married Miss C. Gibson, daughter of the Rev. T. G. Gibson, rector of Holybourne, Hants; in green dress, with loose white frilled collar; seated on a bank, turning his head to the left, resting his right hand upon his knee, and holding his cap in his left hand. Foliage and landscape background; 56½ × 44. On the death of Mrs. Bisland (Mrs. Leach by second marriage) this picture was left by will to the mother of Major H. P. Trechy, of Willow Grange, Worpledon, Surrey. Agnew, 1909 (c). Messrs. Knoedler, New York.

Black, John, M.D., of Kirkaldy. Raeburn Exhibition, 1876

38

LIST OF PICTURES—*continued.*

Black, Dr. J. Full length, seated ; looking at spectator, white wig ; 50 × 40. Engraved by Heath. Reproduced in " Fifty Portraits of Raeburn," 1909, edited by Mr. J. L. Caw. Wallis & Son. Sir George Warrender, Bart.
Blair, Anne, of Avontoun, wife of A. Maconochie Welwood (second Lord Meadowbank). Glasgow International Exhibition, 1901. E. A. Maconochie Welwood, Esq.
Blair, Dr. Hugh (1718-1800). Celebrated Scottish divine, Professor of Rhetoric at Edinburgh University ; three-quarter length, seated, gown, white wig, looks to right. Engraved by Bartolozzi. Raeburn Exhibition, 1876. Henry Temple Blair, Esq., of Avontoun.
Blair, Lord President Robert, of Avontoun (1741-1811). Raeburn Exhibition, 1876, W. S. Society, Edinburgh. Painted in May, 1811 ; engraved by J. Heath. There is another portrait of Lord Blair.
Blair, Master William, of Avontoun, son of Lord President Blair; passed advocate 1821 ; died 1873. Raeburn Exhibition 1876. Miss Cornelia Blair, Scotstoun. Painted about 1814.
Bonar, Alexander. Originally a three-quarter length, this portrait was cut down to its present size because the figure and background were not by Raeburn ; 30 × 25. Presented to Scottish National Gallery by his grand-daughter, Miss S. A. Fleming, Edinburgh, in fulfilment of the wish of her brother, Mr. Alexander Bonar Fleming, of Hillwood, Corstorphine, 1900.
Bonar, Mrs. Miss Sarah M'Call, daughter of John M'Call, of Glasgow, and wife of Alexander Bonar, of Ratho. Bust, middle aged ; she wears a black gown, a white fichu, and a white muslin cap, from under which her brown hair hangs in curls on each side of her brow ; 30 × 25. Like the companion portrait of Mr. Bonar, this was originally a three-quarter length, and was cut to its present size for a similar reason. The canvas is under an oval slip. Presented to Scottish National Gallery by her grand-daughter, Miss S. A. Fleming, Edinburgh, in fulfilment of the wish of her brother, Mr. Alexander Bonar Fleming, of Hillwood, Corstorphine, 1900.
Bonar, The Children ; 82 × 55. Fraser (c) 1901.
Bonar, John Andrew Macdonnel, of Kimmingham and Warriston. Painted in 1820. Seated in an arm chair, turned to the right, looking at spectator ; arms rest on the arms of the chair. Three-quarter length, life size ; 49½ × 39½. Sedelmeyer, 1905. M. Kann sale, June 9, 1911.
Boothby, Sir Brooke, Seventh Bart., author of " Fables and Satires " ; died 1824. 30 × 25. R.S.A., 1863. Raeburn Exhibition. James T. Gibson-Craig, Esq. Lord Melville, Melville Castle.
Boswall, Thomas, of Blackadder. Lent to Raeburn Exhibition, 1876, by Sir George A. F. Houston Boswall, Bart. Painted about 1822.
Boswall, Mrs., of Blackadder. Lent to Raeburn Exhibition, by Sir George A. F. Houston Boswall, Bart. Painted about 1822.
Boswell, Mrs. Irvine J., of Kingussie. Margaret, daughter of Mr. Christie, of Durie ; 30 × 25. Painted about 1820. Engraved by Norman Hirst. Wallis & Son. Col. Walter Brown, of Renfrew.
Bouhl, Miss. A. E. Huntingdon, Esq., America.
Bower, Miss ; 30 × 25. A. G. Murray, Esq. Blair (c) 1905. Mr. H. E. Huntingdon, America.
Boy with Cherry ; 29 × 24½. (c) 1908.
Boy in Green Coat ; 29 × 24. Marler (c) 1904.
Boy in red coat, white vest and lace collar ; member of the Russell family (Duke of Bedford) ; 11 × 10. Heyman.
Boy, A Little. Cunliffe Brooks, Esq. B/I. 1901. (Phillips).
Boy, A.
Boy, A. Forbes and Paterson's Exhibition, 1901.
Boy and Rabbit. Full length, seated ; 41 × 31. Diploma Gallery.
Boyle, Lord President David, 1772–1853. Painted when Lord Justice Clerk. Earl of Glasgow.
Boys, Two. Supposed to be members of the family of Allen, of Errol. Dressed in brown and buff, standing in a landscape ; 60 × 45. Birmingham Art Gallery, 1903. Century of Art Exhibition, 1911. Leopold Hirsch, Esq.
Braidwood, William, first manager of Caledonian Insurance Co. Lent by the directors of the Caledonian Insurance Co. to Raeburn Exhibition, 1876. 30 × 25. Painted about 1819.
Braxfield, Lord Justice Clerk. Robert Macqueen suggested " Weir of Hermiston " in Stevenson's novel. Three-quarter length ; seated ; hands clasped in lap ; wig ; 35 × 26½. Engraved by C. Dawe.
Braxfield, Lord Justice Clerk. In official robes. In Parliament House, Edinburgh. The property of Faculty of Advocates. Painted after 1819. Engraved by D. Lizars.
Breadalbane. The first Marquis of. The Hon. Mrs. Baillie Hamilton.
Bremner, James, first President of Society of Solicitors before the Supreme Court ; died 1826. Lent to Raeburn Exhibition, 1876, by S.S.C. Society, Edinburgh.
Brewster, Sir David, D.C.L. (1781–1868). Principal of Edinburgh University, 1860 ; invented polyxonal lens for lighthouses, the kaleidoscope and lenticular stereoscope. Author of several books on science. Engraved by W. Hall. Raeburn Exhibition, 1876. Raeburn family.
Brown, Miss Isabella ; 29 × 24. 1903 (c) Colnaghi & Co. Knoedler & Co.
Brown, John, of Westernhaugh ; 50 × 40. Fischoff Blahensen sale, New York, March 10, 1900. Curtis.
Brown, Mrs. John ; 38½ × 49. Miss Brown, 1898 (Dowells, Edinburgh).
Brown, Robert. Engraved by W. H. Lizars. H. Brown, Esq.
Bruce, Lady Christian. W. J. Hay, Esq., Duns Castle.
Bruce, James, historiographer.
Bruce, John. Engraved by E. Mitchell.
Bruce, Robert of Kennet, as a youth, afterwards M.P. (1795–1864) for Clackmannan. His son, Alexander Hugh, became Lord Balfour of Burleigh by the removal of the Attainder. Lord Balfour of Burleigh, K.T. Raeburn Exhibition, 1876 ; Glasgow International Exhibition, 1901.
Bruce, Colonel Robert. (?) Mrs. R. T. Hamilton Bruce.
Buchan, David Steuart, Eleventh Earl of ; 29½ × 27. Exhibition of Raeburn's works, 1876, National Gallery of Ireland. Reproduced in the Edinburgh edition of Lockhart's " Life of Sir Walter Scott, Bart.," 1902.
Buchan, Robert. Lent to Raeburn Exhibition, 1876, by Buchan's niece, Mrs. Henderson. Painted about 1823.

39

Buchanan, George, the poet. (See letters, pages 42–3).
Buchanan, Rev. Walter, D.D., of Canongate, Edinburgh; died 1832. Lent to Raeburn Exhibition by Robert Foulis, Esq., M.D.
Buchanan, Mrs. Lent by Robert Foulis, Esq., M.D., to Raeburn Exhibition, 1876.
Buchanan, Mrs. (*née* Murray Kynynmond Edmonstone), wife of John Buchanan, of Arnprior. Lent to Raeburn Exhibition, 1876, by J. Buchanan Baillie Hamilton, Esq. Painted before 1808.
Burns, the Poet. 23 × 19. Painted in 1803 after Nasmyth's portrait, to the commission of Messrs. Cadell & Davies, publishers of the first London edition of the poet's works conjointly with Creech, of Edinburgh. The holograph letter of Raeburn relating to this portrait is printed in the text.
Burns, the Poet. 50 × 40. Copy of above. Painted for James, Earl of Glencairn, Coates House, Edinburgh.
Burrell, Capt. David. In uniform of East India Company. Three-quarter length; arms folded; 50 × 40. John A. Holms, Esq.
Bute, John Crichton Steuart, Marquis of. Painted about 1820. Engraved by Ward. Marquis of Bute.
Byres, James, of Tonley, who was an eminent antiquarian and resided many years in Rome, where he discovered the famous Barberini or Portland vase, which is now in the British Museum. Author of " Hypogæi." This portrait was painted when he was 77 years of age; 30 × 25. R.A., 1904. Scottish National Exhibition, 1908. D. Scott Moncrieff, Esq. Wallis & Son, 1910.

Cadell, William, of Banton. (c) 1810.
Calderwood, Mrs. 30 × 24. Raeburn Exhibition, 1876.
Cameron, Dr. George, when a boy.
Cameron, Dr. George ; 28½ × 23. Maclean, 1906 (c).
Campbell, of Park. Raeburn Exhibition, 1876. G. Maclachlan, Esq.
Campbell, father of Robert N. Campbell, of Kailzie. G. Maclachlan, Esq. Raeburn Exhibition, 1876.
Campbell, Alexander, of Hallyards. Merchant, Glasgow. Bust portrait, looking to left, in bottle green coat, yellow vest, and white neckcloth ; 29 × 24. Deposited by Glasgow Highland Society, 1903, to Glasgow Corporation Gallery.
Campbell, Mrs. Anne, second daughter of Thomas Campbell, Esq., of Tomperan, Perthshire, and wife of Colin Campbell, of Park, Renfrewshire ; in black dress and bonnet, with white shawl over her shoulders ; 30 × 25. Raeburn Exhibition, Edinburgh, 1876. Dowdeswell, 1898.
Campbell, Colin, of Park. Raeburn Exhibition, 1876. G. Maclachlan, Esq.
Campbell, Mrs. Colin, of Park. Raeburn Exhibition, 1876. G. Maclachlan, Esq.
Campbell, Sir Duncan, of Barcaldine and Glenure. In uniform of 3rd Guards (Scots Fusilier Guards). Sir Duncan Campbell of Barcaldine.
Campbell, Lord Frederick, son of fourth Duke of Argyll. Lord Clerk Register; founded Register House, Edinburgh ; 93 × 59. Engraved by J. Heath. General Register House.
Campbell, General, of Loch Nell. Engraved by J. B. Bird. R.S.A., 1863. Duke of Argyll.
Campbell, General, of Loch Nell. In scarlet coat and buff breeches, his arms crossed, holding his bearskin hat in his right hand ; standing in a landscape under some trees. Painted when an officer in the Guards. 48 × 39. Sir Rodney Stewart Riddell, Bart. Agnew (c) 1911.
Campbell, Rev. George, D.D., Minister of Cupar ; distinguished as a preacher and author ; was the father of Lord Chancellor Campbell, died 1825. Bust to left, looking at spectator ; black gown and white bands ; dark background ; 29 × 24. A. G. Campbell, Esq. R.A., 1907.
Campbell, Lady Hume, of Marchmont, and child. Full length ; the lady seated in a red covered chair to the right, holds her half naked child ; 79 × 60. Painted in 1813. Bequeathed to Scottish National Gallery, by her son, Sir Hugh Hume Campbell, of Marchmont, Bart, 1894.
Campbell, Mrs. James. Marion, daughter of John Muirhead, of Croy Leckie, Killearn, Stirlingshire; born 1739, married James Campbell, of Glasgow ; died 1815. She was first cousin of James Watt, the engineer ; 30 × 25. Lionel B. C. Muirhead. Cent Portraits des Femmes, Paris, 1909. Japan-British Exhibition, 1910, etc.
Campbell, Sir John. Painted about 1795. (?) Miss Halkett.
Campbell, John, portrait of, of the Bank of Scotland, Edinburgh. In brown dress with deep roll collar ; white stock and vest. 29 × 24½ (c) 1911.
Campbell, John, of Clathick. Mrs. Atherton.
Campbell, John, of Kilberry (1760–1838). Three-quarter length, standing ; dark grey coat, yellow waistcoat and trousers ; right hand in yellow glove, holding stick and hat ; thumb of left hand in trouser pocket ; 50 × 40. Wallis & Son, 1910.
Campbell, Mrs. John, of Kilberry, daughter of William Rankine, of Dudhope. Three-quarter length, standing in a landscape ; black hair, white dress, right hand holding yellow shawl ; left hand resting on branch of tree. 50 × 40. Wallis & Son, 1910.
Campbell, John, of Saddell, when a child, 1726–1823. Full length, seated. Agnew.
Campbell, John, of Saddell, 39 × 49. Rear-Admiral C. Campbell, 1902 (Fosters). Bought in.
Campbell, John, sen., G. Maclachlan, Esq., Raeburn Exhibition, 1876.
Campbell, Miss Lilias, of Inverawe, Argyleshire, seated in a landscape, leaning against a tree, her hands folded, in white dress, mauve sash, and powdered hair ; 29 × 24. A. C. Thornhill, Esq. 1902 (R. and F). Wallis & Son.
Campbell, Mrs. Louise.
Campbell, Miss Margaret, 47½ × 39. Lawrie & Co., 1905.
Campbell, Miss. Scottish National Exhibition, 1908. J. J. Mowbray, Esq.
Campbell, Mrs., sen. G. Maclachlan. Raeburn Exhibition, 1876.
Campbell, Mrs. 29 × 24. 1901 (c) Colnaghi & Co. Dowdeswell.
Campbell, Mrs. Elderly lady, half figure, seated, dark dress, white fichu, patterned white shawl, white satin cap, hands gloved. 30 × 25. M. Kann. Sale 9 June, 1911.
Campbell, Mrs., of Ballyards, seated three-quarter length. A. R. Don, Esq., Broughty Ferry.

Campbell, Alex. ; 29 × 24. Agnew, 1902.
Campbell, Colonel Alexander, of Possil. Mrs. Atherton. Raeburn Exhibition 1876. G. Maclachlan, Esq.
Campbell, Mrs. Alexander, of Fossil. Half length, to right ; face almost full.   Raeburn Exhibition, 1876.
    G. Maclachlan, Esq. Mrs. Atherton.
Campbell, Mrs., of Ballimore. Miss Christina Lamond Drummond, wife of Colonel Dougald Campbell, of
    Ballimore. An elderly lady, seen three-quarter length, seated to the right in a green garden seat,
    beneath a grey tree trunk and russet foliage, in white dress with an overgown of greenish grey, and
    black shoulder cape, the ends of which fall in front, one hand is gloved in grey; her eyes are brown,
    and on her grey hair is a white kerchief; 50 × 40. Painted about 1795. Bequeathed to National
    Gallery of Scotland by Lady Riddell, 1897. Photographed by Annan.
Campbell, Mrs. and Son. 30 × 25. Gooden & Fox.
Campbell, Mungo Nutter Campbell, of Ballimore.
Carlisle, Mr. 36 × 28. Bonner Sale, New York.
Carlisle, Mrs. 36 × 28. Bonner Sale, New York, 1900. Laffan.
Carmichael, Eleanor Margaret Gibson, as a child, in a landscape, wife of Mr. Begbie, and daughter of Sir
    John Gibson-Carmichael 6th Baronet ; 46½ × 36¾. Sir T. D. Gibson-Carmichael. Shown at Colnaghi &
    Co.'s Gallery, 1905.
Carmichael,-Miss Eleanor. Replica of foregoing. 30 × 25
Carmichael, Sir John Gibson. Forbes and Paterson's Exhibition, 1901.
Carmichael, Lady, *née* Janet Maitland-Dundas, wife of Sir Thomas Gibson-Carmichael, seventh Baronet;
    30 × 25. Sir T. D. Gibson-Carmichael. Shown at Colnaghi & Co.'s Gallery, 1905. Engraved by H. Scott
    Bridgwater.
Carmichael, Sir Thomas Gibson-Carmichael, seventh Baronet, of Skirling. 30 × 25.
Carnegie, Lady Agnes. Painted about 1810.
Carnegie, David.
Carnegie, Lady. Full length; standing, leaning against tree in landscape, with water ; 96 × 59. Earl of
    Southesk, K.T.
Carnegie, Lady ; 50 × 40 (c) 1810.
Cathcart, Master, and Dog. Agnew.
Cathcart, Robert of Drum, W. S. Painted about 1813 Engraved by C. Turner. L. Hirsch, Esq
Cay, Mrs John, *née* Frances Hodshon, wife of John Cay, Esq., of North Charlton, mother of Judge Cay.
    In brown dress with white fichu, and yellow shawl; powdered hair; seated in a red chair, holding a book
    and her pince-nez ; 34½ × 26½. Raeburn Exhibition, 1876. Agnew, 1910 (c).
Cay, Sir Robert Hodshon, of North Charlton, Judge of Admiralty Court. In dark dress, scarlet gown, bands
    and wig, and holding papers in his right hand; 49 × 39. Raeburn Exhibition, 1876. Colnaghi & Co.,
    1910 (c). Messrs. Knoedler, New York.
Chalmers, George, of Pittencrieff. Full length, seated by window showing view of Dunfermline Abbey.
    Painted 1776. Lent to Raeburn Exhibition in 1876 by Dunfermline Town Council.
Chalmers, Mrs., of Gadgirth, in white dress with yellow shawl, white lace cap with blue riband; 30 × 25.
    Partington, 1902.
Charteris. (See Elcho).
Chantrey, Sir Francis, R.A. Three profile sketches ; the head in each case turned towards the left.
    Inscribed, F. Chantrey, R.A. Sketched by H. Raeburn in Princes Street, Edinburgh, 1818, W. C.
    (Pencil ; paper 6¾ × 10¾). On the other side of the paper is a sketch of Raeburn by Chantrey, done at
    the same time. Formerly in the possession of Wilkie Collins the novelist. Presented to Scottish
    National Portrait Gallery by C. Fairfax Murray, Esq , 1901.
Chantrey, Sir F. Half length, body to right, face almost full; 36 × 28. Engraved by J. Thomson. Col.
    Walter Brown
Cleghorn, Dr. Glasgow Royal Asylum.
Cleghorn, Dr. Glasgow International Exhibition in 1901. Robert M. Mann, Esq.
Cleghorn, Miss ; 25 × 30. Wallis & Son.
Clephane, Major-General Douglas McLean. Forbes and Paterson's Exhibition, 1901
Clephane, Mrs. McLean.
Clerk, John, father of Lord Eldin. Author of "Essay on Naval Tactics " and inventor of naval tactics of
    breaking the enemy's line, employed by Rodney's fleet in the West Indies in 1782. Died 1812. Raeburn
    Exhibition, 1876. Sir G. D. Clerk.
Clerk, John, Advocate, afterwards Lord Eldin, an earlier portrait than the following. Raeburn Exhibition,
    1876. Sir G. D. Clerk, Bart.
Clerk, John. Nearly whole length to right ; seated at table on which he rests a book, beside a " Crouching
    Venus." Engraved by C. Turner, 1815. Raeburn Exhibition. Sir G. D. Clerk, Bart.
Clerk, Sir John, fifth Baronet of Penicuik, and Rosemary Dacre, his wife, in a landscape ; 57 × 82. Painted
    about 1790. R.A. 1910. Sir George D. Clerk. Otto Beit, Esq. (The *Morning Chronicle* of May 31,
    1792, says that this picture arrived too late for the Royal Academy, and was exhibited in the Shakespeare
    Gallery instead).
Clerk, Mrs. Isabella. See Wedderburn.
Clunes, Major William. Native of Sutherlandshire ; Colonel of the Sutherland Fencibles, Aide-de-camp in
    India to Sir Hector Munro, and Captain (1809) in the 50th Regiment. He served in the Peninsular War.
    Full length, in scarlet tunic with stand-up collar and stock ; lace ruffle at the neck ; fur-trimmed military
    cloak, dark grey breeches and Hessian boots ; stands with head turned slightly to the right, looking
    straight out. The right hand is at the waist, and the left rests upon the back of the chestnut coloured
    charger, which, with flanks turned towards the spectator, occupies the right. Conventional landscape
    background, with tree trunk crossing the sky from left to right. Light falls from the right front;
    96 × 60. Bequeathed to the Royal Scottish Academy by Lady Siemens, 1902. Scottish National
    Gallery.

41

Cochrane, Mrs. Miniature. Miss Cochrane.

Cockburn, Henry, Lord (1779–1854). Born Edinburgh, educated High School and University. Solicitor-General, 1830; Lord Rector Glasgow University, 1831, raised to the Bench, 1834. Contributor to *Edinburgh Review* and author of "Memorials" of his times. Engraved by R. Bell, and W. Walker. Raeburn Exhibition, 1876.

Colquhoun, Sheriff Archibald Campbell. Exhibited Glasgow, 1863.

Colt, Robert, of Auldhame, Haddingtonshire, and Lady (Miss Dundas). Lent to Raeburn Exhibition by Mrs. Jane Colt, sen., of Gartsherrie.

Colville, General. Engraved by Payne. (?) Lord Colville of Culross.

Compton, Lady, Marchioness of Northampton. 50 × 40. Marquis of Northampton. Painted about 1814.

Compton, Lady. Replica.

Compton, Earl, Marquis of Northampton. Marquis of Northampton.

Constable, Archibald. Publishers of *Edinburgh Review* and Scott's Novels. Painted about 1822; 50 × 40. Engraved by Payne. Raeburn Exhibition, 1876. Thomas Constable, Esq., Queen's Printer. Christie's 1904, Moray. There is also a sketch of Constable.

Contemplation. See Mrs. Johnstone.

Copeland, Jacobina, of Collieston, Dumfries-shire. Wife of Sir William Dunbar, sixth Baronet of Mochrum, Wigtonshire. The Copelands claimed descent from the English Squire, John Copeland, who took David II., King of Scots, prisoner at the battle of Durham or Deville's Cross, 17th October, 1346; 30 × 25. Agnew, 1903.

Cowley, J., R.A., 1816.

Cowlishaw, The Brothers, the Young Fishermen. The young boys are depicted, one with a rod, the other with a landing net, starting for a days fishing, on the banks of a Scotch Loch. 40 × 35. Mr. Heyman, 180 New Bond St. W.

Craig, Sir James Gibson, Bart., of Riccarton, Midlothian (1765–1850) Engraved by R. Bell. Raeburn Exhibition. Sir W. Gibson-Craig, Bart.

Craig, Lady Gibson. Raeburn Exhibition, 1876. Sir W. Gibson-Craig, Bart.

Craig, Mrs. Raeburn Exhibition. Rev. John Weir.

Craig, William. Lord of Session, Senator of the College of Justice; died 1813. Painted about 1810. Raeburn Exhibition, 1876. Andrew Hay Wilson, Esq. Faculty of advocates, Edinburgh.

Craig, Sir W. Gibson, second Baronet (1797–1878). Lord Clerk Register, and Keeper of the Signet; M.P. for Edinburgh. Painted about 1818. Raeburn Exhibition, 1876. Sir W. Gibson-Craig.

Craigie, Dr. Half length, seated. Messrs. Knoedler, New York.

Craigie-Halkett. (See Halkett).

Crawford, Captain James. J. C. Crawford, Esq.

Crawford, Mr., merchant, Glasgow. Raeburn Exhibition, 1876, the Lord Justice General.

Crawford, Mrs. Patrick George. Lent to Scottish Exhibition, Glasgow, by Mrs. J. G. Ure.

Creech, William, Publisher. Engraved by W. and D. Lizars, as frontispiece to "Edinburgh Fugitive Pieces." Mrs. Watson.

Crichton, Lady Elizabeth Penelope, with her mother, Countess of Dumfries. Her elder son, John, inherited the earldom of Dumfries in 1803, and became Marquis of Bute in 1814. In flowing robes walking in a landscape; 94½ × 58½. Reproduced in "Fifty Portraits of Raeburn." Raeburn Exhibition, 1876. Marquis of Bute.

Crombie, Mrs. Mrs. Paul, Edinburgh.

Cruikshank, James, the astronomer. Seated, turned to right, looking at spectator, his left arm resting on the back of his chair. Black coat, white necktie and buckskin trousers. Nearly full length, 49¼ × 39¼. Exhibited in Berlin, 1903, Sedelmeyer, 1905. M. Kann.

Cruikshank, Mrs. Three-quarter length, seated; fur-lined cloak, white dress, white collar; large hat in right hand. Arthur Sanderson, Esq. J. A. Holmes, Esq.

Cumming, Miss. Mr. Callander, of Ruston Park.

Cumming, Mrs. Raeburn Exhibition, 1824.

Cuninghame, of Fairlie. J. C. Cunningham, Esq.

Cuninghame, John, of Craigends. J. C. Cunningham, Esq.

Cunningham, Alexander. J. C. Cunningham, Esq.

Curran, J.P. 30 × 25. Ehrich sale, New York, 1906.

Dalrymple, Lady, of Hailes. 29½ × 24½. Bust, white cap, white dress, short black coat. Salting Bequest, National Gallery.

Dalrymple, Elizabeth. (See Leith).

Dalzel, Rev. Professor Andrew, F.R.S., an eminent scholar. Born 1742, at Kirkliston. He was educated at Edinburgh University, and travelled as tutor to Lord Maitland, afterwards Earl of Lauderdale. Professor of Greek in the University of Edinburgh. Principal clerk to the General Assembly of the Church of Scotland. Died 1806. Three-quarter length, seated to right in red covered chair; right hand holds calf bound book on right knee, left arm rests on chair back; black dress and professor's gown, white cravat; white hair; yellowish-brown eyebrows, dark blue eyes, shaven face; books on green covered table to left; dark greenish background; 49½ × 39. Engraved by R. C. Bell, in Dalzel's "History of the University of Edinburgh," 1862. From the collection of J. T. Gibson-Craig, Esq., who acquired the portrait at the Dalzel Sale on May 7, 1877. Purchased April, 1887, for S.N.P.G.

Davidson, Rev. Thomas, D.D., of Muirhouse; died 1827. Raeburn Exhibition, 1876. Mr. Davidson, of Muirhouse.

Deans, Admiral Robert; 36 × 28. Half length to waist, in uniform, right hand resting on telescope, left hand not seen, face turned to right; stormy sky and sea. Shepherd Bros., Melbourne National Art Gallery. The uniform is not that of an Admiral, and as Deans was not gazetted Admiral until February 14th, 1799, it must have been painted before that date. Very little is known of the Admiral and his exploits. The *Gentleman's Magazine* simply records the fact that he was Admiral of the White, and that he died at his seat at Huntingdon, N.B., in January, 1815. The portrait, with that of his wife, remained in the possession of the family until quite recently. That of the latter was on view at Messrs. Shepherd's last year, but was sold some time since.

Deans, Mrs., wife of Admiral Deans (1756–1823). Three-quarter length, seated. Brown curly hair, white head-dress; white gown, red shawl; left arm rests on back of chair, right hand lies in her lap; 36 × 28. Painted about 1800. Messrs. Shepherd.

Deuchar, David, of Morningside (Miniature). To Raeburn Exhibition, 1876. Miss Deuchar.

Dickie, William (copy). Caledonian Insurance Co.

Dickson, The Rev. Dr., of Leith; 27¾ × 36   E. Schulte, of Berlin.

Dickson, The Rev. Dr., of Leith. Engraved by C. Turner. Kirk Session, of South Leith.

Dog. Study of a. Exhibition of artist's works, Edinburgh, 1876.

Dougal, Mr., of Castle Temple, with dog; 35 × 45½. Charles Hosmer, Esq., of Montreal.

Douglas, Lord. Earl of Home.

Douglas, Mrs. (See Elizabeth Graham).

Douglas, Margaret, of Brigton, afterwards Mrs. Hunter, of Burnside; 35 × 26¾. Seated, three-quarter length, life-size, in a landscape; turned to left and looking in same direction. Powdered curly hair. Low white dress, with blue waistband; her hands folded in her lap. Purchased from the family. Sedelmeyer (1905). Wallis & Son, 1910.

Douglas, Rev. Robert, D.D., of Galashiels; died 1820. Painted about 1813. Raeburn Exhibition, 1876. Miss Thomson.

Drummond, General Andrew John, of Strathallan; 29 × 24¼. Third son of James, fifth Viscount Strathallan. In scarlet uniform, with purple facings and gold epaulettes; white stock. Ex. Earl of Perth. Christie's, 1910. Colnaghi & Co. Messrs. Knoedler, New York.

Drummond, General, of Machanay. Painted about 1817. Lent to Raeburn Exhibtion, 1876, by J. Buchanan Baillie Hamilton, Esq., of Arnprior and Cambusmore.

Drummond, George, his sister Margaret, and his foster brother. George Drummond, Esq.

Drummond, Harley. Raeburn Exhibition. T. Macknight Crawford, Esq., of Cartsburn.

Drummond, Henry Home. Col. Home Drummond.

Drummond, Mrs Home, of Blair Drummond. 34½ × 27   Engraved in mezzotint by H. Scott Bridgwater, R.A., 1908. Lieut -Col. Home Drummond.

Drummond, Captain J. R., R N. Raeburn Exhibition, 1876. Sir J. H. Williams Drummond.

Drummond, Lady, of Hawthornden, wife of Capt. John Forbes-Drummond, who was created a baronet in 1826 for distinguished naval service. Raeburn Exhibition, 1876. Sir James H. Williams Drummond, of Hawthornden.

Duff, Captain, afterwards Admiral Norwich; 34½ × 27. Painted about 1822. Engraved by G. Dawe, 1810. E. Alexander Duff, Esq.

Duff, Colonel and wife. (R. & F.), 1895. Messrs. Colnaghi & Co. M. Th. Duret, Paris.

Duff, Mrs., wife of Colonel Duff, of Fetteresso, several members of whose family were painted by Raeburn; 30 × 25. Birmingham Art Gallery, 1903. Leopold Hirsch, Esq.

Duff, Mrs. 50 × 40. Sir J. B. Robinson.

Duff, wife of General. Lesser (R. & F.), 1895.

Dudgeon, Miss or Mrs   Full length. National Gallery.

Dumfries, Margaret Crawford, Countess of (with her daughter, Lady Elizabeth Penelope Crichton, *see* Crichton).

Dumfries, Patrick Macdowal, fifth Earl of, with Flora, Countess of Loudan. Raeburn Exhibition, 1876. Marquis of Bute.

Dunbar, Sir Archibald. Glasgow International, 1901. Sir Archibald H. Dunbar.

Duncan, Admiral Adam, Lord, second son of Alexander Duncan, Provost of Dundee (1731–1804). Distinguished himself under Rodney at Cape St. Vincent; defeated the Dutch at Camperdown, 1797; thanked by both Houses of Parliament; created Baron Lundie and Viscount Duncan of Camperdown; City of London gave him the freedom and a sword. Full length, standing at table. Painted, 1798. Trinity House, Leith.

Duncan, Alexander, W. S., of Restalsig and St. Fort; 74 × 60. Victoria Art Galleries, Dundee. Property of Mrs. Anstruther-Duncan, Naughton, Fife.

Duncan, Andrew, sen. (1744–1828). President College of Physicians, 1790; Professor of Medicine Edinburgh University; first Physician to the King for Scotland, 1821; wrote "Annals of Medical Science," etc. Painted about 1819. Royal College of Physicians, Edinburgh.

Duncan, Andrew, sen. Royal Medical Society, Edinburgh.

Duncan, Mrs. Half figure in front, head turned slightly to right; black dress, cut low; dark background; 29½ × 24½. Ernest G. von Glehn, Esq., R A., 1906.

Dundas Colonel, First Earl of Zetland. Marquis of Zetland.

Dundas, Sir David, K.C.B., 1735-1820. Painted 1809. 30 × 25. Exhibited Edinburgh, 1824.

Dundas, Henry. (See Lord Melville).

Dundas of Arniston, Lord Chief Baron of Court of Exchequer in Scotland (1758–1819). Seated to left; in official robes; table and curtain; 49 × 40. Painted about 1795. Engraved by F. Woolnoth, 1834. Raeburn Exhibition, 1876. Robert Dundas, Esq., of Arniston. Sir Robert Dundas, Bart.

Dundas, Lady Eleanor. Sir T. D. Gibson-Carmichael, Bart.

Dundas, General. Sir T. D. Gibson-Carmichael, Bart.

Dundas, Mrs., of Arniston. Painted about 1793. Raeburn Exhibition, 1876. Robert Dundas, Esq., of Arniston.

Dundas, Mrs., of Linlithgow, wife of George Dundas, of Dundas. Second daughter of Sir Wm. Stirling, of Ardoch. 34½ × 26½ (1762–1832). Raeburn Exhibition, 1876. Sir William Stirling-Maxwell, Bart., of Keir and Pollock. Wallis (o), 1911.

Dundas, Mrs. Philip, R.S.A., 1863.

Dundas, Robert, of Arniston, second Lord President of the Court of Session (1713–1787). Painted about 1787. There is a copy in Parliament House. Engraved by W. Sharp, 1797. Raeburn Exhibition. Sir Robert Dundas, Bart.

Dundas, Second Lord President. 30 × 25.

Durham, Mrs. Thomas, wife of General Durham, third son of James Durham, of Largo. Raeburn Exhibition. Mrs. Dundas Durham. Sir Robert Dundas, Bart.

Dunlop, John. Lord Provost of Glasgow, and a poet. Misses Donald.

Dunsinnany, Sir William Nairne, Lord of Session ; died 1811. Faculty of Advocates.

Dyce, Rev. Alexander, when a boy (1798–1869). 29¼ × 24⅝. Bequeathed by Mrs. Donald Campbell to the nation. Victoria and Albert Museum.

Edgar, Alexander, of Auchingrammont ; died 1820. Lieut.-Col. Edgar. Raeburn Exhibition, 1876. A. J. Forbes-Leith.

Edgar, Ann. See Lady Raeburn.

Edgar, Dr. Handasyde ; died 1810. Lieut.-Col. James Handasyde Edgar. Raeburn Exhibition, 1876. Humphrey Roberts. 1900 (c) Reid.

Edgar, James, of Auchingrammont ; died 1813. Lieut.-Col. James Handasyde Edgar. Raeburn Exhibition, 1876. Agnew, 1901 (c). Scottish National Exhibition, 1908. J. J. Mowbray, Esq.

Edgar, James, infant son of James Edgar ; died in 1794. 30 × 25. Lieut.-Col. James Handasyde Edgar. Raeburn Exhibition, 1876. John F. Talmage, Esq., New York.

Edgar, Mr. Raeburn Exhibition, 1876. Raeburn Family.

Edgar, Miss.

Edmonstone, Murray Kynynmond, wife of John Buchanan, of Arnprior. Painted before 1808. Raeburn Exhibition, 1876. J. Buchanan Baillie Hamilton, Esq.

Egerton, Sir Thomas (Earl of Wilton). (R. & F.) 1906. Langton Douglas, 1906.

Eglinton, Archibald, thirteenth Earl of. Full length ; about 84 × 60. Representing him as a boy with Eglinton Castle in background. Earl of Eglinton.

Elcho, Lord, and Mr. Charteris. Earl of Wemyss.

Elder, Right Hon. Thomas, of Forneth (1737–1799), Lord Provost of Edinburgh and Postmaster General for Scotland. Painted in 1798 for the University of Edinburgh, the new buildings of which were erected mainly owing to his efforts. Exhibition of Artists' Works, Edinburgh, 1876. Engraved by R. Earlom.

Elder, Thomas. David MacRitchie, Esq., on loan to S.N.P.G. Replica of the picture in Edinburgh University.

Eldin, Lord. (See Clerk).

Elliot, Cornelius, of Wolfelee. Raeburn Exhibition, 1876. Sir Walter Elliot, of Wolfelee.

Elliot, Margaret (Miss Rannie) wife, of above ; died 1796. Raeburn Exhibition, 1876. Sir Walter Elliot.

Elliot, William Elliot, Major 1st Madras Cavalry ; eldest son of Cornelius Elliot ; died in India, 1805. Raeburn Exhibition, 1876. Sir Walter Elliot.

Elphinstone Children, The. 1.99 m. × 1.53 m. Exhibition of British Art, Berlin, 1908. Charles Wertheimer, Esq.

Erskine, Anne, daughter of John Erskine, of Dun, and wife of John Wauchope ; died 1811. Raeburn Exhibition, 1876. Sir John Don Wauchope, Bart.

Erskine, Lady Christian (Lady Christian Bruce), daughter of Lord Elgin and Kincardine ; died 1810. Wife of James Erskine, Esq., of Cardross. French Gallery, Edinburgh, 1909.

Erskine, Colonel. Head engraved by G Dawe.

Erskine, Hon. Henry (1746–1817), of Amondell, Linlithgowshire. Distinguished advocate and brilliant wit, second son of fifth Earl of Buchan ; his son, Henry David, by his first wife, Christian Fullerton, became seventh Earl of Buchan. Painted about 1805. Engraved by James Ward. Raeburn Exhibition, 1876. Exhibited, Edinburgh in 1884.

Erskine, Henry ; 30 × 25. Painted about 1805. Exhibited, Edinburgh, 1884. Miss Fullerton.

Erskine, Hon. Henry. Three-quarter length, standing ; brown hair, grey coat and breeches, white scarf ; right hand rests on a book lying on green covered table ; red curtain. Painted about 1795. 16 × 13. Sold in the sale of John Clerk, of Eldin, in 1813. Shepherd Brothers, 1910. Lord Lucas.

Erskine, Hon. Henry. 29 × 34. Farmer, 1902 (c).

Erskine, James. W. J. Hay, Esq., Dunscastle.

Erskine, James. Erskine of Cardross.

Erskine, Rev. John, D.D., of Carnock (1722–1803). Described in Scott's "Guy Mannering." Raeburn Exhibition, 1876. Engraved by G. Dawe. Miss Burnett, of Kenmay, and family.

Erskine, William. (See Lord Kinnedder.)

Erskine, Mrs. John. Raeburn Exhibition, 1876.

Eskgrove, Lord, Sir David Rae, Bart., Lord Justice Clerk (1724–1804). Faculty of Advocates, Edinburgh.

Farmer's Wife, A (Mrs. Somerville). White cap with black ribbon, white apron reaching to the throat and almost concealing her black gown ; a black and white spotted shawl ; wearing fingerless gloves ; 36 × 30. Stirling Art Exhibition, 1910. Stephen Mitchell, Esq., of Boquhan. Illustrated in " Portraits by Raeburn," edited by Mr. James L. Caw, and published by Schulze & Co., Edinburgh, 1909.

Farquhar, Sir Walter. Nearly whole length, seated in arm chair, with hands clasped. Engraved by W. Sharp.

Farquharson, Archibald, of Finzean. Dr. Farquharson.

Female, Study of a. Painted in Rome. Exhibition of Artist's Works, Edinburgh, 1876.

Ferguson, Dr. Adam, LL.D., Professor of Moral Philosophy at Edinburgh University (1723–1816). In dark coat, vest and breeches with white stock, seated in a crimson armchair ; a table with books by his side ; red curtain background ; 49 × 39. Raeburn Exhibition, Edinburgh, 1876. Scottish National Portraits Exhibition, 1884. Gooden & Fox (c), 1906. Engraved by J. B. Lane, half-length only. The portrait is a whole length.

Do. do. University of Edinburgh.

44

Ferguson, Sir Adam Ferguson, of Kilkerran.   Sir James Ferguson, Bart.
Ferguson, Hugh Munro, of Raith.   R. C. Munro Ferguson, Esq., M.P.
Ferguson, Robert, M.A., of Raith.   R. C. Munro Ferguson, Esq., M.P.
Ferguson, General Sir Ronald, G.C.B., M.P. (1773-1841).   R C. Munro Ferguson, Esq., M.P.   Hunting costume, gun in hand, dog at his feet.   Reproduced in " Fifty Portraits of Raeburn," 1909.
Ferguson, William, of Kilrie, as a boy.   Oval ; head to left ; frilled shirt, open ; 30 × 25.   Raeburn Exhibition, 1876 ; Glasgow International Exhibition, 1901.   R. C. Munro-Ferguson, Esq., M.P.
Fergusson, Mrs., of Monkhood (*née* Hutcheson).   In white dress with yellow fichu over her shoulders, and white cap with blue bow ; 30 × 25.   Miss E. C. F. Pollock.   Agnew (c), 1906.   .
Fergusson, Mrs., daughter of William Petrie, Esq., and wife of John Hutcheson Fergusson, Esq., of Trochraigne.   Three-quarter length.   In green dress, with scarlet shawl over her arms, white kerchief over her hair and fastened under her chin ; seated, resting her left arm upon a table ; 35 × 27.   Miss E. Portal.   Sully & Co. (c), 1908.
Fergusson, Mrs., of Raith, and her Children, Ronald and Beatrice.   Lady in white seated ; girl leaning on her lap, boy by her side with dog ; landscape background ; 48¼ × 39.   Raeburn Exhibition, 1876 ; reproduced in " Fifty Portraits of Raeburn," 1909.   R. C. Munro Ferguson, Esq., M.P.
Fettes, Sir Wm., Bart (1750-1836).   Founder of the Fettes College, and uncle of Sir. Wm. Fettes Douglas, the eminent Scottish artist.   Raeburn exhibition, 1876.   Trustees of Fettes College.
Fettes, William, only son of Sir William Fettes (1787-1815).   Raeburn Exhibition, 1876.   Trustees of Fettes College.
Fife, Alexander, Earl of.   Duke of Fife, K.T.
Fife, James, fourth Earl of.   Duke of Fife, K.T.
Finlay, Mrs. Alexander.   (Miss Justine Camilla Wynne), of Glencorse, near Edinburgh.   Raeburn Exhibition, 1876.   Lieut-Col. J. E. Sharp.   Mrs. Glassford Bell.
Finlay, E. (c), 1908.   Gooden and Fox.
Forbes, James.
Forbes, John Stuart (afterwards 8th Baronet of Pitsligo), with Dog.   Second son of Sir William, 7th Bart., b. 1804 ; m. 1834, Lady Harriet Louisa Anne Kerr, third daughter of William, 6th Marquis of Lothian.   Assumed the additional surname and arms of Hopburn, as heir of entail to the Barony of Invermay, and as heir-at-law to the estate of Balmanno, both in Perthshire ;   died 1866.   Raeburn Exhibition, 1876.   Lord Clinton.   Hon. C. F. Trefusis.
Forbes, Lady.
Forbes, Miss.   F. Fleischmann, Esq.
Forbes, Sir William, 6th Baronet of Pitsligo, Aberdeen.   An eminent banker in Edinburgh.   Sir Walter Scott says in his notes to " Marmion," that he " was unequalled, perhaps, in the degree of individual affection entertained for him by his friends, as well as in the general esteem and respect of Scotland at large."   He was also, of considerable literary ability, and wrote a " Life of Beattie," m. 1770, Elizabeth, daughter of Sir James Hay, Bart., of Haystone.   Sir William died in 1806.   Bust : long straight grey hair, grey blue coat, yellow silk band, bearing enamel medallion ;   grey background ; 30 × 25.   Engraved by S. Freeman.   On loan to Brighton Art Galleries by the Trustees of the late C. J. Mackenzie, of Portmore, Scotland.
Forbes, Sir Wm. ; 30 × 25.   Mrs. Stewart Forbes.   Wallis (c), 1905.
Forbes, Sir William, 7th Baronet of Pitsligo ; 49 × 39.   Picture unfinished.   Married 1797, Williamina, sole child and heiress (by Lady Jane Leslie), of Sir John Stuart, Bart., of Fettercairn.   Sir William died in 1828, and was succeeded by his second son, John Stuart.   Seated, three-quarter length ; right elbow rests on arm chair placed by table at window ; left arm hangs at the other side of the chair, his fore-finger on green-covered chair ; full face, iron-grey hair, black coat, white collar and cravat ; red curtain.   On loan to Brighton Art Galleries by the Trustees of the late Colin J. Mackenzie, Esq., of Portmore, Scotland.
Forbes, William, with dog ; eldest son of 7th Baronet, died unmarried, 1826.   Raeburn Exhibition, Edinburgh, 1876.   Lord Clinton.
Ford, Mrs. Robert.   Sir Lewis Molesworth.
Forsyth, Wm., horticulturist ; 24½ × 29½.   G. F. Hearn, Esq., gift to Metropolitan Museum, New York.
Fox, Charles James (1749-1806).   R. A. Oswald, Esq., of Auchencreive.
Fraser, Alexander Charles, Jun., of Reelig, fourth son of Edward Fraser ;   born 1789, served in the Hon. East India Company Civil Service ; died at Delhi in 1816.   In green and blue plaid coat, white waistcoat, frill open at the neck ; full face, body to the right ; 30 × 25.   Painted (1803) at the age of fourteen.   Agnew, 1897.   Adolph Hirsch, Esq.   R.A., 1907.
Fraser, Edward Satchwell, third son of Edward Fraser of Reelig.   Born in 1786, served in the Hon. East India Company Civil Service, died at St Helena in 1813.   In green and blue plaid coat, white waist-coat and stock, turned slightly to the left ; 30 × 25.   Painted at the age of seventeen in 1803.   A. Wertheimer, Esq., 1897.
Fraser, Miss Eliza, of Castle Fraser.
Fraser, George John, of Reelig, fifth son of Edward Fraser.   Born in 1800, served in the Hon. East India Company Army, married in 1832, died at Delhi, in 1842.   In brown coat and waistcoat, with white frill loose at the neck ; full face. body slightly to the right ; 30 × 25.   Painted (1815) at the age of fifteen.   Agnew, 1897.
Fraser, James Baillie, of Reelig, eldest son of Edward Fraser.   Born in 1783, an accomplished writer of fiction and of travels in the east, he was a great traveller in India, Persia and Mesopotamia about the year 1836, see obituary notice in the Journal of the Geographical Society, vol. xxvi. ; he married in 1823, Jane Tytler, daughter of Lord Woodhouselee, and died in 1856 at Moniack, N B.   In claret-coloured coat and yellow waistcoat, white stock, head slightly to the left ; 30 × 25.   Painted (1809) at the age of twenty-six.   Gooden (c), 1897.
Fraser, James.   36 × 28.   Renton, R & F., 1903.

Fraser, Jane Anne Catherine, of Reelig, daughter of Edward Fraser. Born 1797, married in 1816, died 1880. In purple dress, with white lace collar and cords; full face, body to the right; 30 × 25. Painted (1816) at the age of nineteen. A. Wertheimer, Esq. Wm. Beattie, Esq. M. Kann sale, 9 June, 1911.

Fraser, General Mackenzie, of Castle Fraser, Ross-shire; 49 × 39. Portrait unfinished. He was M P. for Ross-shire. Lieut.-Gen. in the Army and Colonel of the 78th Highlanders. Derived from his mother the estate of Inverallochy, and that of Castle Fraser from her younger sister, Elizabeth, and assumed the name of Fraser. Married, in 1786, Helen, Sister of Lord Seaforth; died 1809. Three-quarter length, scarlet coat, gold epaulettes and buttons, black collar and lapels, white cravat; Thumb of right hand in belt, left hand holding hilt of sword, scarf round waist, buff trousers, grey background. Raeburn Exhibition, Edinburgh, 1876. On loan to Brighton Art Galleries, by the Trustees of the late C. J. Mackenzie, Esq., of Portmore, Scotland. Fraser, Lieut.-Colonel Mackenzie, of Castle Fraser.

Fraser, William, Jun., of Reelig, second son of Edward Fraser. Born in 1784, served in the Hon. East India Company Civil Service, was assassinated by a native while Commissioner of Delhi in 1835; see account in *Blackwood's Magazine*, January, 1878. In claret-coloured coat, white waistcoat and stock, head slightly turned to the right; 30 × 25. Painted (1801) at the age of sixteen. Agnew (c) 1897. Sedelmeyer Galerie, 1908. M. Eveil Picard, Paris. M. Kann, Paris.

Fraser-Tytler, Jane. (See Tytler-Fraser).

Fullerton, Mrs. Francis; 35 × 27. Colnaghi & Co. Agnew & Son.

Fullarton, William, of Skeldon, Ayrshire, advocate. Painted about 1805. Raeburn Exhibition, 1876. Miss Fullarton.

Galloway, Baillie Wm. Merchant Company, Edinburgh.

Gardiner, Dr. Miniature. Miss Lee.

Gellion, Ch.F. Bust of a young man.

George IV., Head of, engraved on plate of Dr. Thomas Charles Hope, (which see, and also text).

Gevine, Mrs. In white dress with blue sash, and blue ribbon in her powdered hair. 29 × 24½. Dr. Farquharson (c) 1911.

Gibb, Mr. A pastel.

Gifford, St. Thomas; 29 × 24½. A. Smith (c), 1904.

Gilbert, John. Half figure, turned slightly to right, dark dress, dark background; 29 × 24. Rev. W. H. Wayne, R.A., 1906.

Gilchrist, Ebenezer. John McCulloch, Esq.

Gladstone, Mrs. Sir J. R. Gladstone, Bart.

Gladstone, Thomas. Grandfather of W. E. Gladstone. Died 1809. Sir J. R. Gladstone, Bart.

Glencairn, Lord, friend of Robert Burns, the poet. Painted Canongate, Kilwynne Masonic Lodge No. 1, Edinburgh. 30 × 25. Wallis & Son; now in America.

Glenelly, Earl of. Grace (c), 1898.

Glengarry. (See MacDonell).

Glenlee, Lord of Barskimming and Glenlee, Lord President of the Court of Session. In dark dress with white stock, seated in an armchair by a table, on which are papers and books, red curtain background; engraved by Walker. Raeburn Exhibition, 1824. Holder, 1902 (c) 1904. Colnaghi & Co. Knoedler & Co.

Gordon, Alexander, fourth Duke of (1743.1827); 30 × 25. Manchester Art Gallery.

Gordon, Chas., fourth Earl of Aboyne; 50 × 40. J. H. Brass, Esq. Turner (c), 1906.

Gordon, George, fifth Duke of. (1770-1836). Ensign in 35th Regiment, 1790; with Duke of York in Flanders; raised regiment of 92nd, or Gordon Highlanders, Colonel, 1796; served in Ireland and Holland; General, 1819, G.C.B., 1820; succeeded to the title, 1827. Head to right, grey powdered hair, brown eyes; 12 × 11. Miss Raeburn, on loan to S.N.P.G.

Do. 30 × 25. Agnew, 1904.

Do. Raeburn Exhibition, 1876. The Lord Justice General.

Gordon, Jane, Duchess of; 30 × 25. Wife of fourth Duke, died 1812. Agnew (c), 1901.

Gordon, John, of Aikenhead; 50 × 40. Painted 1816. Raeburn Exhibition, 1876. John Gordon, Esq.

Gordon, Mrs., of Aikenhead; 50 × 40. Painted 1816. Raeburn Exhibition. John Gordon, Esq.

Gordon, Mrs. (Christian Forbes), wife of Charles Gordon of Buthlaw and Cairness; 35 × 27. Painted in 1790. Agnew, 1910.

Gow, Neil, violinist and composer. Born at Inver, near Dunkeld, in 1727. He was self-taught till the age of thirteen, when he received some lessons from John Cameron, a follower of the Stewarts of Grandtully, and he soon became unrivalled in Scotland as a performer on the violin; his " up bow " being especially distinguished for strength, and his rendering of Scottish dance music, full of spirit, vigour, and expression. He was patronised by the Scottish nobility, and was in great request at balls throughout the country. He composed many admirable Scottish reels, strathspeys, and other pieces of dance music. The first collection of these was published at Dunkeld in 1784, and three others were issued during his lifetime. Several of his sons were well known musicians. Neil Gow was a man of great worth, prudence, and humour. He died at Inver, in 1807. Nearly full length, seated playing the violin; almost full face to right; dark brown hair touched with white, greyish hazel eyes, dark eyebrows, shaven face, mouth dimpled at corners, double chin; dark bluish coat and vest with grey buttons, knee breeches, and hose of red and green tartan; yellowish brown background; 48½ × 38½. Formerly in the possession of Henry Raeburn, Esq., J.P., of St. Bernards, who in an autograph letter, now in the hands of the Trustees of the Gallery, certifies that this "is the original portrait painted by the late Sir Henry Raeburn, my father, and that the other portraits of Neil Gow, painted by him, were copies thereof." Mr. Raeburn presented the picture to Robert Salmond, Esq., who lent it to the National Gallery of Scotland from 1871 to 1883. Engraved in mezzotint by Wm. Say, in stipple by Scott, and as a vignette in line by Croll. Purchased, April, 1886, S.N.P.G. NOTE :—Dear Sir, I am quite in extremity for cash ; would you oblige me with the balance for the plate of Neil Gow ? It would be of the greatest service to me at this time ; or if not convenient for the whole, if you would favour me with ten pounds for the present, it would more than oblige me. Yours very truly, W. Say. *March 19th, 1816.* To Mr. T. Mackdonald, 39 Fleet Street (Frame maker, and publisher).

Graeme, John, of Bakbank. Raeburn Exhibition, 1876. Miss Graeme, Maxtone Graham, Esq.

Graeme, Mrs., of Bakbank. Raeburn Exhibition, 1876. Maxtone Graham, Esq.

Grahame, of Whitehill.

Graham, Anne Cunningham, of Gartmore; married Thomas Durham, of Largs in 1820. Dressed in black, her hair in ringlets. Oval; 30 × 25. Birmingham, 1903 ; French Gallery, 1910. C. A. Barton, Esq.

Graham, Elizabeth, of Fintry, afterwards Mrs. Douglas of Brigton. Seated in an armchair in front of a tree, turned to right and looking in same direction ; white dress, blue waist-band, muslin frill round neck ; her right arm rests on arm of chair, her hands lie folded in her lap ; three-quarter length, life-size ; 35 × 26. Purchased from the family; Sedelmeyer, 1905. E. R. Bacon, Esq., New York. Sedelmeyer ; Wallis & Son, 1910.

Graham, Right Hon. Sir James. Painted before 1800. Sir Richard Graham, Bart

Graham, John, of Gartin. H. D. Erskine, Esq.

Graham, Mrs., of Gartin. H. D. Erskine, Esq.

Graham, Miss Nancy, afterwards the wife of her cousin, Captain Alexander Gordon Graham, Hanovarian Grenadier Guards, of Cromarty, Scotland. White muslin dress with short sleeves and red shoes ; seated, in a landscape, holding a bunch of pansies and wallflowers in her hand; full length ; life-size. Sedelmeyer, 1900.

Graham, Robert Cunningham, of Gartmore (1730–1798). It is said to have been begun by David Martin, the artist's master, and finished by Raeburn.

Graham, Walter, merchant, Glasgow.

Grant, Alan, Esq.; 29 × 24. Sully (c), 1908.

Grant, Sir James, twenty-third Laird of Grant. Countess Dowager of Seafield.

Grant, Sir John Peter, M.P., of Rothiemurchus, Inverness-shire ; held high judicial post in India; died, 1848 (miniature). Raeburn Exhibition, 1876. James T. Gibson-Craig, Esq.

Grant, Sir J. P. Three-quarter length. Painted about 1796.

Grant, Lady. J. P. Grant, Esq.

Grant, Hon. Mrs., of Kilgraston. Margaret, second daughter of Francis, Lord Gray; 30 × 25. Agnew, 1905. Col. Walter Brown, of Renfrew.

Gray, Lord Francis. Earl of Moray.

Gray, Lord Francis. Earl of Moray.

Gray, Hon. John. Engraved by T. Hodgetts. Earl of Moray.

Gray, Baron John. Engraved by Bond. Full length.

Gray, John of Newholm (1731–1811) ; town clerk of Edinburgh. Three-quarter length, seated. Engraved by G. Dawe, 1806. Raeburn Exhibition, 1876. Alexander Cunningham, Esq , W.S.

Gray, John Hamilton, afterward Rev. (1800–67).

Gregory, Prof., James (1753–1821) ; 36 × 28. Seated in armchair, and looking to left. Engraved by G. Dawe. Ehrich Sale, New York, March 24, 1904. Rutherford.

Gregory, Prof. Replica. Royal College of Surgeons, Edinbugh.

Gregory, Mrs., second wife of Prof. James Gregory (1770–1847); 49 × 39. Three-quarter length, seated. Engraved by J. B. Pratt.

Greig, Mrs.

Griffith, M.P., Mr. Baron Gustave de Rothschild, Paris.

Greenwich Pensioner. Louvre.

Guthrie, H. (1768–1834) ; 35 × 27½. Miss E. Wright. Verity (c), 1908.

Guthrie, John, of Carbeth (1768–1834). Guthrie Smith, Esq.

Haddington, Countess of. Glasgow International Exhibition, 1901. Dr. Paton.

Haig, James, Esq., aged eighteen, in dark green coat, with white stock; 30 × 25. Painted in 1812. Colnaghi & Co. D. H. King, Esq., sold at his sale in New York, to Mr. Hollins.

Haliburton, David, of Bushey, in brown coat and vest with white stock; 23½ × 19½. Lord Tweedmouth. Charles Davis (c), 1905.

Halkett, Mrs. Craigie. Scottish National Exhibition, 1908. Mrs. Lindsay.

Halliburton, Lord D ; 50 × 40. Sold at Christie's in 1906 to Herr Heinemann, who presented it to the Alte Pinokethec, Munich. This picture, however, is by Sir William Beechey. See letter in the life of Beechey by Mr. W. Roberts.

Hamilton and Brandon, Duke of. Lord Rossmore.

Hamilton and Brandon, Duke of, with horse. Duke of Hamilton.

Hamilton, Douglas, eighth Duke of. Duke of Hamilton.

Hamilton, Elizabeth, Authoress. Engraved by H. Meyer and W. T. Fry.

Hamilton, Miss Harriet Wynne, daughter of Richard Wynne, and wife of James Hamilton of Kames. Full length, dressed in a high waisted and simple white gown cut low at the throat, and wearing round her shoulders a red shawl with a narrow border and patterned corners. She stands with her right arm resting on a tree trunk ; her figure is turned to the left, and her left arm swathed in the shawl which falls to the ground on the left side. The face is lit from above on the right ; background of low toned sky, with a dark, woody, landscape low down on the left; 94 × 60. Presented to Scottish National Gallery by Sir William Stirling Maxwell, Bart., K.T., 1876.

Hamilton, Mrs., daughter of Richard Wynne, and wife of James Hamilton of Kames ; 23½ × 32. Sir William Ingram, Bart. Westgate-on-Sea.

Hamilton, Lady Jane Montgomerie. Earl of Eglinton.

Hamilton, sen., Dr. James (1749–1835). Physician to Royal Infirmary, Edinburgh; said to have been the last to wear eighteenth century costume. Half length to right. Engraved by C. Turner and J. Burnet. Raeburn Exhibition, 1876. Lord Moncreiffe of Tullibole.

Hamilton, sen., Dr. James. A miniature.

Hamilton, General John, of Orbitson and Dalzell. Lord Hamilton of Dalzell.

Hamilton, John, of Pencaitland. Sir Robert Dundas, Bart.

Hamilton, John, of Pencaitland. Replica. Mrs. Hamilton Ogilvy.

Hamilton, Mrs. John, of Pencaitland. Sir Robert Dundas, Bart.

Hamilton, John, of North Park. Mr. Hamilton.

Hamilton, Mrs., of North Park. Mr. Hamilton.

Hamilton, Master John; 50 × 40. Abel (c), 1904.

Hamilton (Margaret Stirling) Lady, wife of Sir Hugh Hamilton, of Rosehill. Half length to right, seated holding speaking trumpet. One of a set of portraits of the Stirling family. See engraved portraits in British Museum.

Hamilton, William, eleventh Duke of. Duke of Hamilton.

Hardewicke, Earl of. Raeburn Exhibition, 1824.

Harrower, James, of Inzievar, with his wife and son; 51 × 41. Birmingham Art Gallery, 1903. Charles George, Esq., W.S. Raeburn also painted a half-length portrait of Mr. Harrower seated in an armchair with his hands clasped in front of him, which may be the portrait sold at Christie's in 1903; 35½ × 26½.

Hart, Mrs., daughter of Sir J. Montgomery, of Stanhope, Lord Chief Baron of Scotland, and wife of Major Hart, of Castlemilk, Dumfries-shire. Painted about 1810. Plate to Conway's Great Masters, 1905. Full length, standing in a garden; head turned to left; right arm resting on wall, left hanging by her side; 94 × 60. Agnew, 1908. Sedelmeyer, of Paris.

Harvey, John, of Castle Semple. Full length, standing; 94 × 59. J. W. Shand Harvey. Sulley (c) 1906. Sedelmeyer Galerie. 1908. E. M. Hodgkins.

Harvey, Col. Lee. J. W. Shand Harvey. Agnew (c) 1906.

Harvey, Mrs. Lee, and daughter; 94 × 59. J. W. Shand Harvey. Exhibition British Art, Berlin, 1908. A. Wertheimer.

Hastings, Warren.

Hay, Chas. (See Lord Newton).

Hay, Sir James, fourth Baronet of Haystone. Painted about 1806. The baronetcy having been dormant since 1683, he preferred his claim to it in 1762, which was allowed by a jury assembled at Peebles in the same year; married Dorriel, youngest daughter and co-heiress of Daniel Campbell, of Greenyards; died 1810; succeeded by his son John. Three-quarter length, to right; looking at spectator; blue black coat, yellow waistcoat, white collar and cravat; red curtain and glimpse of landscape. Engraved by T. Hodgetts. Lent to Raeburn Exhibition, Edinburgh, 1876, by Sir Robert Hay, Bart., of Haystone. On loan to Brighton Art Galleries by the trustees of the late C. J. Mackenzie, of Portmore, Scotland.

Hay, John, Master of Trinity House. Painted about 1820. Lent to Raeburn Exhibition, Edinburgh, 1876, by Incorporation of Shipmasters, Trinity House, Leith.

Hay, Sir John, of Haystone, fifth Baronet. Born 1755; married 1785, Mary Elizabeth, youngest daughter of James, sixteenth Lord Forbes, by whom he had, with other issue, John, the sixth baronet; died 1830. Painted about 1818. Raeburn Exhibition, Edinburgh, 1876.

Hay, Master; 29½ × 24. John A. Holms, Esq. Wallis & Sons, 1910. Reid (c) 1905.

Hay, of Spot, Captain R.; 94 × 58. Agnew, Louvre.

Hay, Mrs., of Spot. Three-quarter length; 49 × 40. Bristow (c) 1908. Exhibited in Paris, 1908, as property of A. Sanderson. W. A. Coates, Esq.

Head, Study of a. Sir John Stirling Maxwell, Bart.

Head, unnamed. Raeburn Exhibition, 1876.

Henderson, Mr. Bust.

Henderson, Mrs. Bust.

Hepburn, James. Half length, young man in grey suit, white stock; curly powdered hair. 30 × 25. M. Kann Sale, 9th June, 1911.

Hepburn, Lady, of Smeaton-Hepburn. Unfinished. Seated, three-quarter; white dress, red chair, powdered hair set with pearls; 50 × 40. Wallis & Son, 1910.

Hepburn, Nellie. Earl of Haddington.

Hill, Principal George (1750–1819). Sheriff Hill, of Dingwall; bought at Inverness, in 1900, by Messrs. Wallis & Son.

Hill, Mrs., wife of Principal Hill; 38 × 30. Sheriff Hill; bought in his sale at Inverness, 1900, by Messrs. Wallis & Son. Messrs. Knoedler & Co., of New York.

Hill, Dr. John, and son. Professor of Classics Edinburgh University, and brother of Principal George Hill, of St. Andrews. Painted about 1801. Raeburn Exhibition, 1876. John Cook, Esq. Wallis & Son.

Hodgson, Miss Jane, afterwards Mrs. William Giles. Miss Jane Hodgson was a cousin of Lord Ellenborough, and, like him, was descended from William Christian, of Ewanrigg Hall, Cumberland, and was related to most of the leading families of that county. She was sister to Colonel James Hodgson, of the East India Company, and married Captain William Giles; 30 × 24½. Birmingham Art Gallery, 1903. Lockett Agnew, Esq.

Home, George, of Branxton. Col. Milne Home.

Home, Miss Jean. Col. Milne Home.

Home, John, Dramatist and Historian (1724–1808); 29 × 24. Engraved by C. Watson, and others. National Portrait Gallery. There are two other portraits of him.

Honyman, Lady, wife of Lord Armadale. Painted about 1800. Raeburn Exhibition, 1876. Mrs. Catherine Dallas.

Honyman, Bart., Sir William (Lord Armadale). Senator of College of Justice; married 1777, Mary, daughter of Robert Macqueen, Lord Braxfield; died 1825. Painted about 1800. Raeburn Exhibition, 1876. Mrs. Catherine Dallas.

Hope, Right Hon. Charles Hope, of Granton, Lord President; born 1763; son of John Hope, and great grandson of the first Earl of Hopetoun. Held the office of Lord President of Court of Session for thirty years; Lord Justice General, 1836; died 1851. He was a man of fine appearance, with a splendid voice, which Lord Cockburn said was only surpassed by that of Mrs. Siddons. Three-quarter length, life-size, seated in a chair on the left, facing to the right wig and robes of Lord President; dark red curtain; 50 × 40. Engraved by G. Dawe. Raeburn Exhibition, 1876. Loan collection of portraits, Birmingham, 1900. The Earl of Hopetoun, K.T.

Hope, the Right Hon. Charles, Lord President. Painted about 1803; 39 × 49 Charles Cook, Esq , of Edinburgh.

Hope, General, the Hon Charles, son of the second Earl of Hopetoun, by his third wife Lady Elizabeth Leslie; married Lady Louisa Anne, eldest daughter of George Finch Hatton, afterwards Earl of Winchelsea; died in 1828. Bust, life-size, facing spectator, in uniform, scarlet tunic, gold shoulder knot, black collar; 29 × 24. Engraved by William Miller. Raeburn Exhibition, 1876. Loan collection of portraits. Birmingham, 1900. Earl of Hopetoun, K.T.

Hope, Lady Charlotte, wife of Lord President Hope. 30 × 25. Painted about 1811. Adrian Hope; Arthur Sanderson, Esq., Gooden & Fox (c), 1904. Messrs Knoedler, New York.

Hope, Hugh, son of Sir Archibald Hope. Sir Alexander Hope, Bart., of Pinkie.

Hope, Major. Mr. Horsburgh.

Hope, Mrs. John. Sir Henry Cook.

Hope, Dr Thomas Charles, Professor of Chemistry, Edinburgh University; died 1843. Seated in easy chair, with book in right hand. Engraved by T. Hodgetts. Raeburn Exhibition, 1876. John Hope.

Hopetoun, General John, G.C.B., fourth Earl of (1765–1823). Remarkable for his stature; served with distinction in Peninsular War; elevated to peerage of United Kingdom as Baron Niddry, of Niddry Castle, Linlithgowshire. Painted about 1817. Engraved by W. Walker. Raeburn Exhibition, 1876. Commissioners of Supply of the County of Linlithgow.

Hopetoun, G.C.B., General John. Replica. County Hall, Cupar. Raeburn made a copy of Ramsay's portrait of the second Earl of Hopetoun for the Earl of Hopetoun.

Horner, Francis, M.P., political economist; born 1778; died 1817. In 1802 he removed to London, and five years later was called to the English Bar. In 1806 he entered Parliament in the whig interest. He was one of the earliest contributors to the *Edinburgh Review*. Bust portrait, face slightly to right; square forehead, brown hair and eyebrows, short, ruddy whiskers; grey eyes; light coming from above to left, throwing strong shadows over eyes; black coat, high in the collar; white cravat; dark background, greenish grey in tone behind the figure; 30 × 24. Engraved by S. W. Reynolds, 1818. Bequeathed by Lady Murray, S N.P.G.

Horner, Francis, politician and political economist. Born in Edinburgh; died at Pisa. Seated, three-quarter length; face to the left; 49½ × 39½. Painted in 1812. Presented to National Portrait Gallery, July, 1877, by his nieces, daughters of Leonard Horner, Esq., F.R.S., in fulfilment of their father's wishes.

Horner. Replica. Speculative Society, Edinburgh.

Horner. Replica of part. Earl of Rosebery.

Houston, Governor Alexander, of Clerkington, Haddingtonshire. Raeburn Exhibition, 1876. Robert Alexander Houston, Esq.

Houston, Mrs., of Clerkington. Raeburn Exhibition, 1876. Robert Alexander Houston, Esq.

Hume, David (1756–1838). Professor of Scots Law in Edinburgh University, 1786. Sir Walter Scott attended his class. Nephew of famous historian, David Hume. Engraved by C. Turner, in 1822. Raeburn Exhibition, 1876. Faculty of Advocates, Edinburgh.

Hume, David (1756–1838). Painted in 1822. Raeburn Exhibition, 1876. W.S. Society, Edinburgh.

Hume, Joseph, son of Professor David Hume. Lord Kingsburgh.

Hunt, William, of Pittencrieff, Fifeshire. Painted in 1810, Raeburn Exhibition, 1876. James A. Hunt, Esq.

Hunt, William. Replica.

Hunter, Dr. Andrew, of Barjarg. Professor of Divinity Edinburgh University, and minister of Troon Church; died 1806. Half length, in wig and gown and bands. Engraved by Dawe and Hodgetts. Raeburn Exhibition, 1876. W. F. Hunter Arundell, Esq., of Barjarg.

Hunter, Mrs., of Burnside. Seated, three-quarter length. Mrs. Cox. (See Mrs. Douglas of Brigton).

Huntly, Marquis of. (See Duke of Gordon).

Hutton, Dr. James (1726–1797). Geologist; Published " Investigations of the Principles of Knowledge," 1794 and other works. Raeburn Exhibition, 1876. Sir George Warrender, Bart.

Hyndford, Thomas, Earl of. Seated, red coat, white trousers; 50 × 40. Wallis & Son, 1910. Mrs. Shute.

Hyndford, Countess of. Copy by Raeburn, after Allan Ramsay. Raeburn Exhibition, 1876.

Inglis, Admiral Charles, brother of Sir Patrick Inglis. Raeburn Exhibition, 1876. Sir J. D. Don Wauchope, Bart.

Inglis, Henry David. Half length to left. Engraved by C. Turner. Bust of same by S. Freeman.

Inglis, Rev. Harry (copy). A. W. Inglis, Esq.

Inglis, Henry Raeburn. See " Boy and Rabbit."

Inglis, Lady (Anne Cockburn), mother of Admiral Sir Charles and Sir Patrick Inglis. Wallis & Son, 1910.

Inglis, Sir Patrick, of Sunnyside, son of Sir John Inglis, of Cramond, and Anne Cockburn, of Ormiston. Raeburn Exhibition, 1876. Sir J. D. Don Wauchope, Bart

Inglis, William.

Innocence. Young girl in muslin; 34 × 27. Sedelmeyer, 1899.

Ironside, R. A., of Tannochside; 25 × 30. Wallis, 1906.

Jackson, James. Commissioner of Excise. Raeburn Exhibition, 1876. Alexander Jackson, Esq., M.D.

Jaegar, J. M. Bucklitsch and pony. Earl of Kintore.

James, Mrs. (Doubtful). Christie's, 1910.

Jameson, John. John Jameson, Esq.

49

Jameson, Mrs. John Jameson, Esq.
Jamieson, jun., William. Merchant in Glasgow; died, 1826. Half length, life-size figure, slightly to the left; 30 × 25. Painted in 1805 as a gift to Jamieson's god-daughter, Catherine Rowand. Purchased by Glasgow Corporation in 1897.
Jardine, Professor George, of Hallside. Engraved by Hodgetts. Mr. Jardine.
Jardine, Mrs., wife of Professor G. Jardine. Mr. Jardine.
Jardine, Sir Henry (1776–1821). Bust; 30 × 25. Miss Cullen. Col. Home Drummond. Wallis & Son, 1910.
Jeffrey, Francis, Lord (1773–1850). Lord Advocate, 1830; M.P. for Edinburgh, 1832; raised to Bench in 1834; one of the projectors of the *Edinburgh Review.* Engraved by Freeman. Raeburn Exhibition; Raeburn Family. Earl of Rosebery, K.G., K.T.
Jeffrey, Patrick, uncle of Francis Jeffrey of the *Edinburgh Review.* Shepherd Brothers, 1910.
Johnstone, Dr. David (1734–1824). Minister of North Leith, and founder of Blind Asylum, Edinburgh; 25 × 30. Painted about 1809. Engraved by G. Dawe. Wallis & Son, 1910. Mrs. Uzielli. Fisher (c), 1911.
Johnstone, Dr. David. Replica in Blind Asylum, Edinburgh.
Johnstone, Commodore George. Raeburn Exhibition, 1876. Mrs. Ferguson.
Johnstone, Commodore George. Replica. Agnew.
Johnstone, Admiral George. Half length, clean shaven, in naval dress, blue coat, cream coloured waistcoat, with gold facings; 35 × 27. From the Raeburn Family. R. and F., 1901. Lesser, 1905.
Johnstone, Mrs., wife of Commodore George Johnstone. In white dress, with a black lace scarf over her hair, and falling over her shoulders; seated looking at a miniature which she holds in her left hand; red curtain and landscape background. Dated on the back, 1791; 35 × 27½, Raeburn Exhibition, 1876. Scottish National Portrait Exhibition, 1884. Wallis & Son
Johnstone, James, of Straiton. Painted about 1800. In blue coat, white vest, and white stocks; seated in a crimson chair, turning over leaves of a book. 34½ × 26¼. Raeburn Exhibition, 1876. Sir William Baillie, Bart., of Polkemmet. Knoedler and Co. (c), 1911.
Johnstone, Mrs., wife of James Johnstone, of Straiton; second daughter of William Baillie, Lord Polkemmet. Painted about 1800. In white high-waisted dress with short sleeves; maroon cloak thrown over her shoulders; seated on a stone seat, in a landscape. 34½ × 26¼ Raeburn Exhibition, 1876. Sir William Baillie. Baillie Family. Knoedler and Co. (c), 1911.
Johnstone of Alva, John, Dame Betty, and Miss Wedderburn; 39 × 46. Major Johnstone. Wood (c), 1906.
Johnstone, Lucy. (See Mrs. Oswald).
Johnstone, Mrs., of Baldovie.
Johnstone, Mrs. Raeburn Exhibition, 1876. Mrs. Ferguson.
Johnstone, Sir William Pulteney. Miss Johnstone

Keith, Alexander, of Ravelston, Midlothian. Raeburn Exhibition, 1876 John Murray Gartshore, Esq., of Ravelston. The Murray Gartshore family.
Kennedy, Thomas, of Dunure and Dalquharan; 50 × 40. Painted about 1812.
Kennedy, Rt. Hon. Thomas F., of Dunure; 50 × 40. Raeburn Exhibition, 1876. Rt. Hon. T. F. Kennedy.
Kennedy, Mrs., of Dunure. Wife of Thomas Kennedy of Dunure, and daughter of John Adam, architect. Three-quarter length, seated to the left, in a red covered arm chair; long green cloak with a white lining, open in front, green gown, and a close-fitting white cap, almost covering her hair; the right elbow rests on the arm of the chair, and the left hand lies on her lap A crimson curtain is looped up on the right to show a distant view of Dunure Castle. Painted about 1811; 50 × 40. At Dalquharan Castle, Ayrshire, the seat of the Kennedy family, there is another version of this portrait. Presented to the Royal Scottish Academy, National Gallery of Scotland, by Mr. John Heugh, 1877.
Kennedy, Master. Earl of Iska.
Kent, Portrait of the Duke of (doubtful); 30 × 25. Mr. Heyman, 180 New Bond Street, W.
Ker, Sir James Innes, of Roxburghe; 30 × 25. Ichenbeuer sale, New York, February 27. Gillespie.
Ker, Lady Innes. Duke of Roxburghe.
Kerr, Charles, Mrs., of Calderbank. Colonel Stevenson. Colnaghi & Co. George Salting. This picture was one of those rejected by the National Gallery Trustees, in making their selection of the Salting bequest.
Kerr, Mrs. (*née* Wardrop); 30 × 25. Cottier & Co. Bought in (c) 1908.
King, Hon. Mrs., of Duniva. In grey dress with black lace fichu and a flowered cloak round her arms, white cap; 29 × 24. Agnew (c), 1905.
King, Thomas, of Drums; 50 × 40. Dowager Lady Napier. Agnew, 1899. Forbes and Paterson's Exhibition, 1901.
Kinnear, Mrs. George. Etched by Murdoch, and re-produced in *Studio*, 1908. Lord Kinnear.
Kinneder, Lord, William Erskine, friend of Sir W. Scott; 36 × 27.
Kinnoull, The tenth Earl of. Thomas Robert Hay; born 1785. Succeeded his father as 10th Earl, 1804; died 1826. Full length, standing in front in a room, head turned to left; in uniform, bare headed, his shako on table beside him; curtain and sky background; 93¼ × 59. Earl of Kinnoull. R.A., 1906.

Lamb, Charles (?). *Aet* 30; 28 × 24. Marquand Sale, New York, January 23, 1903. Laurie.
Lamont, Mrs. (*née* Lang), wife of Captain Lamont; 24½ × 29 R. W. Paterson, Esq., of Mass., U.S.A.
Lauzun, Mrs. H. W. (1776–1861); 29½ × 24¾. Painted in 1795. National Gallery.
Law, Agnes. See Makgill.
Law, James, F.R.C S E., of Elvingston, son of William Law; died 1830. Engraved by A. Hay. French Gallery, Edinburgh, 1909.
Law, Mrs. Jane Robinson, wife of James Law, F.R.C.S.E., of Elvingston; died 1846. French Gallery Edinburgh, 1909.
Law, Janet, of Kembach House, Fifeshire. Seated, in landscape, looking to spectator. J. A. Holmes, Esq.
Law, John, of Elvingston. Engraved by G. Dawe.

Law, Miss Margaret. Seated, three-quarter length. John A. Holmes, Esq.
Law, William, of Elvingston, Sheriff of Haddingtonshire (1714-1806). Raeburn Exhibition, 1876. James T. Gibson-Craig. French Gallery, Edinburgh, 1909.
Lawrie, Mrs. Kennedy. Seated to right, looking at spectator; short black hair; low black velvet dress, with short sleeves. Half length; 29 × 24½. Sedelmeyer. Fischoff-Blakensen sale, New York, 1900. Brandus.
Leith, Mrs. George, of Overhall (*née* Elizabeth Dalrymple). Sir E. H. Dalrymple-Home-Elphinstone, Bart.
Leslie Boy, The; 30 × 24½. This portrait represents one of the artist's step-children. When Raeburn was twenty-two in 1778, he married a lady of some fortune, who was several years his senior. This was Ann, daughter of Peter Edgar, factor to the Earl of Selkirk, and laird of Bridgelands, in Perthshire. She was the widow of " Count " James Leslie, one of the Leslies of Balquhun in Aberdeenshire. His foreign title of nobility was gained by proceedings not strictly directed to the prosperity of the House of Hanover. He left her a widow with three children, and the house and property of Deanhaugh, to the west of Edinburgh, near the present Dean Bridge, which spans the deep gorge of the Water of Leith. Raeburn treated her children as though they were his own, and won their love and regard in a very unusual degree. Sir Edward Tennant.
Lewis, W. T., comedian, in buff coat and red vest, seated ; 34½ × 26½. Christie's, 1906. (Doubtful).
Liddell, Mrs., (*nee* Jane Hobbuck), mother-in-law of Judge Cay. In white dress with yellow sash, and black shawl ; powdered hair; 29 × 24. Raeburn Exhibition, 1876. Cay. Agnew (c), 1910.
Liston, Sir Robert, K G., C.B., Bart. Sir James Liston-Foulis, Bart.
Liston, Lady, wife of Sir Robert Liston. Sir James Liston-Foulis, Bart.
Lindsay, Alexander of Pinkieburn. Painted about 1807. Raeburn Exhibition, 1876. Rev. W. Lindsay-Alexander, D.D.
Lindsay, Rev. James, of Pinkieburn, minister of Kirkliston, Linlithgowshire ; died, 1796. Raeburn Exhibition, 1876. Rev. W. Lindsay-Alexander.
Lindesay, Colonel, John Scott (when a boy). Raeburn Exhibition, 1876. Miss Sands.
Liston, Sir Robert, K.G.C.B. ; 30 × 25.
Liston, Lady; 30 × 25.
Livingstone, Rev. Archibald, minister of Cambusnethan. Raeburn Exhibition, 1876. Dr. James Livingstone.
Livingstone, E.
Loch, Miss. Mrs. Atherton.
Lockhart, John Gibson, Novelist writer, son-in-law of Sir Walter Scott, and author of a life of the latter. Born, Glasgow, 1793 ; died Abbotsford, 1854. Seated to the right, looking at spectator ; black hair ; white necktie, yellow waistcoat, and blue coat with gold buttons ; right arm rests on back of chair, and he holds a book in his left hand. Half length. Sedelmeyer, 1900. Forbes and Paterson's Exhibition, 1901.
Lockhart, Mrs.
Loudon, Flora, Countess of, in her own right (with Patrick, Earl of Dumfries) ; married in 1804, to Francis, First Marquis of Hastings ; died, 1840. Raeburn Exhibition, 1876 ; Marquis of Bute.
Lothian, Baillie Walter, Treasurer of George Watson's Hospital. Raeburn Exhibition, 1876 Merchant Company of Edinburgh.
Lothian, K.T., William, sixth Marquis of; died in 1824. Raeburn Exhibition, 1876. Marquis of Lothian.
Low, Adam, of Fordel, Provost of Dunfermline ; 1787-89. Raeburn Exhibition, 1876. Magistrates and Town Council of Dunfermline.
Lyon, Lieut.-Col. Raeburn Exhibition, 1876. David Smith. Esq.
Lyon, Mary, daughter of the Earl of Strathmore, 89 c. × 69 c. ' Gallerie Charles Brunner, Paris, 1908.

Macartney, Miss, daughter of Sir John Macartney, and Anne Scriven, daughter of Edward Scriven, who was descended from the Barclays of Urie ; 50 × 40. Gooden, 1889. Forbes and Paterson's Exhibition, 1901. Pawle. D. H. King sale, New York. Pulitzer.
Macartney, Miss ; 36 × 28. Wallis & Son, 1910. Major Thorburn.
Macdonald, of Clanranald. Turned to the right, looking at spectator; green coat, red vest, and white necktie. Half length ; 29 × 24½. Purchased from the family. Raeburn Exhibition, 1876. Sedelmeyer, 1902.
Macdonald, Colonel, of St. Martins. Full length seated ; book in right hand ; left resting on desk at window curtain, dark background. Fairmount Park Art Gallery, Philadelphia, U.S.A.
Macdonald, William, of St. Martins ; 83 × 59. Highland and Agricultural Society. Edinburgh.
Macdonald, Jean ; 30 × 25. Bass, 1903.
Macdonald, Miss. Miniature. Glasgow International Exhibition, 1901. T. S. Robertson, Esq.
Macdonald, Reginald George, of Clanranald (1788-1873) ; and his two younger brothers. Reproduced in " Fifty Portraits of Raeburn," 1909. Mrs. Ernest Hills.
Macdonald, Colonel Robert ; 50 × 40. Fischoff, 1908.
Macdonald, William, of St. Martins, Perthshire (1732-1814). Painted, 1803. Raeburn Exhibition, 1876 Highland and Agricultural Society of Scotland.
Macdonall, Alastair, Chief of Glengarry, said to have been the original of " Fergus McIvor " in " Waverley " ; died 1828. Full length, in Highland costume ; right hand holding gun ; left at his side ; shield, horn, etc., in background ; 96 × 60. Painted about 1800. Engraved in mezzotint by Thomas Hodgetts. R.A. 1812. lent by John Cunninghame, Esq., of Balgourie, to Scottish National Gallery.
Macdonell, Admiral Somerled. In uniform ; body to right ; face almost full Lent to Scottish National Exhibition, 1908, by John Cunninghame, Esq.
Macdougall, Allen, of Gallanach, Argyleshire (1768-1807) ; 34½ × 26½. Wallis, 1900. Sir J. Stirling Maxwell, Bart.
Macdowell, General Hay. H. D. Erskine, Esq.
Macgregor, Major. 48 × 38. Wyker (c) 1907.
Macintosh, J. 30 × 25 1898.

Mackenzie, Colonel Alexander, the younger, of Rodmore. Painted about 1800. Full length; he leans against a horse in a landscape; blue grey coat, light trousers, top boots; right hand gloved holds glove and hilt of sword; busby on head. On loan to Brighton Art Galleries by the Trustees of the late C. J. Mackenzie, Esq., of Portmore, Scotland.

Mackenzie, Alexander, of Portmore. Painted 1822. Half length; seated in red chair; grey coat, white scarf, grey wig; red curtain and glimpse of landscape; 35 × 27. On loan to Brighton Art Galleries by the Trustees of the late C. J. Mackenzie, Portmore, Scotland.

Mackenzie, Mrs. Alexander, of Portmore. Raeburn Exhibition, 1876. Colin J. Mackenzie, Esq., of Portmore.

Mackenzie, Sir Alexander, fifth baronet of Coul. Sir Arthur G. R. Mackenzie, Bart.

Mackenzie, Lady, wife of above.

Mackenzie, Colin, the younger, of Portmore. A lad about twelve or fourteen years of age; fresh smiling face; grey coat, white ruffled collar and yellow waistcoat; grey background; 29 × 25. On loan to Brighton Art Galleries by the Trustees of the late C. J. Mackenzie, Esq., of Portmore, Scotland.

Mackenzie, Sir Alexander Muir, of Delvine (1764-1835); 49 × 40. Sir Alexander Muir Mackenzie, Bart. Agnew (c) 1904.

Mackenzie, Lady Muir.

Mackenzie, Colin, of Portmore, Scotland. Three-quarter length, seated, in a landscape; short grey hair, black coat, grey riding breeches, top boots; left leg crossed over right; 49 × 39. On loan to Brighton Art Galleries by the Trustees of the late C. J. Mackenzie, Esq., of Portmore, Scotland.

Mackenzie, Mrs. Colin, wife of Colin Mackenzie, of Portmore, Clerk of Session, and a friend of Sir Walter Scott. Seated, in a landscape; white dress, brown hair, full face; arms lying in her lap; 49 × 38½. On loan to Brighton Art Galleries by the Trustees of the late C. J. Mackenzie, Esq., of Portmore, Scotland.

Mackenzie, The Hon. Francis John, of Seaforth, supposed to be a brother of the last Lord Seaforth. (?) Raeburn Exhibition, 1876. The Misses Mackenzie.

Mackenzie, Sir G. S., when a boy. Sir Arthur G R. Mackenzie, Bart.

Mackenzie, Sir George Steuart, Bart., of Coul (1780-1848); Vice-President of the Royal Society of Edinburgh. Painted about 1811. Raeburn Exhibition, 1876. Rev. John Mackenzie.

Mackenzie, Lady (1754-1829), mother of Sir George Steuart Mackenzie, seventh Baronet of Coul. Painted about 1794. Raeburn Exhibition, 1876. Rev. John Mackenzie.

Mackenzie, Henry (1745-1831). Sir Walter Scott called this writer the "Scottish Addison." A lawyer by profession, he wrote the "Man of Feeling," and was among the first to study German literature, and in 1788, published a "Memoir on German Tragedy," and in 1791, "Translations from Lessing"; 29½ × 24¾. Purchased in May, 1877, by the Trustees of National Portrait Gallery Half length; face three-quarters to the right. Engraved by B. Smith.

Mackenzie, Henry. Forbes & Paterson, 1901. (There is another portrait of Mackenzie by Raeburn).

Mackenzie, Master, and his Dog; The boy is seated on a stone bench, looking to the right. His right hand holds his whip, while his left one is resting on a fine Newfoundland dog. Landscape background; 43¼ × 33½. Sedelmeyer, 1895.

Mackenzie, Mrs. Three-quarter, seated in green garden chair, set in a landscape; black bodice and white dress; 50 × 40. Sedelmeyer Galerie, 1908. A. Sanderson, Esq. Agnew's, 1908.

Mackenzie, Mrs. Lewis. (See Ross, Grace Lockhart).

Mackenzie, The Hon. William, of Seaforth. Colonel Mackenzie Fraser.

Macleod, Donald, of Geames, Sheriff of Ross-shire (1753–1834). Painted about 1800. Raeburn Exhibition, 1876, Rev. John Mackenzie.

Macleod, General Norman, of Macleod. Macleod of Macleod. Wallis & Son, 1911.

Macleod, Mrs., second wife of General Norman Macleod of Macleod.

Macleod, Sir William. (See Lord Bannatyne).

Macnab, The, Head of the Clan and twelfth laird. The Hon. Mrs. Baillie Hamilton.

Macneil, Jean; 48 × 40. Wigzell, 1895.

Macneil, Roderick, of Barra, Chief of the Clan, in blue coat and white frill, holding a gun in his right hand. Three-quarter length; 50 × 40. Christie's, 1898.

Maconochie, The Hon. Allan of Meadowbank, first Lord Meadowbank, Judge of Court of Sessions. Painted about 1814. Raeburn Exhibition, 1876; Allan A. Maconochie Wellwood, Esq.

Maconochie, Mrs., wife of the Hon. Allan Maconochie. (See Wellwood).

Machonochie, Mrs., and child. Louvre. Not the picture lent to Exhibition of artist's works, Edinburgh, 1876, but probably the picture sold at Christie's in 1902-03

McCall, Mrs., of Ibroxhill. Half length to left, almost full face. Reproduced in "Fifty Portraits of Raeburn," 1909. T. Denroche Smith, Esq.

McCormick, Edward, Sheriff of Ayrshire; 49½ × 39¼. Raeburn Exhibition, 1876. Faculty of Advocates Edinburgh.

McCrae, Portraits of the Family. Mrs. Alexander McCrae, Alexander McCrae, jun., Thomas Ann McCrae. Mother and girl in white, boy red jacket, white frilled collar, yellow trousers and waistcoat; red curtain; landscape; 50 × 40. Captain Spender Clay, of Lingfield. Wallis & Son, 1910.

McMurdo. Lieut.-Colonel Bryce; 94 × 58. National Gallery.

Macqueen, Robert. (See Lord Braxfield).

Macqueen, Mrs. (See Ord, Elizabeth).

Madonna, Head of a. A miniature.

Mair, Mrs. Margaret (*née* Thompson), of Plantation, near Glasgow. In green silk dress with white fichu, and white lace cap; seated to the right, in a red chair, before a spinning-wheel, which she is working with her foot; she draws a thread from the distaff with her left hand. 58¼ × 46¼. Mrs. Sarah Hadden, Pearson (c) 1911.

Maitland, Rear-Admiral, eldest son of Colonel the Hon. Richard Maitland, and grandson of the sixth Earl of Lauderdale; died 1836. Raeburn Exhibition, 1876. Naval and Military Exhibition, Edinburgh, 1889. Misses Raeburn.

52

Maitland, Lady Catherine, daughter of Daniel Connor, Esq., of Ballybricken, co. Cork, and Orme Square, London; married at Cork, April, 1804, Sir Frederick Lewis Maitland (grandson of the sixth Earl of Lauderdale), Rear-Admiral and K C.B., Admiral Superintendent of Portsmouth Dockyard, Captain of the *Bellerophon* on the surrender of Napoleon Bonaparte on board that ship, July 15, 1815. Lady Maitland died at Lindores, co. Fife, in 1865. Nearly whole-length figure, seated, in a landscape under a tree, directed to left, and looking at spectator, nearly full face; in white dress cut to V-shape at neck, slate-coloured shawl round shoulders, wearing gold neck-chain from which is suspended a pearl (or very small locket); brown hair falling in ringlets over forehead and bound with dark velvet ribbon; hands folded in lap, blood-colour signet ring on index finger of left hand; landscape and hills in distance to left; 50 × 40. Painted about 1817. Engraved by Norman Hirst. Exhibited Raeburn Exhibition, Royal Academy, Edinburgh, 1876. No. 215 (Rear-Admiral W. H. Maitland-Dougall, of Scotscraig). Agnew's Eleventh Annual Exhibition, November–December, 1905, No. 15. Wallis & Son, 1910. J. Pierpont Morgan, Esq.

Maitland, Judge. 24½ × 29. Wallis & Son.

Makgill, Captain George, of Kembach House, Fifeshire. Three-quarter length, seated in green chair in landscape; red coat, yellow lapels, yellow waistcoat and trousers; 30 × 25. French Gallery, Edinburgh, 1909. Wallis & Son, 1910. Major Thorburn.

Makgill, Mrs. (Agnes Law, a descendant of Law, the banker), wife of Captain George Makgill, of Kembach House, Fifeshire. Three-quarter length, seated, in landscape; brown hair, powdered and bound in white band; white dress, grey blue sash; brown shawl on chair; 50 × 40. Wallis & Son, Edinburgh and London, 1910. Major Thorburn.

Malcolm, K.C.B., Colonel Sir James. Naval and Military Exhibition, Edinburgh, 1889. W. E. Malcolm, Esq., of Burnfoot.

Malcolm, Mrs., of Burnfoot.

Mar, John Francis, seventh Earl of. Lent to Glasgow International Exhibition, 1901, by the Earl of Mar and Kellie.

Mar, John Francis, Earl of. Earl of Mar and Kellie.

Marcet, Dr. Alexander. Engraved by H. Meyer.

Maxwell, Miss, Harriet, of Pollock (1789–1841); daughter of Sir John Maxwell, seventh baronet. Raeburn Exhibition, 1876. Sir William Stirling Maxwell, Bart.

Maxwell, Sir John, Bart., of Pollock (1791–1865). Unfinished. Sir John Stirling Maxwell, Bart.

Maxwell, General Sir William, of Calderwood, seventh baronet (1754–1837). Raeburn Exhibition, 1876. Sir William Maxwell, Bart. Colonel Neilson.

Maxwell, Sir William, sixth Baronet of Calderwood, Lanarkshire; born in 1748; married 1807, Hannah Leonora, daughter of Robert Pasley, of Mount Annan; died without issue in 1829; 50 × 40. Three-quarter length; almost full face; in uniform, red coat, gold epaulettes, black collar and cuffs, buff trousers; right thumb in sash; left hand grasps sword hilt; dark brown background; 50 × 40. Reproduced in colour in *Studio*, 1908. Captain Gill. W. Lockett Agnew, Esq. (c) 1908.

Meadowbank, the Hon. Alexander Maconochie Wellwood, second Lord, of Meadowbank and Garvoch (1771–1861). Engraved by Dick. Raeburn Exhibition, 1876. Allan A. Maconochie Wellwood, Esq.

Meadowbank, the Hon. Allan Maconochie, First Lord of Session (1748–1816). (See Maconochie).

Meath, the Right Rev. Lord Bishop. (See O'Beirne).

Melville, Henry Dundas, Viscount; born 1742. A distinguished lawyer and statesman; filled several high offices; created Viscount Melville, 1802. Impeached for alleged malversation as Treasurer of the Navy, 1805, but acquitted; died 1811. Three-quarter length, to right, in wig and gown, right hand on table; left at side. Curtain. Engraved by S. Freeman in line, 1831, and by G. Dawe. Raeburn Exhibition, 1876. Bank of Scotland.

Melville, Viscount. Replica. Half figure to right, in robes and wig. Curtain in background; 29 × 24½. Sir William Agnew, Bart. R.A., 1903.

Melville, Viscount. M. Colnaghi (R. & F.), 1908. Ichenhauser.

Melville, John Whyte, of Bennochy. Balfour Melville. Esq.

Melville, General Robert, of Strathkinness. Balfour Melville, Esq.

Menzies, Sir Robert, fifth Baronet. Painted about 1802. Sir Robert Menzies, Bart.

Mercer, Mrs. (*née* Wilson); 20 × 25. Herr D. Heinemann, of Munich.

Millar, Patrick, of Dalswinton. Three-quarter length, with horse, in uniform of Dumfries-shire Yeomanry. Wallis & Son, 1910.

Miller, Sir Thos. (See Glenlee).

Miller, Lady, of Glenlee, Kirkcudbright; died 1846. Raeburn Exhibition, 1876. A. W. Miller, Esq.

Mills, William, Lord Provost of Glasgow (1834–1337). Half length, head to right, white necktie and ruffled shirt; 30 × 25. Presented by the trustees of George Mills, in 1892, to the Corporation Galleries, Glasgow.

Milne, Admiral Sir David, G.C.B. (1763–1845). Full length, standing in uniform; Algiers in the background. Colonel Milne Home. (See letter in text).

Minto, Anna Maria, Countess of, wife of first Earl of Minto, Governor-General of India, and daughter of Sir George Amyand, Bart.; 24½ × 29. W. G. Elliot. Wallis & Son (c), 1905. A. Baumgarten, Esq., of Montreal.

Moir, Miss Annie. R. W. C. G. Henderson, Esq.

Molesworth, Sir Arscott Curry, Baronet, of Pencarrow, Cornwall. Mrs. Ford.

Moncrieff, Margaret, afterwards Mrs. Pattison. Seated to the left on a green garden chair, looking at the spectator, her hands crossed in her lap; she wears a white kerchief over her dark hair, and a white muslin dress with a black mantilla round her body. Landscape background. Three-quarter length, life-size; 49½ × 39½. Laurie. Duveen (c), 1904. Sedelmeyer, 1906.

Moncrieff, Rev. Sir Henry Wellwood, D.D., eighth Baronet; an eminent divine, author of a work on the "Constitution of the Church of Scotland" and "Life of Dr. Erskine"; in black coat with white stock, figure to the left; 30 × 25. Engraved by E. Scriven and Charles Turner. Mentioned in Andrew's "Life of Sir Henry Raeburn." Raeburn Exhibition, 1876. Sir Daniel Macree, P.R.A. S. G. Morrison, Esq. Harvey (c), 1900. James Orrock, Esq. Agnew (c), 1904.

Moncrieff, Rev. Sir Henry Wellwood, Bart. Church of Scotland Widows Fund Trustees.
Moncrieff, Rev. Sir Henry Wellwood, Bart. Lord Moncrieff.
Moncrieff, Robert Scott. Orphan Hospital, Edinburgh.
Moncrieff, Mrs. Scott, Miss Margaritta MacDonald, wife of Mr. R. Scott Moncrieff (afterward Scott Moncrieff Welwood). Head and shoulders, the figure is turned towards the spectator, the head looks to the right, and is tilted backwards. Her hair clusters in a big wavy curl on each brow, shadowing her eyes, the light falls from the left front, over her low square-cut gown of mellow-white; she wears a loose red cloak, which envelops her shoulders, and, hanging open in front, is caught together again near the bottom of the canvas; 30 × 25. Etched by C. O. Murray, for the " Portfolio," 1879. Engraved in Mezzotint, by Thomas G. Appleton, 1887. Photographed by Annan. Bequeathed to the Royal Scottish Academy, National Gallery of Scotland, by Mr. R. Scott Moncrieff Welwood, of Pitliver, 1887.
Moncrieff, Mrs. Robert Scott, of Wellwood and Pitliver. Replica. Thomas J. Barratt, Esq.
Monro, Dr. Alexander. Engraved by J. Heath.
Monro, Alexander Binning. (See the sons of D. M. Binning).
Monro, Mrs. Katherine, younger daughter of David Inglis; born, 1741; married Dr. Alexander Monro (Secundus); died, 1803. Painted 1799; 30 × 25. Agnew (c), 1908.
Monteith, Sir Charles Granville Stuart, of Clowburn and Mansfield. Seated three-quarter length. At Mansfield, Old Cumming.
Monteith, Henry, when a boy; in green coat and black tie. (R. and F.), 1903. Gamble.
Monteith, Henry, M.P.; 1765-1848. Mr. Monteith.
Monteith, Mrs. James (Miss Margaret Thomson, of Camphill). Painted about 1820. Raeburn Exhibition, 1876. Mrs. Walter C. Smith.
Monteith, Rev. James Stuart. Seated three-quarter length. Painted, 1792. At Mansfield, Old Cumming.
Monteith, Ludevina Stuart. Seated three-quarter length. Painted about 1792 or 3. At Mansfield, Old Cumming.
Montgomery, Right Hon. Sir James, Bart. Trustees of William Campbell Walker, Esq., on loan to S.N.P.G.
Montgomery, Sir James, Bart. (1721-1803). Lord Chief Baron of Exchequer; Solicitor-General, and Lord Advocate. In black dress and gown, white wig and bands, seated at a table on which are a mace and some papers. Replica; 90 × 59. Raeburn Exhibition, 1876. Buttery (c) 1. Kaiser Frederick, Museum, Berlin.
Montgomery, Sir James, Bart.
Montgomery, Sir James, second Baronet of Stanhope, Peebles-shire, Lord Advocate, 1804. Three-quarter length; seated against a tree in a landscape; blue coat, white collar and scarf, buff riding trousers, top boots; 49 × 39. On loan to Brighton Art Galleries by the Trustees of the late C. J. Mackenzie, Esq., of Portmore.
Montgomery, Sir James. Replica.
Montgomery, Lady, wife of Sir James Montgomery, second Baronet; and daughter of Dunbar, fourth Earl of Selkirk; died 1814. Painted about 1810. Raeburn Exhibition, 1876. Sir G. Graham Montgomery, Bart ; Sir Basil Montgomery, Bart., Kinross.
Montgomery, Lord. (See Earl of Eglinton).
Montgomery, Robert, Advocate, was born in 1774, and died in 1854. He was son of Sir James Montgomery, chief Baron of Exchequer, and father of Dean Montgomery. Three-quarter length; seated towards left, the figure almost front, the crossed legs turned towards the right, the hands lying clasped on the knee; the face seen almost front is shaven, except for a small side whisker; the hair and eyebrows are iron grey, the eyes a warm brown. His double-breasted blue coat is partially buttoned, and he wears tight buff riding breeches and top boots; plain grey brown background; 48½ × 38½. Bequeathed by Dean Montgomery, S.N.P.G.
Montgomery, Robert.
More, Miss Hannah. Seated three-quarter length; cap, and white dress; right arm resting on cabinet, left in her lap. Louvre.
Morrison, Susanna; 30 × 25. Laking, 1901.
Morrison, Lieut.-Col. William. Painted in 1811; 35 × 25. Agnew, 192.0
Morrison, Lieut.-Col.; 31½ × 27. P. Smith, 1894.
Muirhead, Robert, of Cory Leckie; 29 × 25. Lionel B. C. Muirhead, Esq.
Muirhead, Mrs. Robert, daughter of Mr. Dunlop, of Househill; 29 × 25. Lionel B. C. Muirhead.
Munro, Sir Thomas, of Lindertis. The Munro Family.
Munro, Mrs., mother of Sir Thomas Munro. The Munro Family.
Munro, Mrs. 30 × 25. White dress, and cloak tied at neck with ribbon; hair hanging in curls on forehead. Victor Morawitz, Esq ; New York.
Murchison, Miss Barbara. Three-quarter length; seated dressed in white, short-waisted gown; hands in lap; brown curling hair; landscape background; 36½ × 27½. Reproduced vol. XII , page 250, *Burlington Magazine*. R. F. Murchison. Colnaghi & Co. (c); 1903. Buda-Pest Musee des Beaux Arts. (See letter in text)
Murdoch, George, Lord Provost of Glasgow. Mr. Yuille.
Mure, Thomas, of Warriston. Miss Mure.
Mure, Mrs., of Warriston. Miss Mure.
Murray, Miss Janette; 30 × 25. Willson (c), 1903.
Murray, Sir John Archibald, Lord of Session (1779-1859). Advocate; first M.P., for Leith, after the Reform Act; one of the founders of *Edinburgh Review*. Raeburn Exhibition, 1876. Engraved by W. Walker Right Hon. T F. Kennedy, of Dunure. The Family.
Murray, John, and his brother. John was an eminent engineer, and built the Sunderland Docks. The two boys are walking in a landscape to the right. The elder in a brown dress carries a fishing rod on his shoulder, the younger in green dress, and wearing a tartan cap, holds on to a large dog that is walking between them. Three-quarter length, life-size; 48½ × 38. Sedelmeyer, 1906.

Murray, Mary and Grace; 60 × 25. Mawson (c), 1902.
Murray, Sir William, fifth Baronet of Ochtertyre, Peebles-shire. Married in 1770, Augusta, daughter of George, third Earl of Cromartie; died 1800. Raeburn Exhibition, 1876. Sir Patrick Keith Murray, Bart.

Naesmyth, Lady; 35 × 27½. Eleanor, second daughter of John Murray, Esq., of Philiphaugh; married, 1785, Sir James Naesmyth, of Rosso, fourth baronet; died 1807. Half figure, seated to right at a table, holding a book in right hand; white dress, with coloured scarf; fair hair. General D. Anderson, R.A., 1906.
Nairne, Captain Alexander, H.E.I.C.S. Painted about 1813. Raeburn Exhibition, 1876. Rev. Spencer Nairne, rector of Hunsdon.
Nairne, Sir William. (See Dunsinnan).
Napier, Sir William. In red hunting costume, buff breeches and top boots; standing in a landscape, looking to left, his left arm resting on a pedestal, and holding his hat in his left hand; in his right hand he holds a riding whip, which he supports on his hip. Full length, life-size; 90 × 56½. Sedelmeyer, 1906.
Newbiggin, James, of Whitehouse. In green coat and white stock; powdered hair. 29 × 24. Raeburn Exhibition, 1876. Adam Rolland, Esq., of Gask. Weekes (c) 1911.
Newbiggin, Mrs. Three-quarter length. In white dress, with black shawl over her arms; powdered hair; landscape background. 28½ × 24. Painted about 1795. Raeburn Exhibition, 1876. Adam Rolland, Esq., of Gask. Mrs. Rainy. Agnew's, 1910. C. Davis, Esq. (c) 1911.
Newton, Lord, Charles Hay, of Newton; born 1740; called to the Bar, 1768; he became a Lord of Session in 1806; died 1811. Bust portrait. The round, clean-shaven face looks straight out; the shoulders, enveloped in the red of a judge's robe, are turned slightly to the left; light falls from the left front, and is concentrated upon the face and upper part of the white bands; the background is dark brown, the lower part of the figure obscured in shadow; 30 × 25. Engraved in mezzotint by Charles Turner, 1814. Photogravure in "Portfolio," 1887. Engraved on wood by Timothy Cole for *The Century,* 1898. Photographed by Annan. Bequeathed by Mrs. Malcolm Laing, 1864, to Scottish National Gallery.
Newton, Lord. Lent to Glasgow International Exhibition, 1901, by R. C. Munro-Ferguson, Esq., M.P.
Newton, Lord. Henry Graves.
Newton, Lord. Three-quarter length, in robes, head and shoulders similar to bust portrait in National Gallery, Scotland, formerly in Craig House, Forfarshire. Sir G. Macpherson Grant (?)
Nicoll, Rev. Francis, D.D., Principal of the United College, St. Andrews; died 1835. Raeburn Exhibition, 1876. Ministers' Widows' Fund, Church of Scotland.
Nisbet, Jane, as a child, afterwards Mrs. Jordon, of Harperfield. Half length, oval; dressed in white; 30 × 25. Wallis & Son, 1910. Mrs. Shute.
Northampton, Margaret, wife of the second Marquis of, and daughter of Major-General and Mrs. McLean Clephane. Forbes & Paterson's Exhibition, 1901.
Northampton, Marquis and Marchioness of. (See Earl and Countess of Compton).

O'Beirne, Rev. Lucius, Bishop of Meath, 1796, and Private Secretary to the Lord-Lieutenant of Ireland. Seated in armchair turned to the right nearly full face; black dress and powdered wig; dark background. Three-quarter length, life-size; 50 × 40. E. H. Willett Collection; R.A., 1888, ascribed to J. Hoppner. Sedelmeyer, 1896. Now in Dresden Art Gallery.
O'Beirne, Mrs., wife of Rev. Lucius O'Beirne.
Oliphant, David, March (c), 1907. Colnaghi & Co. Alexander Reid, Esq.
Ord, Miss Elizabeth, wife of Robert Macqueen, Lord Braxfield, and daughter of Robert Ord, chief Baron of Exchequer in Scotland. Painted about 1790. Raeburn Exhibition, 1876. John Ord Mackenzie, Esq., of Dolphinton.
Orde, Colonel. In dark coat, with white stock. 29½ × 24½. Colnaghi & Co. (c) 1911.
Oswald, Mrs., of Auchincruive (*née* Lucy Johnstone), daughter of Colonel Johnstone, of Hutton Hall, Berwickshire, Burns' Ballad, "Wat ye wba's in your toun?" was written in her praise. In white dress open at the neck, gold earrings, figure to the left; 29½ × 24½. Raeburn Exhibition, Edinburgh, 1876. Engraved by Ryall. From the collection of J. T. Gibson-Craig, Esq., 1887. Christie's, 1902. Colnaghi and Co. Tooth. There is a replica.

Paterson, children of Mr. and Hon. Mrs. Paterson, of Castle Huntly. Reproduced in "Fifty Portraits of Raeburn," 1909. Charles J. G. Paterson, Esq.
Paterson, George, of Castle Huntly. C. J. G. Paterson, Esq.
Paterson, Mrs. Moncrieff, (Dowells, Edinburgh); 50 × 40. Paterson. Lawrie, 1904.
Patterson, J., Esq., Engineer of the Leith Docks and Caledonian Canal. From the collection of Captain Maitland, of the Hussars, a great-grandson of Mr. Patterson; 40 × 50. Wallis & Son.
Pattison, John, of Kelvingrove (1755–1807). Mr. Pattison.
Pattison, Mrs. Mr. Pattison.
Peat, Mrs., and daughters; Janet Ewart, wife of John Peat, S.S.C. of Edinburgh, with her two youngest daughters, Janet and Anne. The latter became a poetess and died in 1885, aged ninety-five. From the collection of Rev. Alex. C. H. Anderson, B.D., great-great-grandson of Mrs. Peat; 39½ × 51. T. Agnew and Sons.
Perth, Lady, and daughter, Lady Willoughby d' Eresby. Lady, three-quarter length, seated in landscape; girl standing on seat; 50 × 40. Engraved in "Fifty portraits of Raeburn," 1909. Earl of Ancaster.
Phillips, Mrs. John, of Stobcross, Glasgow, in grey dress and gloves, with white shawl, white gauze scarf, and cap with bow; seated; 28 × 24. Exhibited Grafton Gallery. Asher Wertheimer (c) 1898.
Pillans, Professor James (1778–1864). Engraved by C. Turner. Edinburgh Institute, 1822, and Raeburn Exhibition, 1824.
Pitcairn, John. National Gallery of Scotland.
Pitcairn, Mrs. National Gallery of Scotland.
Pitcairn, John Provost, of Dundee; 35 × 26. Wallis (c) 1904.

Pitcairn, Mrs. 35 × 26. Wallis (c) 1904.
Playfair, Professor John, Professor of Natural Philosophy in the University of Edinburgh; died 1819;
    holding his spectacles in his right hand, seated at a table on which are a globe and books; 50 × 40.
    Agnew (c) 1890.
Playfair, John, F.R.S. 49¾ × 39½. National Portrait Gallery.
Playfair, John.
Polkemmet, Lord. (See William Baillie).
Portland, Duke of. 44 × 33. D. H. King's sale, New York, March 31, 1904, £500, Dehne.
Portrait of an Artist at his Easel. 89 c × 68 c. Gallerie Charles Brunner, Paris, 1908.
Portrait of a Boy. W. A. Coats, Esq.
Portrait of a Child in White. 30 × 25. Sir W. Cunliffe Brooks. Morton, 1902.
Portrait of a Child. Vokins, 1888.
Portrait of a Lady and Children. The Children by Raeburn. The lady (Mrs. Raeburn, Sir Henry's
    daughter-in-law) painted by Sir J. Watson Gordon.
Portrait of a Divine. Forbes & Paterson's Exhibition, 1901.
Portrait of a Gentleman. An engraving of this work is to be found in the Anderton Collection of Royal
    Academy Catalogues in the Print Room of the British Museum.
Portrait of a Gentleman. Duke of Fife.
Portrait of a Gentleman. (Doubtful). Christie's, 1910.
Portrait of a Gentleman. Half length figure; white powdered hair, white cravat, and brown coat; 24 × 19.
    Ewing Collection, Glasgow Corporation Galleries.
Portrait of a Gentleman. The Sir George Drummond Collection, Montreal.
Portrait of a Gentleman (?) 35½ × 28½. Christie's, 1910.
Portraits of Gentlemen (unnamed). Nos. 121, 123, 124, in the exhibition of the artist's works, Edinburgh, 1876.
Portrait of a Gentleman. 0.91m × 0.71m. Half length; right arm resting on back of chair; left hand
    partly seen. Lent by the Royal Gallery of Stuttgart, to Exhibition of British Art, Berlin, 1908.
Portrait of a Gentleman. Christie's, 1902. Colnaghi & Co. E. H. Hodgkins, Esq.
Portrait of a Gentleman. 35 × 27½. Turned to left looking at spectator; green coat, white stock, seated;
    resting right arm on the back of his chair. Half length, life-size. Ex artist's sale, 1877. Sedelmeyer,
    1902.
Portrait of a Gentleman; 21 × 17. D. H. King sale, New York, March 31, 1904. Pulitzer.
Portrait of a Gentleman (miniature). J. L. Caw, Esq.
Portrait of a Gentleman. (R. and F.) Colnaghi & Co. Wallis & Son.
Portrait of a Gentleman; 0.73 × 0.61. Bust, full face, blue eyes, fair hair, dark grey coat, gold buttons, and
    white waistcoat. Brussels National Gallery.
Portrait of a Gentleman. The Sir George A. Drummond Collection, Montreal.
Portrait of a Gentleman; 28 × 36. Wallis & Son.
Portrait of a Gentleman, in dark dress. Christie's, 1901. Colnaghi & Co. Dr. Magin.
Portrait of a Gentleman, in dark coat; 30 × 25. A. Wertheimer, Esq., 1902.
Portraits of a Gentleman, and Son, in a landscape. Webb, 1907.
Portrait of a Gentleman, wearing spectacles; 29 × 24. Gregory. (R. and F.), 1897.
Portraits of a Gentleman and Lady. Colnaghi & Co. R. H. McCormick.
Portrait of a Girl; 31½ × 25, oval. Three-quarter figure; seated facing spectator; white dress, white scarf
    crossed over bosom; long brown mittens; dark background. Hamilton McCormick, Esq. R.A., 1906.
Portrait of a Little Girl. Glasgow International Exhibition, 1901. James Coats, Esq.
Portrait of a Girl Sketching; 30 × 24. Glasgow International Exhibition, 1901. Mrs. George Holt,
    Birmingham, 1903.
Portrait of a Young Girl, sitting, leaning on a portfolio. Raeburn Exhibition, 1876. James T. Gibson-Craig, Esq.
Portrait of a Young Girl in White; 27 × 20½.
Portrait of a Young Girl, seated. Agnew, 1887.
Portrait of a Lady, full length. Raeburn Exhibition, 1876 (182). Raeburn Family.
Portrait of a Lady, bare to shoulders; face turned to spectator; long curly hair. Exhibited in New Gimpel,
    and Waldstein Galleries, New York, 1909; and reproduced in "Fifty Portraits of Raeburn," and
    American Art News, 1909. This portrait is very doubtful. Etched by George Aikman, A.R.S.A.
Portrait of a Lady (doubtful). Christie's, 1910.
Portrait of a Lady. 93½ × 59. National Gallery.
Portrait of a Lady. Earl of Mansfield.
Portraits of a Lady and Gentleman. 49 × 38. Agnew, 1889.
Portrait of a Lady in green. 30 × 25. Wallis, 1902.
Portrait of a Lady in grey. 29 × 24. Wigzell, 1901.
Portrait of a Lady in grey. 30 × 25. E. M. Denny. Robson (c) 1906.
Portrait of an Old Lady. Graves, 1887.
Portrait of an Old Lady with large cap. Raeburn Exhibition, 1876. Sir James T. Gibson-Craig.
Portrait of a Lady in white. 35½ × 28. Martin (c) 1905.
Portrait of a Lady in white and yellow. 33½ × 26. Colnaghi & Co., 1902.
Portrait of a Young Lady in white. 29 × 24. F. Mackenzie, Esq. C. Davis, Esq., 1902.
Portrait of a Young Lady. Half length to waist; white dress; face to right; curling hair set with jewels.
    Reproduced in "Fifty Portraits of Raeburn," 1909.
Portrait of an Officer. 93 × 57. E. Tayler, Esq. (F) 1905.
Portrait of an Officer with a Dog. Exhibition of artist's works, Edinburgh, 1876. Raeburn.
Portrait of an Officer in Uniform. 35½ × 27. Huggins (c) 1905.
Preston, Mary, daughter of Sir George Preston; married, in 1774, to Robert Wellwood, of Garvoch. Her
    daughter, Elizabeth, married the Hon. Allan Maconochie. Painted at age of 92, in 1808. Raeburn
    Exhibition, 1876. Allan A. Maconochie Wellwood, Esq., of Meadowbank.

Preston, Sir Robert.   J. A. Maconochie Wellwood, Esq.
Pringle, Anne, of Crichton.   Professor A. S. Pringle Pattison.
Pringle, Miss Violet, daughter of Lord Haining.   Professor A S. Pringle Pattison.
Pulteney, Bart., Sir William.   Lord Grantley.

Rae, Sir David, Bart.   (See Lord Eskgrove).
Raeburn, Portrait of Sir H., in dark coat with roll collar, yellow vest and white stock; his left hand raised
    to his chin, and the elbow supported by his right hand.   Red curtain background ; 35 × 27   International
    Exhibition, 1862 ; National Portrait Exhibition, 1868 ; Raeburn Exhibition, Edinburgh, 1876 ; Burlington
    House, 1877 ; Scottish National Portraits Exhibition, 1884 ; From the sale of the artist's works, 1877 ;
    From the collection of Sir William Patrick Andrew, 1887.   Purchased at Christie's, from the collection
    of Lord Tweedmouth, for Scottish National Gallery.   Painted about 1815.   Engraved in stipple, by W.
    Walker.   Etched by W. Nicholson, 1818.   This work was offered by the artist as his Diploma work on
    his election as R.A., in 1815, it was declined on the ground that members' own portraits were inadmissible,
    and he subsequently (in 1821) presented the "Boy and Rabbit," now in the Diploma Gallery, Burlington
    House.   Purchased for the National Gallery of Scotland from the Tweedmouth collection for 4,500
    guineas.
Raeburn, Portrait of.   Agnew, 1887.
Raeburn, Portrait of ; 27 × 23.   Tooth, 1899.
Raeburn, Portrait of ; 35 × 27.   Agnew, for Scott M. Gatty, Esq., 1905.
Raeburn, Sir Henry, R.A.   By Sir Francis Chantrey, R.A.   Head and shoulders, in profile, to left ; rounded
    head, bald and fringed with thin hair ; shaven face, with long upper lip and slight double chin.   Inscribed
    Portrait of H. Raeburn, R.A.   Drawn by F. Chantrey, R.A., in Princes Street, Edinburgh, 1818 (Pencil ;
    paper ; 10¾ × 6¾).   On the other side of the paper are three slight sketches of Chantrey by Raeburn, done
    at the same time.   Formerly in the possession of Wilkie Collins, the novelist.   Reproduced in
    lithography, in R. A. M. Stevenson, Sir Walter Armstrong, and J. L. Caw's "Sir Henry Raeburn."
    Presented by C. Fairfax Murray, Esq., 1901.
Raeburn, Sir Henry.   Bust by Thomas Campbell.   Head slightly raised and turned to left ; bald and
    prominent forehead, shaven face, with small whiskers at ears ; eyeballs marked, firmly compressed
    mouth and thin lips ; drapery, edged with fringe, thrown over shoulders.   Inscribed on back, in incised
    letters.   Marble Bust, circular base, height 26 ins.   Thomas Campbell, Roma, 1822.
Raeburn.   Medallion by James·Tassie (?).   We have it on the authority of Miss C. Raeburn that her father
    Henry Raeburn, son of the painter, was accustomed to state that this medallion was modelled by his
    father himself.   Probably the exact facts may be that it was executed in the modelling room of Tassie
    and at least substantially retouched by Sir Henry.   Its style shows affinity to Raeburn's handling in
    painting and it is not signed or initialed by Tassie, as is most commonly the case in his portrait medallion.
    Small Bust, in profile, to right ; firm mouth, resolute face, hair tied behind, frill at breast.   Inscribed on
    truncation, in incised letters.   H. Raeburn, 1792.   White enamel paste, oval ; 3½ × 2½.   Miss Raeburn.   On
    loan to S.N.P.G.
Raeburn, Lady, wife of the artist (*née* Ann Edgar), daughter of Peter Edgar, of Bridgelands.   In white and
    brown dress and white head-dress. seated in a landscape with her arms folded on her lap ; 58 × 44.
    Raeburn Exhibition, Edinburgh, 1876 ; Burlington House, 1877 ; Scottish National Portrait Exhibition,
    1884 ; Burlington House, 1888.   From the sale of the artist's works, 1887 ; From the collection of John
    Heugh, Esq., 1878 ; From the collection of Sir William Patrick Andrew, 1887 ; From the collection of
    Lord Tweedmouth.   Now the property of Sir Ernest Cassel.
Raeburn, Henry, with grey horse.   The horse painted by Raeburn, the boy by John Syme, Raeburn's pupil
    and imitator.
Raeburn, Henry (1784-1863) second son of the artist, mounted on a grey pony.   Painted about 1796.   Scottish
    National Exhibition, 1908.   The Earl of Rosebery.   Wallis & Son, 1910.   Insurance Co.
Raeburn, Henry.   Study for above portrait.   16 × 12.   S.N.P.G.
Raeburn, Eliza, daughter of the artist's son, Henry Raeburn.   She died at the age of six years.
Raeburn, Mrs., and her children.   Mrs. Raeburn by Sir J. Watson Gordon, P.R.S.A. ; the two children by
    Raeburn.   The mother is seated, holding youngest child on her knees, the other girl is standing by her
    side in front, her face turned towards the spectator.   Landscape, column, and curtain background.
    48 × 38½.   Sedelmeyer, 1895.
Raeburn, Peter.   19 × 23.   V. G. Fischer, Esq., of Washington.
Ramsay, The daughters of Allen, afterwards Mrs. Malcolm and Lady Campbell.   A little girl in white dress
    with pink sash and cap, embracing her baby sister.   17 × 14.
Ramsay, Colonel and Mrs.   Signed R. 1790.   The figures are seated in a landscape ; on the left, the lady,
    placed to the right, looking at the spectator ; she wears a white dress and white head-dress, and holds a
    glove in her hand ; behind her, on the right, stands the Colonel, in red coat, looking to the right, his arm
    resting on the back of the seat.   Three-quarter length, life-size ; 48 × 38½ ; signed R. 1790.   R.A. 1895.
    Paris Exhibition, 1900.   Ex Sir William Agnew Collection.   Sedelmeyer, 1906.
Ramsay, Lady.   29¾ × 24½.   Sedelmeyer, 1905.
Ramsay, Robert, of Camno.   Sir Arthur G. R. Mackenzie, Bart.
Ramsay, William.   50 × 40   Wallis, 1903.
Ramsey, Peter, of Charlotte Square, Edinburgh, and Gogan House, Banke ; 40 × 50.   D. Heinemann, Esq.,
    of Munich.
Rannie, James, wine merchant, Leith.   Raeburn Exhibition, 1876.   Lord Torpichen.   Mr. Swinton.
Rannie, Miss Margaret.   (See Mrs. M Elliot, of Wolfelee).
Reid, Robertson, Mrs. F., of Gallowflat ; 30 × 25.   A. Wertheimer, Esq., 1899.
Reid, Dr. Thomas, Professor of Moral Philosophy, Aberdeen ; 29½ × 25½.   National Portrait Gallery of
    Scotland.   Other versions of this portrait are in the Hunterian Museum, and at Fyvie Castle,
    Aberdeenshire.

57

Reid, Dr. Thomas (1710–98). Lent to Glasgow International Exhibition, 1901, by Mark Bannatyne, Esq.

Reid, Rev. Thomas, D.D. (1710–1796). Professor of Moral Philosophy, Aberdeen; succeeded Adam Smith as Professor of Logic, Glasgow, 1764; wrote "Enquiry into the Human Mind," and other works. Raeburn Exhibition, 1876. Mrs. Gregory, Canaan Lodge.

Rennie, John, F.R.S., Civil Engineer, who built Waterloo Bridge, London Docks, and East and West India Docks, at Blackwall; he also designed the breakwater at Plymouth, and London Bridge, which were afterwards constructed by his son, Sir John Rennie. In dark blue coat with brass buttons, white stock; 30 × 25. National Portrait Exhibition, 1868. Formerly the property of Sir George Rennie, grandson of John Rennie, the engineer. Christie's, 1905. Now in the collection of G. B. Rennie, Esq.

Rennie, John. Raeburn Exhibition, 1876.

Richardson, Mrs. (Elizabeth Ann Stewart), of Urrard, Perth, wife of James Richardson, of Pitfour; their son John became thirteenth Baronet.

Riddell, Thomas Milles. In scarlet coat, with buff breeches and top boots, holding his hat and rifle in his right hand, and resting his left hand on his hip; standing in a landscape, under a tree, turned slightly to the left. 94 × 58. Sir Rodney Stuart Riddell, Bart. A. Wertheimer, Esq. (c), 1911.

Ritchie, Miss. A miniature.

Robertson, Andrew (c), 1901.

Robertson of Edinburgh. Almost full face; white collar and scarf. Mr. Andrew Reid, Glasgow. Illustrated in "Portraits by Raeburn." Edited by J. L. Caw.

Robertson, Mrs. George.

Robertson, Mrs., of Alt-na-Skiach (*née* Inglis). In red dress with white lace collar and mob cap; 30 × 25. Christie's, 1906. Colnaghi & Co. Colonel Brown.

Robertson, Patrick of Gallowflat.

Robertson, Mrs., of Gallowflat.

Robertson, William (1721–1793). Principal of Edinburgh University; wrote a "History of Scotland," 1759. "History of America," etc. Famed for his eloquence. Raeburn Exhibition, 1876. University of Edinburgh.

Robinson, Jane, wife of James Law, of Elvington. French Gallery, Edinburgh, 1909.

Robinson, Master; 30 × 24½. Standing in a landscape, turned to the right, holding a hoop and a short stick in his right hand; half length figure, life-size. Ex. the Morgan family, Lord Tredegar's family name. Sedelmeyer, 1897.

Robison, John (1739–1808), Professor of Moral Philosophy, Edinburgh. Secretary Royal Society, Edinburgh. Striped red dressing gown, and white cap; 50 × 40. Engraved by C. Turner. Raeburn Exhibition, 1876. Royal Society, Edinburgh.

Robison, John, Professor. Edinburgh University.

Rolland, Adam, of Gask; advocate, supposed to have suggested "Pleydell" in Sir Walter Scott's "Antiquary." Raeburn Exhibition, 1876. Miss Abercrombie. Two other versions were lent to the same exhibition by Adam Rolland, of Gask. Scottish National Exhibition, 1908. Miss Bruce and the Trustees of the late Miss Agnes Abercrombie.

Rolland, Adam, of Gask. Advocate. Born 1734; died 1819. Full length; in black coat, waistcoat, knee breeches and stockings; he sits facing the spectator, leaning his elbow (the fingers are raised to the cheek) on the writing table to the right; his right hand hangs over the arm of the blue-covered chair; a blue curtain forms the background except to right and left, where patches of yellow sky are introduced; 78 × 60. Three versions of this picture exist. Deposited by the Society in Scotland for the Propagation of Christian Knowledge. Scottish National Gallery.

Rolland, James. Raeburn Exhibition, 1876. Adam Rolland, Esq., of Gask.

Rosebery, Neil, third Earl of Rosebery, K T. (1728–1814); succeeded his father in 1756; married, first, 1764, Susan, sister and heiress of Sir Randall Ward, Bart.; and second, 1775, Mary, daughter of Sir Francis Vincent, Bart., by whom he had, with other children, Archibald, his successor. Raeburn Exhibition, 1876. The Earl of Rosebery.

Ross, Grace Lockhart, of Balnagown, daughter of Sir James Lockhart Ross, and grand-daughter of the twelfth and last Lord Ross; married, in 1794, Lewis Mackenzie, Esq., in which year the portrait was painted; 95 × 59. Agnew, 1904.

Ross, Miss Isabella (1756–1823), wife of George Bell, M.D. Nearly whole length figure, seated in a landscape, under a tree, looking to right; in white dress cut low, with slate-coloured overdress trimmed with black lace; brown hair falling in ringlets over forehead; trees in the distance; 50 × 40. Painted in 1801-2. Engraved by J. B. Pratt. Exhibited Messrs. Agnew's Annual Exhibition, November-December, 1906. Wallis & Son, 1910. J. Pierpont Morgan, Esq.

Ross, Mrs. Jean, wife of John Cockburn Ross, and heiress of William Ross, of Shandwick; 50 × 40. Agnew, 1902. J. B. Joel, Esq.

Ross, John Cockburn, of Rochester and Shandwick; died 1827; 40 × 50. J. Crathern, Esq., of Montreal.

Ross, Miss. Three-quarter length, standing in a landscape; left arm resting on a wall; right hanging at her side. Lord Glencomer.

Ross, Walter, as a boy. Son of John Ross, W.S. Painted about 1822. Raeburn Exhibition, 1876. John Cook, Esq., W.S. Henry Cook, Esq.

Ross, Miss Wilhelmina, of Shandwick; died in 1849. Agnew, 1901.

Ross, Wm., of Shandwick, killed in a duel by Lieut. David Reed, on Hounslow Heath, 1791; 41 × 50. W. Ross, Esq.

Rosslyn. Earl of. Alexander Wedderburn, Lord Chancellor, 1733–1805.

Russell (Bedford) Family. A Boy. In red coat, white vest, lace collar; 11 × 10. Heyman.

Russell, Mrs. Mary, daughter of Sir Alexander Bannerman, fourth baronet, of Elsick, Kincardine. Raeburn Exhibition, 1876. Charles M. Barstowe; Esq.

Russell, Miss. (See Mrs. Andrew Wood).

Russell, Lord W. Grandson of John, fourth Duke of Bedford; born 1767; married 1789, Charlotte Anne, daughter of George, fourth Earl of Jersey; was murdered by his valet in May, 1840; 50 × 40. Raeburn Exhibition, 1876. W. P. Adam, Esq., M.P. Mr. Glaisher, 1896.

Rutherford, Professor.

Sailor, A Disabled. Louvre.

Sands, Major W. J., H.E.I.C.S. Raeburn Exhibition, 1876. Miss Sands.

Scott, Colonel Francis, of Horsely Hill, in red uniform with epaulettes, his left hand on his hip, his right hand resting on his sword; a landscape background; 50 × 40. Agnew (c) 1899. R.A., 1906. Franco-British Exhibition, 1908. M. Trevalyn Martin, Esq.

Scott, Mrs. Hugh. Colnaghi & Co. Knoedler & Co.

Scott, Mrs. 28½ × 23½. Half-length, life-size. Ex Scott collection. Sedelmeyer, 1900.

Scott, Sir Walter. As a Boy in Highland Costume; 30 × 28. Biddulph, 1897.

Scott, Sir Walter. When a Young Man, in brown coat, with pink vest and white stock; 29 × 24. Formerly in the possession of Campbell, the poet. From the collection of William Russell, Esq., 1884. Gooden & Fox, 1905. Now in America.

Scott, Sir Walter, Bart. of Abbotsford, born in Edinburgh, 1771, son of a writer to the *Signet*; educated at High School and University of Edinburgh; called to the Scottish Bar, 1792; Sheriff depute of Selkirkshire, 1799; published *Waverley* in 1814; created baronet in 1820; died Abbotsford, 1832. Full length, painted 1808; 72 × 58. Engraved by C. Turner and E. Pickett. Raeburn Exhibition, 1876, Duke of Buccleugh and Queensberry, K.T. The *Gentleman's Magazine* for Dec. 1809, says that "Mr. Cromek will shortly publish a whole length portrait of Sir Walter Scott, from the admired picture painted by Raeburn, for Constable, of Edinburgh; which appeared in the last Exhibition of Scottish Paintings. The print will be 20 × 14." This no doubt refers to the Mezzotint by C. Turner, 1810.

Scott, Sir Walter, Bart. Replica of full length, 71 × 58. Collection of Baroness Burdett-Coutts.

Scott, Sir Walter, Bart. Mrs. Bishop, of Richmond. Judging from the print after this portrait which appeared in the *Morning Leader*, in 1907; this version cannot be accepted as genuine.

Scott, Sir Walter. 1809. Hon. Mrs. Maxtone Scott, of Abbotsford.

Scott, Sir Walter. 1822-23. Engraved by W. Walker. Earl of Home.

Scott, Sir Walter, Bart. Bust size, 29½ × 24½. Raeburn Exhibition, 1876. Raeburn Family. Arthur Sanderson, Esq. Colnaghi and Co., 1911. This portrait is doubtful.

Seafield, Lord.

Seaforth, Lord. 29½ × 24. Vokins (c) 1910.

Selkrig, Alex., Accountant, born 1764, died 1845. 25 × 30. D. Morrice, Esq., of Montreal.

Selkrig, Charles. Raeburn Exhibition, 1876. James Hay, Esq.

Seton, Lady. Miss Innes, daughter of Mr. Innes of Cathlaw. Lady Seton's husband's title was a Swedish one, and they both lived at Preston, near Linlithgow; 23 × 28. Col. Walter Brown, of Renfrew. Wallis & Son, 1910. Col. Walter Brown.

Shaw, Alex. 29 × 24. W. L. Graham, 1905.

Shiriff, Lieut.-Colonel, H.E.I.C.S, of the Madras Army. Painted about 1800. Full length in uniform Raeburn Exhibition, 1876. James D. Gillespie, Esq., M.D. Wallis & Son, 1910. Mrs. Gillespie.

Shuttleworth, Mrs. Lady Marjoribanks, Lees.

Siddons, Mrs. (R. & F.), 1905.

Siddons, Mrs. (probably). Bust side view, face turned to spectator; white cap, and ruff, dark jacket. Shepherd, 1910.

Simpson, Mrs. Three-quarter length; seated in a landscape; 48½ × 38½. William McEwan, Esq.

Sinclair, Sir George, Bart., of Ulbster, as a boy. Born 1790; married 1816. Lady Catherine Tollemache, daughter of Louisa, Countess of Dysart, and sister of the Earl of Dysart; died 1868; 57 × 42½. Painted about 1794. Full length, fair haired, seated in a landscape on a rock, looking at spectator; red jacket and frilled collar; left hand rests on rock, his right holds his cap. Landscape background. Viscount Iveagh. R.A., 1907.

Sinclair, Sir John, Bart, of Ulbster. Political economist and philanthropist, born at Thurso, 1754; educated at Edinburgh; first President of Board of Agriculture; wrote among other important works, "A Statistical Account of Scotland;" raised two battalions, each of 1,000, in readiness for the expected French invasion; died at Edinburgh, and was buried at Holyrood Abbey. Seated, face three-quarters to left; 48½ × 38½. S. N. G.

Sinclair, Sir John, of Ulbster (1754-1835), as Colonel of the Caithness and Rothesay Fencibles. In the Uniform of a Field Officer of Highland Militia, over the scarlet coatee and trews of Sinclair Tartan, he wears two sashes, a buff and a red, a large plaid, a sporran, and a heavy cavalry sabre; standing in a landscape, his left hand resting on his hip; 94 × 60. Painted about 1790. Glasgow Exhibition, 1901. Christie's, 1909. Lent to R.A. 1910, by the Trustees of Archibald H. M. Sinclair, Esq. On loan to Scottish National Portrait Gallery.

Sinclair, the Rt. Hon. Sir John, Bart. 60 × 93½. The Archdeacon of London.

Sinclair, Sir John, Bart. National Portrait Gallery.

Sinclair, Sir John, Bart, of Ulbster. Bust, dark coat, grey hair, paper in left hand; 30 × 25. Wallis & Son, 1910. Archdeacon Sinclair.

Sinclair, William, fifth son of Sir John Sinclair, Bart; 49 × 39. Painted in 1808, at the age of four years. R.A., 1910. Wallis & Son, 1910. Archdeacon of London.

Skene, James, of Rubislaw; advocate, 1797; born, 1774; died, 1864. Raeburn Exhibition, 1876. Miss Skene.

Skene, Mrs., wife of James Skene, and daughter of Sir William Forbes, Bart., of Pitsligo. Raeburn Exhibition, 1876. Miss Skene.

Skirving, Archibald, son of Adam Skirving, author of "Johnnie Cope," &c. (1749-1819); studied art in Rome, and settled in Edinburgh as a portraitist in crayons. His likeness of Burns, the poet, is well-known. Raeburn Exhibition, 1876. Raeburn Family.

Smith, Archibald, of Jordanhill. T. D. Smith, Esq.

Smith, Archibald. Replica.

Smith, Mrs. Alexander. Raeburn Exhibition, 1876. David Smith, Esq. Hallam Murray, Esq.

Smith, Donald, banker, Edinburgh. Raeburn Exhibition, 1876. David Smith, Esq.

Smith, George, Master of Trinity House. Painted about 1807. Raeburn Exhibition, 1876. Incorporation Trinity House, Leith.

Smith, James, of Jordanhill. Painted 1823. International Exhibition, Glasgow, 1901. Mrs. Archibald Smith.

Smith, Mrs. (*née* Wilson), wife of above. Painted 1823, and engraved by J. W. Chapman in 1890. Mrs. Archibald.

Smith, John, of Craigend. Painted in 1790. 30 × 25. J. S. Rankin, Esq. S.N.G.

Somerset, Miss. 25 × 30. Sedelmeyer. Exhibited Berlin, 1903. D. Morrice, Esq., of Montreal.

Somerville, Mrs., of Airhouse, Berwickshire. (See Farmer's wife).

Speirs, Archibald, of Elderslie. Mr. Speirs.

Spiers, Mrs. Archibald (Margaret Dundas). Marquis of Zetland.

Spens, Dr. Nathaniel (1728–1815). Son of Thomas Spens, of Lathallan; President of Royal College of Physicians, Edinburgh, 1794–1796; President Royal Company of Archers, 1809; Adjutant-General, 1810. Married Mary, second daughter of James Millikin, of that ilk. In uniform, full length; standing in a landscape; shooting with bow and arrow. Painted for the Archer's Hall, Edinburgh, and engraved by Bengo, 1796. Raeburn Exhibition, 1876. Royal Company of Archers, Edinburgh.

Spenser, Edmund. (Copy). Earl Spencer. Painted in 1820 from the original portrait in the possession of the Earl ot Kinnoul.

Stanhope, Lady. Colnaghi & Co. (c) 1896. Madame Andre, Paris.

Steuart, David. (See Earl of Buchan).

Steuart, Sir Henry, Bart., lent to Scottish Exhibition, Glasgow, by Sir Alan L. Seton-Steuart, Bart.

Steuart, of Coltness and Westshields, Sir James; 49 × 38½. National Gallery of Ireland.

Steuart. Lady Seton. Three-quarter length; brown eyes; dark hair in ringlets on either side of head; close fitting white robe; full crimson cloak with gold-toned lining; the left hand hangs by her side and holds a soft turban-like hat, the same colour as the cloak; the right hand grasping the cloak is extended and rests on a garden balustrade; 48 × 36. Stirling Exhibition, 1910. Sir Alan H. Seton-Steuart, Bart., of Touch.

Stewart, Lieut.-Col. Alexander, 4th Battalion Royal Scots; Equerry to H.R.H. the Duke of Kent; 24 × 29. Andrew T. Reid, Esq., of Glasgow.

Stewart, Lady Alicia, of Coltness, daughter of William Blackee, of Carrick-Blackee, co. Armagh; born, 1744; married, in 1772, General Sir James Denham-Stewart, of Coltness and Westhills; 50 × 40. Agnew, 1901. Lent to Franco-British Exhibition by Mrs. F. C. K. Fleishmann. Cent. Portraits des Femmes, Paris, 1909, and to Wallis & Son, 1910.

Stewart, Admiral Sir C. Houston Stewart, as a midshipman. Sir H. Shaw Stewart. Illustrated in " Portraits by Raeburn."

Stewart, Daniel, founder of Daniel Stewart's Hospital (1741–1814). Raeburn Exhibition, 1876. Merchants' Company of Edinburgh.

Stewart, Professor Dugald; 46 × 37. Engraved by C. Turner and Lizars. Ex E. G. Fraser Tytler. Ehrich sale, New York, March 21, 1906, £290. Thomas.

Stewart, George and Maria, children of Professor Dugald Stewart. The boy, in green coat, yellow vest with white frilled collar, with his hands holding back a dog; his young sister, in white dress with low neck and short sleeves, by his side, holding a rabbit in her arms. Three-quarter length; 50 × 40. Colnaghi and Co. (c), 1901. Exhibition of British Art, Berlin, 1908.

Stewart, G. H., of Physgill, with horse, R. J. Stewart, Esq., of Glasserton.

Stewart, Mrs., of Physgill. Full length in landscape. Painted about 1823. Engraved in *udio*, 1908 R. J. Stewart, Esq., of Glasserton. Messrs. Duveen. Sir George Cooper, Bart.

Stewart, John, of Garth. Sir Donald Currie, K.C.M.G.

Stewart, Sir Michael Shaw. Engraved by S. Cousins. Sir Hugh Shaw Stewart, Bart.

Stewart, Miss of Ballechin (Dowell, Edinburgh); 38½ × 47. J. Burnet Stewart, 1904.

Stewart, Mrs., of Kirkchrist. Lawson Peacock, Esq.

Stewart, Mrs., wife of Charles Stewart, Esq., of Dalguise; 50 × 40. Agnew, 1904. Cent Portraits des Femmes, Paris, 1909. Sir Edward Stern.

Stevenson, Lieut.-General, Sir James, K.C.B., of Barns; died, 1850. Raeburn Exhibition, 1876. James Hope, Esq., of Belmont.

Stirling, Miss Christian, wife of George Dundas, of Dundas, and second daughter of Sir William Stirling. Archibald Stirling, Esq.

Stirling, Helen, only child of Robert Stirling (1808–1822). Seated in a landscape. Painted, 1811. Raeburn Exhibition, 1876 Sir William Stirling-Maxwell, Bart. Reproduced in " Fifty Portraits of Raeburn." 1909.

Stirling, John, of Kippendavie, and Jane, his youngest daughter. He was an old branch of the baronial family of De Striveling or Stirling, of Keir; his second daughter, Margaret, was married to James, tenth Lord Torpichen. Painted about 1814. Raeburn Exhibition, 1876. John Stirling Esq., of Kippendavie.

Stirling, Robert. Archibald Stirling, Esq.

Stirling, William, of Cordale. Archibald Stirling, Esq.

Stodart, Robert, of Kailzie, Peebles-shire, and of Ormiston Hill, Edinburgh. Raeburn Exhibition, 1876. Robert S. Wyld, Esq., LL.D.

Stothert, William, of Cargen. Painted about 1817. Raeburn Exhibition, 1876. Rev. W. Burton Alexander.

Story, Miss; 30 × 24½. Green, 1897.

Strahan, Renny, Mrs.; 30 × 25. Colnaghi & Co. (c), 1899. A. Tooth.

Stuart, Charles, Esq., of Edinburgh. In black coat with white stock; 30 × 25. Sedelmeyer (c), 1901.

Stuart, Sir James. Engraved by Buxton.

Stuart, Sir John, of Fettercairn, M.P. for Kincardineshire, 1797. Baron of Exchequer; died 1821. Painted about 1805. Raeburn Exhibition, 1876 Lord Clinton. Hon. C. F. Trefusis.

Suttie, George, H.E.I.C.S., son of Sir George Suttie, third baronet of Balgone, Haddingtonshire. Painted about 1795. Raeburn Exhibition, 1876. Sir George Grant Suttie, Bart., of Preston Grange and Balgone.

Suttie, Janet, daughter of Sir James Suttie Bust in oval, turned to right; face three-quarters looking to left. Painted about 1818. Raeburn Exhibition, 1876. Sir George Grant Suttie, Bart. Scottish National Exhibition, 1908.

Suttie, Lady, wife of Sir James Suttie, fourth baronet, of Balgone, who in 1818, succeeded his aunt Janet Grant, Countess of Hyndford, as heir of line in the estates of Preston Grange, and assumed in consequence the surname and arms of Grant. Painted about 1795. Raeburn Exhibition, 1876. Sir George Grant Suttie.

Suttie, Miss Margaret. Painted about 1818. Engraved in mezzotint, by R. C. Clouston, 1893. Glasgow International Exhibition, 1901; Scottish National Exhibition, 1908. Sir George Grant Suttie.

Swanston, William, of Leith-head. Three-quarter length, leaning on wall in landscape; 50 × 40. S. Mitchell, Esq. Illustrated in " Portraits by Raeburn." Edited by Mr. J. L. Caw, 1909.

Sym, Robert, W. S. Born in Glasgow, 1752, came to Edinburgh when young; uncle of " Christopher North " (Professor John Wilson); well-known in literary circles and was the " Timothy Tickler " of the Noctes Ambrosianæ, died 1844. Engraved by R. C. Bell. Raeburn Exhibition, 1876. Mrs. Margaret Anne Ferrier. Miss J. Grant.

Symmington, Miss Janet. 50 × 40. Seated in landscape; in white dress; holds hat in left hand. E. M. Hodgkins, Esq.

Tait, John W. S., of Harvieston, where he was visited by Robert Burns. He saw the battle of Falkirk. Archbishop Tait was one of his grandsons. Mr. Tait died in 1800, aged seventy-three years. Raeburn Exhibition, 1876. Mr. Tait. Mrs. Pitman.

Tait, John W. S., and grandchild John. Painted in 1793. The figure of the boy was introduced after Mr. Tait's death. The latter is seated in rustic chair, in a landscape, face looking to spectator; right elbow rests on arm of chair; he holds a watch in his right hand (his other hand is also a right hand, see text). The child holds fob in left hand. Raeburn Exhibition. Mr. Tait. Mrs. Pitman.

Tattersall. The Family. Lister (R. and F.), 1902.

Taylor, Rev. William, D.D., Principal Glasgow University. Mrs. Monteith.

Telford, Thomas, eminent civil engineer, son of a shepherd in Eskdale, Dumfries-shire (1757–1834). At the age of fourteen years he was apprenticed to a stone mason; in 1780 went to Edinburgh, and studied architecture and drawing; removed to London, and was employed in the erection of Somerset House. His first great work was the Ellesmere Canal; it was followed by the Caledonian Canal, the Menai Suspension Bridge; and St. Katherine Docks, London. He was buried in Westminster Abbey. Painted about 1812. Raeburn Exhibition, 1876. Mrs. Burge.

Thomson, Rev. Andrew, an eminent divine, orator, and controversalist; died 1831. Engraved by W. Walker, Raeburn Exhibition, 1876. The artist's Family. Wallis & Son. Colnaghi & Co. L. Nardus. There was a portrait of Mr. Thomson in St. George's Parish Church, Edinburgh.

Thomson, Christina. (See Mrs. White).

Thomson, George. Engraved by Cochrane. R.S.A., 1863. (See Mrs. Thomson).

Thomson, Rev. John (1778–1840). Won fame as a landscape painter; appointed minister of Duddingston, 1805; was a scholar and excelled in music. Engraved by A. Hay. Raeburn Exhibition, 1876. Raeburn Family. Archibald Stirling.

Thomson, John, Merchant, Edinburgh. In grey coat with roll collar; white vest and stock. Raeburn Exhibition, 1876. Mrs. Bell. Gooden and Fox (c) 1911.

Thomson, Robert. Col. Sir R. White-Thomson.

Thomson, Thomas (1768–1852), Advocate, Principal Clerk of Session, Edinburgh. President Bannatyne Club. Edited several acts of Parliament. Raeburn Exhibition. 1876. Right Hon. T. F. Kennedy, of Dunure.

Tod, Mrs. Eliza, daughter of Sir James Pringle, fourth baronet of Stichell, and wife of Archibald Tod, of Drygrange. Half length; grey dress with white frilled collar, grey and white cap; 30 × 25. Wallis & Son, 1910.

Tod, John, of Kirkhill, writer to the *Signet*. Raeburn Exhibition, 1876. Alexander Tod, Esq.

Torpichen, James, ninth Lord (1759–1815). Lieut.-Colonel; a representative peer; married Anne, daughter of Sir John Inglis, Bart., and died without issue, when the barony descended to his first cousin James. Lord Torpichen.

Torpichen, Lady, wife of Lord Torpichen. Raeburn Exhibition, 1876. Lord Torpichen.

Towers, Professor James. R. Towers, Esq.

Traill, Lady Janet. Daughter of William, tenth Earl of Caithness; married, 1784, James Traill, Esq., of Hobbister and Rattar; died in Edinburgh, and buried at Rosslyn Chapel, 1806. In pale yellow muslin dress, cut low at the neck and turned back with white; yellow sash; her hair semi-powdered, and bound with a pale blue ribbon; seated, to the right, holding the folds of her dress with her left hand, and resting her right hand on her lap; landscape and foliage background. 49¼ × 39¼. The portrait hung for many years in a Scottish box. James Christie Traill, Esq. Duveen (c) 1911. 14,000 gs.

Traill, James, of Hobbister and Rattar. Born 1759; Advocate; Sheriff of the Counties of Caithness and Orkney; married Lady Janet Sinclair, daughter of William, tenth Earl of Caithness. In dark coat, vest and breeches, with white stock and frill; powdered hair; seated, to the left, in a crimson chair, holding some papers in his right hand, and resting his left upon the arm of his chair; a table behind, on which are books and papers. 49¼ × 39¼. James Christie Traill, Esq. Colnaghi & Obach (c) 1911.

Trotter, Archibald, of Bush, Midlothian. Raeburn Exhibition, 1876. Lieut.-Colonel Trotter.

Trotter, Mrs., of Bush. Exhibition of artist's works, Edinburgh, 1876. Lieut.-Colonel Trotter.

Turing, Lady (*née* Miss Campbell, of Saddell). Sir Robert Turing.

Twysden, Lady (Mary, daughter of George Jervis). Nearly full face; white dress with frill; brown hair dressed high and falling over each shoulder; blue eyes. Miniature, 3½ × 2½. J. P. Morgan, Esq. (See Dr. Williamson's Catalogue of Miniatures, No. 307).

Tytler, Alexander Fraser, Lord Woodhouselee, of Woodhouselee. Born, 1747; married, 1776; Senator of the College of Justice, Edinburgh; father of the " Historian of Scotland "; Author of Universal History, Ancient and Modern; died 1812. In black and white stock, with grey hair; full face, body to the left; 30 × 25. Painted in 1804. Engraved by Picart. Exhibited in Edinburgh, about 1877. Christie's, 1897. Colnaghi & Co. A. Tooth. Fischoff-Blakeson sale, New York, 1900.

Tytler, Mrs. Grant Fraser. E. Grant Fraser Tytler, Esq.
Tytler, Jane Fraser, daughter of Lord Woodhouselee; wife of James Baillie Fraser, of Reelig, eldest son of
    Edward Fraser. In white dress, cut low; dark red cloak, trimmed with fur over the shoulders; full
    face, body slightly to the left; 30 × 25. A. Wertheimer. Charles P. Taft, U.S.A.
Tytler, William W. S. Engraved by J. Jones, 1790. E. Grant Fraser Tytler, Esq.

Urquhart, William, Merchant, Glasgow. Half length, life-size, looking towards spectator; 38 × 25. Painted
    about 1815. Presented by his daughter-in-law, Caroline J. Urquhart, in 1900, to Glasgow Corporation
    Galleries.
Urquhart, Mrs. William, wife of William Urquhart. Half length, life-size, looking to left; 30 × 25. Painted
    about 1815. Presented as above.

Veitch, Mrs., of Elisch. Three-quarter length. Miss Graham.
Vere, Mrs. Jacolina Leslie, stepdaughter of Sir Henry Raeburn, wife of Daniel Vere, of Stoneybynes, Sheriff
    Substitute, of Lanarkshire, who was the last representative in the male line of an old English family
    long resident in Lanarkshire. Seated in green garden chair, set in landscape, white dress; brown
    cloak lined with yellow; left arm leaning on wall, right hanging at her side; 50 × 40. Raeburn
    Exhibition, 1876. James T. Gibson-Craig, Esq. Agnew (c), 1887. Mrs. Keiller. Wallis & Son, 1910.
    W. A. Coats, Esq. Dr. John Brown describes a portrait of Mrs. Vere, " lying asleep, her head on a
    pillow—a fine study."
Vernon, Right Hon. Louisa Barbara.
Vismes, Miss de (Lady Murray). Scottish International Exhibition, 1908. Earl of Mansfield.

Wallace, Hugh. Hugh R. Wallace, Esq.
Wallace, Mrs. Miniature. Hugh R. Wallace, Esq.
Walker, Mrs. F. Sir J. Drummond, Bart.
Wardrop, James, of Torbanehill (1731-1830). Bust turned to right; head almost full face, grey hair. Raeburn
    Exhibition, 1876. Mrs. Arthur Shirley. Scottish International Exhibition, 1908. J. C. Wardrop, Esq.
Wardrop, James, of Torbanehill, Linlithgowshire. In dark dress with white stock. 29¼ × 24¼.
    A. Wertheimer, Esq. (c) 1911.
Wardrop, James, of Torbanehill, by Sir Henry Raeburn, R.A. This picture is a very fine replica of the
    beautiful and important portrait in the possession of the Wardrop family, and is said to have been painted
    when the sitter was 92 years old—four or five years before Raeburn's death. It was the property of the
    late Dr. Dyce Brown, London, and is now in the possession of G. S. Davidson, Esq., 8 Kelvingrove
    Terrace, Glasgow.
Wardrop, James, M.D.; (1782-1869). Famous occulist and Surgeon-in-Ordinary to George IV.; had a large
    collection of pictures. Raeburn Exhibition, 1876. Maitland Wardrop, Esq.
Warner, R., of Bath; 25 × 30. Wallis & Son.
Watson, Walter T., son of Captain Andrew Watson, of Hunthill. Portrait in Pastel; executed about 1796.
    Raeburn Exhibition, 1876. Dr. Sidey.
Wauchope, Andrew, of Niddrie; 59 × 45. Lent to R.A. in 1908, by Mrs. Wauchope.
Wauchope, James (1767-1797).
Wauchope, John, Esq., W. S.; born 1751; admitted W.S., 1774; died 1828. To waist, leaning back in chair,
    the figure turned towards the left, the genial face almost full front and slightly inclined to one side. He
    wears a double-breasted white waistcoat and a dark blue coat, the left arm brought across the lower edge
    of the picture, is obscured by a cast shadow. Warm dark grey background; 30 × 25. Presented to
    Scottish National Gallery by Rev. H. B. Sands, 1884.
Wauchope, John (1742-1810), of Edmonstone. Sir John Don Wauchope, Bart.
Wauchope, Colonel John, of Edmonstone, second son of John Wauchope and Anne Erskine (1769-1837).
    Raeburn Exhibition, 1876. Sir John Don Wauchope, Bart., of Edmonstone.
Wauchope, Mrs. John. (See Anne Erskine).
Wedderburn, Alexander. (See Earl of Rosslyn).
Wedderburn, James (1782-1822). Advocate. Solicitor-General for Scotland, 1816. Raeburn Exhibition,
    1876. Colin Mackenzie, Esq., W.S. Mrs. Mackenzie.
Wedderburn, Miss. (See John Johnstone).
Wedderburn, Mrs. Raeburn Exhibition, 1876. Colin Mackenzie, Esq. Mrs. Mackenzie.
Wellwood, Rev. Sir Henry Moncrieff, Bart., D.D.
Wellwood, Mrs. Robert. (See Mary Preston).
Welwood, Hon. Alexander Maconochie. (See Lord Meadowbank).
Welwood, Elizabeth, of Garvock, wife of Allan Maconochie, first Lord Meadowbank; 24 × 29. Painted in
    1818. R.A. in 1910. John A. Maconochie Wellwood, Esq.
Welwood, Mrs. (See Anne Blair).
Wemyss, Francis, seventh Earl of (1779-1853). Painted 1812. Lithograph by Carbonnier. Raeburn
    Exhibition, 1876. Earl of Wemyss and March.
Wemyss, Countess of (Miss Margaret Campbell), wife of seventh Earl. Raeburn Exhibition, 1876. Earl of
    Wemyss and March.
Wharton, Mrs. William. Marquis of Zetland, K.T.
White, Mrs., in white, wife of the Rev. Thomas White, of Lichfield; 30 × 24. Painted about 1822. Forbes,
    1902. Sir R. T. White-Thomson, K.C.B.
White, Mrs., of Howden. Her daughter, Miss Logan White, married Raeburn's son (?). Turned to left,
    looking at spectator; in white dress and cap, black lace shawl; half length, life-size; 30 × 25,
    Sedelmeyer, 1902.
Wilkie, Sir D., R.A. In brown coat and white stock; oval, 30 × 25. Wall (c) 1908.

Williams, Hugh William (Grecian Williams).   Water colour painter, author and traveller.   Half length; face three-quarters to the left ; 29$\frac{1}{2}$ × 24$\frac{1}{2}$.   Presented to National Portrait Gallery, in 1894, by Sir Charles Tennant, Bart.

Williamson, Mrs. Robertson, daughter of William Robertson, Esq., of Lawers; married, in 1814, her cousin, David Robertson Williamson, Esq., of Balgray, Lord Balgray (Lord of Sessions).   In white dress, cut low at the neck, and fastened with a white satin bow at the waist ; pale pink satin coat, with long sleeves and tassels; standing before a tree, resting her left arm upon a branch, and holding her hat, trimmed with roses, dangling from long grey ribbons; landscape and foliage background.   94 × 58$\frac{1}{2}$. (c), 1911.   22,300 gs.

Willoughby d'Eresby.   (See Lady Perth).

Wilson, Professor John, poet, essayist, and moral philosopher.   Born 1785, in Paisley; studied at Glasgow University and at Magdalen College, Oxford; in 1812 published his first volume, "The Isle of Palms," and other poems; in 1816, "The City of the Plague."   In 1815 he passed advocate in Edinburgh on the foundation of *Blackwood's Magazine*.   In 1817 he began his connection with that journal, of which, however, he was never editor, as has been stated.   In 1822 he began to contribute to its pages the celebrated "Noctes Ambrosianæ" of "Christopher North."   In 1820 he was appointed to the Chair of Moral Philosophy in Edinburgh University ; his eloquence and kindliness won the respect and love of his students ; died 1854.   His "Works," in twelve volumes, were edited by his son-in-law, Professor Ferrier, in 1855-58.   Full length figure, turned to the left ; face nearly fronting, with yellowish brown hair and brown eyes; his right hand rests on the neck of a brown horse to the left, and holds a hat and the reins ; his left hand, hanging down by his side, wears a greenish grey glove, and holds another of same ; chocolate brown coat, with brass buttons; white cravat and vest, from beneath which a red ribbon, with watch seals, appears suspended in front; yellow riding breeches and long boots, spurred, and with brown, turned-down tops; background of a mellow sky, with trees and hills in distance, seen between the horse's legs, and large brown tree to right; 93 × 58.   Painted about 1805.   Presented to R.S.A. by his son, John Wilson, Esq., S.N.P.G.

Wood, Alexander, President of Harveian Society.

Wood, Andrew, Surgeon, Edinburgh (1742–1821).   Miniature.   Raeburn Exhibition, 1876.   Dr. Wood.   (?) Miss Edmondstone.

Wood, Andrew; 30 × 25.

Wood, Mrs. Andrew (Miss Russell), wife of Andrew Wood (1754–1845).   Raeburn Exhibition, 1876.   Dr. Wood, Edinburgh.   (c), 1911.

Wood, Neville, when a child.   Seated in a landscape, looking at a spectator, clad in white shirt, a fox terrier lying by his side ; his right hand resting on its back, full length ; 29 × 24.   Ex the widow, Neville Wood.   Sedelmeyer, 1901.

Wood, Peter.

Wood, Thomas.   A. R. Wilson-Wood, Esq.

Woodhouselee, Lord.   (See A. Fraser Tytler).

Wright, Alexander, F.S.A.   Exhibited, Dublin, 1878.

Wyld, Mrs., of Gilston.   Raeburn Exhibition, 1876.   Dr. Robert S. Wyld.

Wynne, Miss Justine Camilla.   (See Mrs. Alexander Finlay).

Wynward, Colonel Harvey.   Colonel Cornwallis West.

Young, Alexander, W.S.   A. Rutherford, Esq.

Young, Mrs.   A. Rutherford, Esq.

Young, Mrs. Graham, and child.   Seated in a landscape, the mother with her left hand supports the child, which stands on her knee ; with her right hand she holds above her head a flower, at which the child looks, and stretches his hand to seize.   Mother and child are dressed in white muslin.   Life-size figures ; 39$\frac{3}{4}$ × 36.   Sedelmeyer, 1899.   Sedelmeyer Gallery, Paris, 1908.   M. H. Rosenheim, Esq.

The following were the property of Sir Henry Raeburn, R.A., and remained in the family until 1902.   A Derby Vase, painted with a wreath of flowers in colours, and gilt with arabesques, by Bloor ; 11$\frac{1}{2}$ in. high; Six Derby white and gold coffee-cups and saucers; A Worcester bowl, enamelled with figures in the Chinese taste on dark blue and gold scale pattern-ground, and with border of foliage in colours and gold ; 9$\frac{1}{4}$ in. diam.   From this bowl Sir Henry Raeburn's grandchildren were christened ; A Coalport dessert service, printed with flowers in colours, and with raised white flowers, consisting of centre-dish, six shaped dishes, and twelve plates.   Believed to have belonged to Sir Henry Raeburn ; A small circular Sheraton mahogany table, with three drawers and shelf beneath, inlaid with patera ornament and chequer borders in satin and other woods ; 15 in. diam.

.

TABLE OF CONTENTS.

LIST OF ILLUSTRATIONS.

Cover Illustration :—Mrs. SCOTT MONCRIEFF, from the Mezzotint printed in Colours by E. Gulland, published by H. C. Dickins, 26 Regent Street.

GEO. PULMAN & SONS, LTD.,
The Cranford Press,
LONDON AND WEALDSTONE

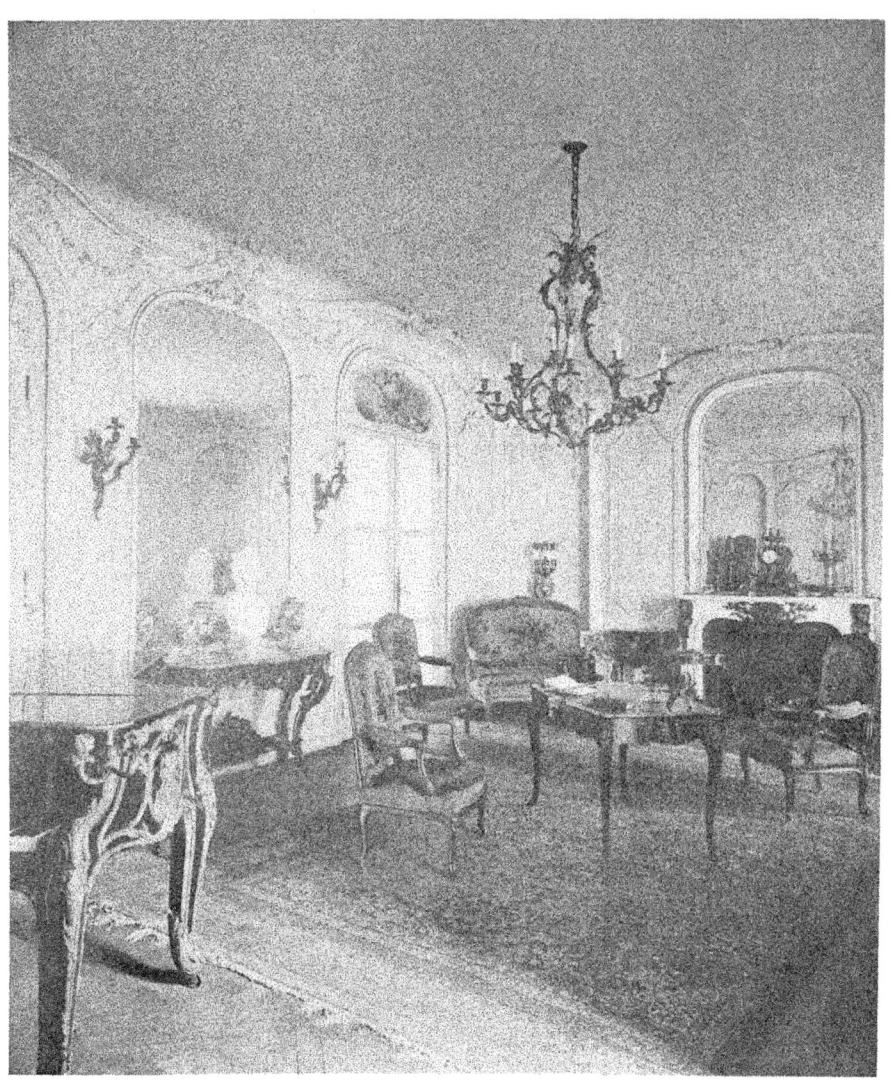

HOS⋮ HALL

DECORATIONS,
FURNISHINGS,
& ANTIQUES .

35 BROOK ST.
(GROSVENOR SQUARE)
LONDON w.

18 GEORGE ST EDINBURG

THE CONNOISSEUR
The Premier Art Magazine
ONE SHILLING NET MONTHLY

FIRST published in 1901, THE CONNOISSEUR, from its inception, has attracted a circle of readers unrivalled in the annals of periodical literature.   Now recognised as the premier art magazine, THE CONNOISSEUR, through its authoritative articles, excellent illustrations, and superb colour plates, has amongst its subscribers all those who require definite information regarding the arts and crafts of other days, and also those to whom the faithful reproductions in colour of the masterpieces of the pictorial and plastic arts of the past five centuries appeal.

ANNUAL SUBSCRIPTION.

Through any Bookseller or Newsagent -   - - - - **12/-**
Post Free from the Publishers : Anywhere in the United Kingdom **16/-**
Canada   - -   **14/-**   To any Country in the Postal Union   **17/-**

Publishing, Editorial, and Advertising Offices   TEMPLE CHAMBERS, TEMPLE AVENUE, E.C , LONDON, ENGLAND.

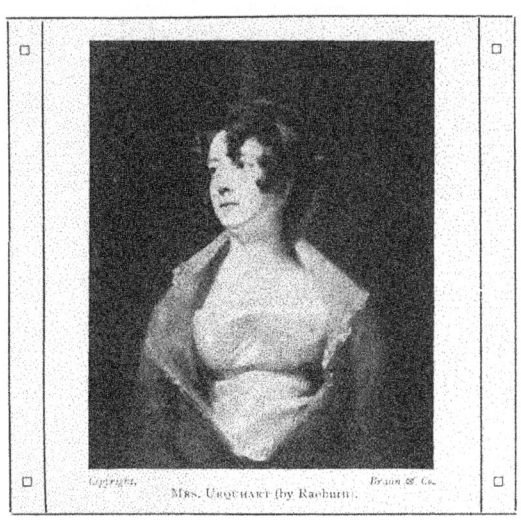

THE HISTORY OF THE SPUR

By CHARLES DE LACY LACY, M.A.

10/6 net. Will be published on October 23rd, 1911

THE History of the Spur is the first book written in the English language on this interesting subject.

Hitherto some articles have been written by Mr. James, many years ago, in the *Archæological Journal*, and there have been letters and short descriptions of Spurs in *Archæologia*, and in several works on Armour.

Here we have the first attempt to trace, link by link, the gradual sequence of change in the long chain that has been handed down to us from the earliest times. Starting from the very small and simple appliances of the Pre-Christian era, Spurs are traced through the Middle Ages, up to the enormous and highly decorated implements of the 15th and 16th centuries, and down to the comparatively simple forms of the present day.

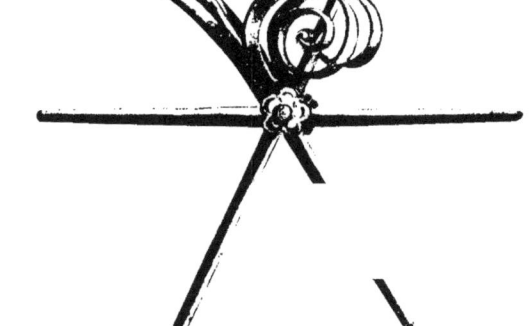

It is hoped that this book will remedy a want long felt by Antiquarians and persons interested in Armour and Equipments.

The volume is illustrated with upwards of 70 drawings taken by the Author from specimens in English and Continental Museums and in private collections.

Orders can now be received, and should be accompanied by remittance for the number required.

Publishers: "**THE CONNOISSEUR**," 1 Temple Chambers, Temple Avenue, E.C.

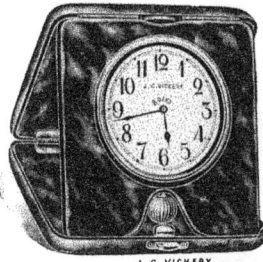 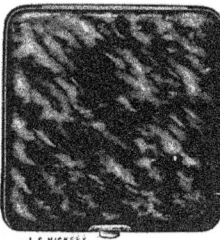 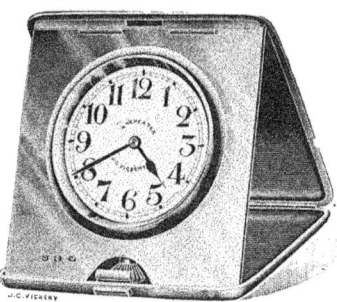

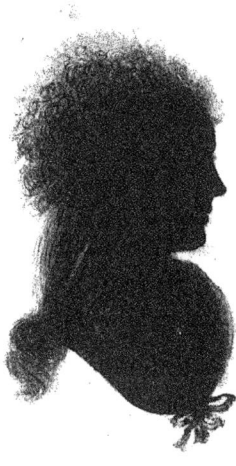
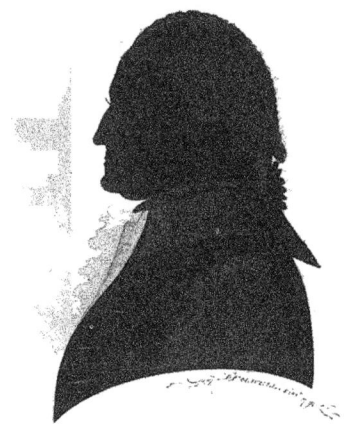

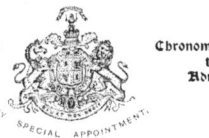
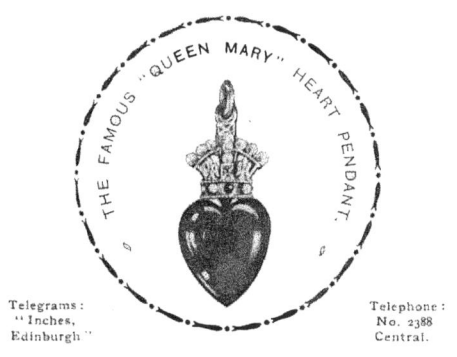
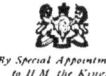
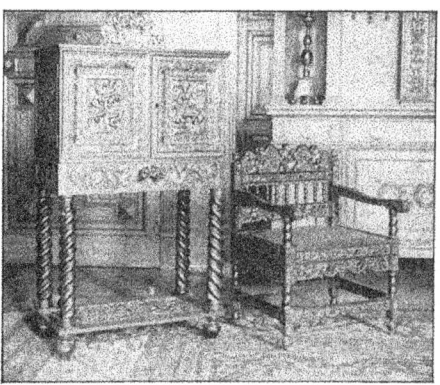

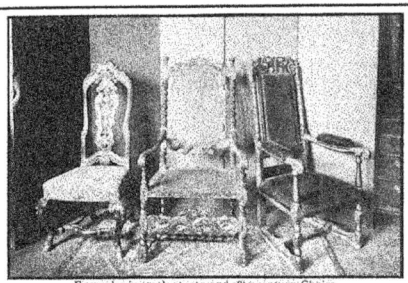
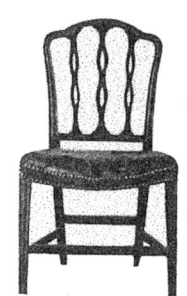

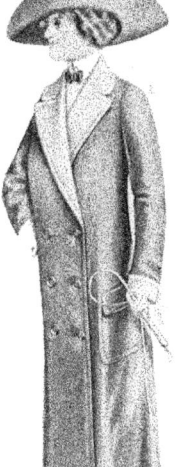
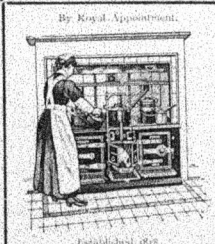

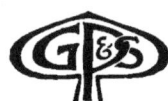

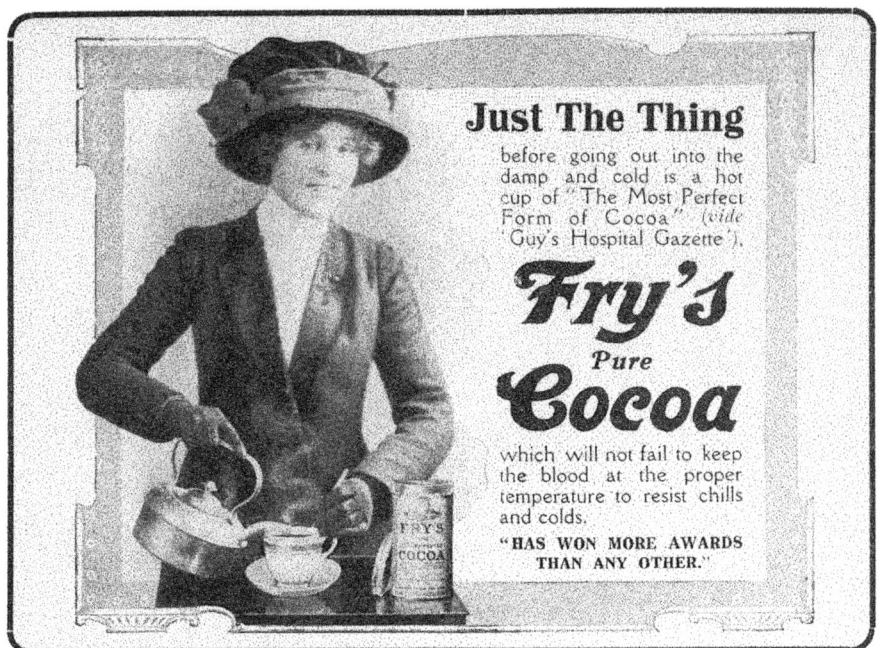

J. SPRATT, The Noted Art & Curiosity Dealer

ESTABLISHED 1835.

14 Northernhay Place (London Inn Sq.), EXETER

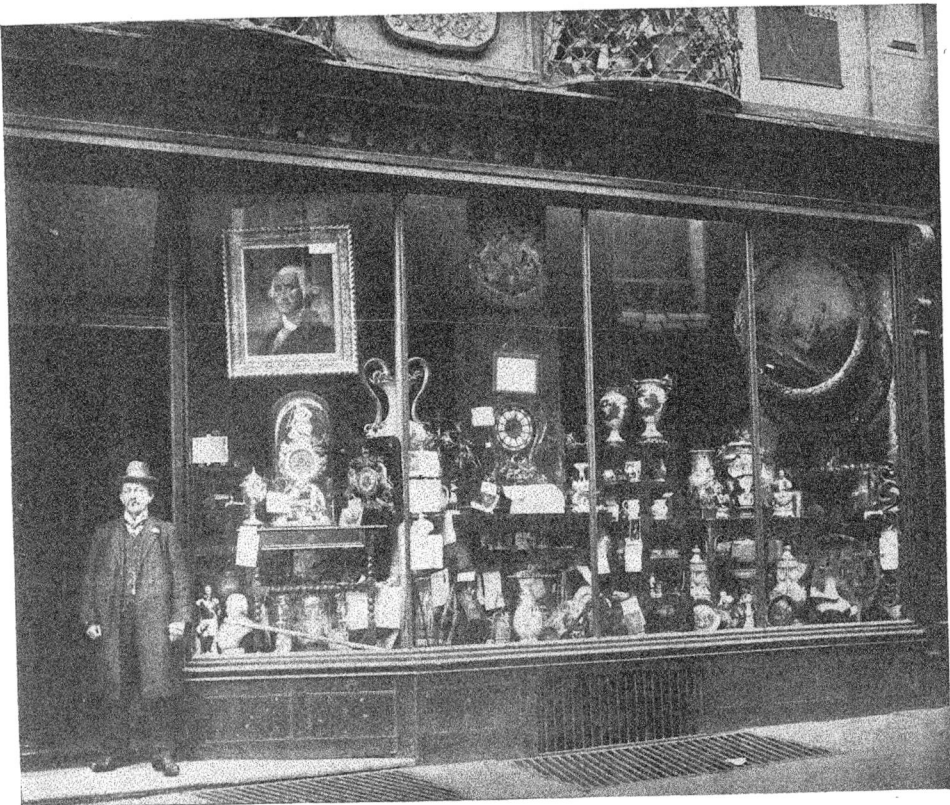

2,500 PICTURES TO SELECT FROM (collected from all leading Auctions and private sources, principally in Devon and Cornwall, Including, LADY HAMILTON (by ROMNEY); BOBBIE BURNS (Early Work by RAEBURN); A PEEP THROUGH THE TREES (GAINSBOROUGH); BARGES ON THE THAMES (Oil Sketch by J M W. TURNER, R A); MRS. FITZWILLIAM as "Individual" in Tom Noddy's Secret (by E HAYES).

And Specimens by COOPER, VAN BLBER, COX, CONSTABLE (P. De-Champagne), GREEN, GRIFFIER, GIRTIN, GREUZE, HALS, HARDING, HOBBEMA, MEISSONIER, MORLAND, PHIL MORRIS, MILLET, NASMYSH, OSTADE, SEBASTIAN, DE-DIOMBO, REMBRANDT, RUYSDAEL, TROYON, WHEATLEY, etc., etc.

Water Colours and Miniatures—BERTEN, BLOCK, COSWAY, DARNEY, ARTHUR HUGHES, etc.
Rare Etchings—REMBRANDT, OSTADE, WHISTLER, etc.
Engravings of every description, including 'EMMA' (by J, JONES), and others too numerous to mention.
Autographs—W. SHAKSPERE, Thynne Sweeteste, Stratforde, March 16, NELSON, W. PENN, and others.

ANTIQUE FURNITURE, OLD CHINA, COINS, SILVER AND CURIOS OF EVERY DESCRIPTION PURCHASED.
VALUATIONS AND COMMISSIONS EXECUTED
CUSTOMERS IN ALL PARTS OF THE WORLD. PLEASE NOTE.—Communicate your wants and I will try to supply them.

Observe the Address : **J. SPRATT, 14 Northernhay Place, EXETER**

ND - #0225 - 211122 - C0 - 229/152/9 - PB - 9781334039119 - Gloss Lamination